The McDonaldization of Society

The McDonaldization of Society

An Investigation Into the Changing Character
of Contemporary Social Life

George Ritzer

University of Maryland

PINE FORGE PRESS
Thousand Oaks ◆ London ◆ New Delhi

For information, address:

Pine Forge Press
A Sage Publication Company
2455 Teller Road
Newbury Park, California 91320

Copy Editor: Paul Dreyfus
Text and Cover Design: Lisa Mirski
Publications Coordinator: Robin Kerns
Proofreader: Chiara Huddleston
Typesetting: Michael Oates
Printer: Malloy Lithographing Inc.

McDonald's is a registered trademark of the McDonald's Corporation.

Printed in the United States of America

3 4 5 6 7 8 9 10—97 96 95 94 93

Library of Congress Cataloging in Publication Data

Ritzer, George
    The McDonaldization of society : an investigation into the
changing character of contemporary social life / George Ritzer
        p.   cm.
    Includes bibliographical references.
    ISBN 0-8039-9000-6 (pb : paper)
    1.Social structure—United states. 2. United States—Social
conditions—1980- 3. Management—Social aspects—United States.
4. Fast food restaurants—Social aspects—United States.
5. Rationalization (Psychology)   I. Title.
HM131.R58   1992
306' .0973—dc20   92-17450
                                                         CIP

To Alan Ritzer, who helped open my eyes to McDonaldization, and to Paul O'Connell, whose gentleness and Shavian wit were inspirations for this book.

About the Author

George Ritzer is an acknowledged expert in the field of social theory and sociology of work and has served as Chair of the American Sociological Association's Sections on Theoretical Sociology and Organizations and Occupations. A distingushed Scholar-Teacher at the University of Maryland, Professor Ritzer has been honored with that institution's Teaching Excellence award. Two of his other most recent books include *Frontiers of Social Theory* (Columbia University Press) and *Sociology: Experiencing Changing Societies* (5th edition) with Kenneth Kammeyer and Norman Yetman.

About the Publisher

Pine Forge Press is a new educational publisher, dedicated to publishing innovative books and software throughout the social sciences. On this and any other of our publications, we welcome your comments and suggestions.

Please call or write us at

PINE FORGE PRESS
A Sage Publications Company
2455 Teller Road
Newbury Park, CA 91320
(805) 499-0721
Internet: sdr@pfp.sagepub.com

Contents

Preface

I have been thinking about the process of rationalization for many years. It has long been believed that bureaucracy represents the ultimate form of rationalization. However, it gradually began to dawn on me that something new was on the horizon, something that was destined to replace the bureaucratic structure as the model for rationalization. That "something" turned out to be the fast-food restaurant, most notably McDonald's, which not only revolutionized the restaurant business, but also American society and, ultimately, the world.

As a New Yorker, I came late to McDonald's because, during my teenage years (the 1950s), the fast-food restaurant had not yet invaded the large cities to any great degree. I can remember the first time I ever saw a McDonald's. It was on an automobile trip to Massachusetts in 1958, and, for some reason, it left an indelible mark on my memory. Retrospectively, I think I realized, at least subliminally, that those golden arches represented something new and important.

About a decade later, and by this time a professional sociologist, I was living in New Orleans and my brother, Alan Ritzer, a lifelong New Yorker, came to visit. We went to McDonald's; that was his first exposure to the fast-food restaurant. He, too, was struck by the significance of this phenomenon and of the problems it posed for society.

Through the 1970s I developed my theoretical orientation, which was heavily influenced by the work of the German social theorist Max Weber and his views about the rationalization process. It was Weber who viewed bureaucracy as the paradigm case of rationality. Although Weber recognized the advantages to be gained from rationalization, he was most animated by its dangers, especially the possibility of what he called an "iron cage" of rationality. Weber felt that rational systems were inhuman and dehumanizing. He dreaded the possibility, indeed the likelihood, that an increasing number of sectors of society would be rationalized; he felt that ultimately society would become a seamless web of rational institutions. Once rational systems proliferated to that extent, we would be faced with an iron cage of rationality; there could be no escape, no exit.

By the early 1980s, I began to put Weber's theory of rationalization together with my interest in, and concern over, the growth of the fast-food restaurant. By this time, McDonald's was far more ubiquitous and its clones in the fast-food business, as well as in many other social settings, were spreading throughout society. I was both struck and alarmed by this trend, and in 1983 I wrote an essay entitled "The McDonaldization of Society."

With the latter essay out of my system, I moved on to other things, including other kinds of applications of Weberian theory. In 1990 I gave a speech in which I touched on McDonaldization in the context of a far broader discussion of the applications of Weberian theory to the modern world. I thought that the most important part of the talk was an effort to explain the rise of Japanese industry, and the decline of American industry, from the point of view of the theory of rationalization. However, when it came time for open discussion, the audience only wanted to talk about McDonaldization. This was clearly an idea with which people resonated. I had been getting similar reactions from students over the years whenever I lectured on McDonaldization. In fact, as McDonaldization became more and more ubiquitous, the level of interest in the phenomenon, and in the problems it generated, increased dramatically.

It seemed clear to me that it was time to write a book on the issue. In the decade since I had written my essay, fast-food restaurants had proliferated to the degree that they were virtually everywhere. Many other businesses were organized along the lines developed by McDonald's. Almost all social institutions (for example, education, sports, politics, and religion) were adapting McDonald's principles to their operations. And McDonaldization was spreading around the world—fast-food croissanteries in Paris (of all places), Kentucky Fried Chicken in Beijing, McDonald's in Beijing and Moscow.

In fact, in May 1992, just as this book was going to press, I was in Moscow lecturing at the Russian Academy of Sciences. I was stunned by the many changes taking place in that society, but drawn particularly to the spread of McDonaldization. There, in the heart of Moscow, stood the new McDonald's. Muscovites are attracted to it in droves for a variety of reasons, not the least of which is the fact that it is *the* symbol of the rationalization of America and its coveted market economy. The rationality of McDonald's stands in stark contrast to the irrationalities of the remnants of communism. Long lines and long waits (so much for fast food) are common, but one sunny Saturday in May the line stretched as far as the eye could see. In fact, teenagers were offering, in exchange for a few rubles, to get you a "Beeg Mek" in no more than 10 or 15 minutes. Russians are in a headlong rush toward McDonaldization, seemingly oblivious to its potential problems.

This book is essentially a work in social criticism. McDonald's clearly has many advantages and they will be mentioned throughout the book. However, McDonald's and its many clones have plenty of opportunity, and spend huge sums of money, to tell you about their good points. This book seeks to give the public discourse a little balance by focusing on the problems created, and the dangers posed, by McDonaldization.

As a theoretically based work in social criticism, this book is part of a historical tradition in the social sciences in which social theory is used to critique society and thereby to provide the base for its betterment. It was this that animated Weber in his work on rationalization, and it also provided the motivation for such great classic and contemporary social theorists as Georg Simmel, Emile Durkheim, Karl Marx, C. Wright Mills, and Jurgen Habermas.

I should point out that I bear no particular animus toward McDonald's. It is no better or worse than other fast-food restaurants and other manifestations of the rationalization process. I have labeled the process of concern here "McDonaldization" because McDonald's was, and is, the most important manifestation of this process. Besides, it has a better ring to it than some of the alternatives— "Burger Kingization," "Seven Elevenization," "Fuddruckerization," "H&R Blockization," "Kinder Careization," "Jiffy Lubeization," or "Nutri/Systemization."

As the preceding list makes clear, a wide array of social phenomena are linked together in this book under the broad heading of McDonaldization. Some have been directly affected by the principles of the fast-food restaurant, whereas in other cases the effect is more indirect. Some have all of the basic dimensions of McDonaldization, but others may have only one or two. In any case, in my view they all are part of what Weber called the rationalization process and what is here, in order to make Weber more timely, labeled McDonaldization.

The major themes of this book, especially the critiques of the irrationalities of McDonaldization, are likely to be highly controversial. My experience in lecturing on this theme is that audiences are generally supportive of McDonaldization and protective of it. Critiques of McDonaldization inevitably spawn heated debate in the lecture hall. It is hoped that this book will spark a similar debate in a larger arena. The generation of such debate, as well as the insights to be derived from it, is not only the essence of good teaching but also of good sociology. Whether or not the reader agrees with my conclusions, I will have succeeded in achieving my goal if the reader has been provoked into rethinking this significant aspect of everyday life.

This book is written for the general reader. Its goal is to be accessible to a wide readership. However, it is firmly based on one of the strongest of social theories, Weber's theory of rationalization. It is also an "empirical" study, albeit one that is highly informal. The "data" are drawn from a wide range of available sources and deal with the full range of social phenomena that can be dealt with under the heading of McDonaldization. However, although it is theory-based and relies on "data," this is not written as a dry theoretical and empirical study; it is not weighted down by the requirements of scholarly monographs. Rather, it is designed to be a book that can be read by many people and inform them of a wide-ranging social development that is occurring all around them. More important, it is written as a warning that the seductions and attractions of McDonaldization should not blind us to its many dangers.

I would like to thank Gladys Martinez, Brian Hoffman, JoAnn DeFiore, and Steve Lankenau for their invaluable help as graduate research assistants on this book. I also want to thank a number of my undergraduate students for many valuable insights into the McDonaldization of society. Their generation is even more enmeshed in our McDonaldized society than mine, and if present trends continue, their children will be still more ensnared. Among these students are Alyson J. Blewett, Carolyn Eddy, Melissa Fireman, Jennifer Gilbert, Wendy Grachik, Anna Kennedy, Tremelle I. Howard, Paula Hutter, Andrew Paradise, Mark C. Polk, Tim Prewitt, Sean Savio, Jamie Schapiro, Keri Sferra, Caroline Smith, Paul Tewksbury, Constance H. Ward, and most notably, Dora Giemza. Also to be thanked are several colleagues, including Conrad Kottak, Larry Mintz, Linda Moghadam, Stan Presser, and, as usual, Ken Kammeyer. Among the reviewers to be thanked are John Walsh, Peter Kollock, Wolf Heydebrand, Marshall Fishwick, Gary Alan Fine, and Robin Leidner, whose comments and critiques were invaluable in shaping this book.

I would like to thank especially Steve Rutter, publisher and president of Pine Forge Press, for believing in this book and for using it as Pine Forge's first publication. Finally, I need to thank Paul Dreyfus for his diligence as a copy editor, and Jeremy Ritzer for his skills as indexer.

I hope that this book offers readers some new insights into the society in which they are in the process of constructing. If they are as alarmed as I am by the dangers posed by McDonaldization, perhaps they can do what Weber thought virtually impossible—act to reverse the trend toward McDonaldization. Although I do not think such a reversal is possible, or even necessarily desirable, I do think that there are steps that people can take to ameliorate the problems, to humanize a McDonaldized society. It is hoped that this book will not only inform, but also serve as a warning, and perhaps most important, point the reader in directions that can help make the "iron cage of McDonaldization" a more human setting in which to work and live.

1

The McDonaldization of Society

An Introduction

Ray Kroc, the genius behind the franchising of McDonald's, was a man with big ideas and grand ambitions. But even Kroc could not have anticipated the astounding influence his creation was to have. McDonald's *is* one of the most influential developments in twentieth century America. Its impact is felt far beyond the confines of the United States and the fast-food business. It has influenced a wide range of undertakings, indeed the way of life, of a significant portion of the world. And that influence is destined to continue to expand at an accelerating rate in the foreseeable future.

However, this is *not* a book about McDonald's, or the fast-food business, although both will be discussed frequently throughout these pages. Rather, McDonald's is treated here as the major example, the "paradigm case," of a wide-ranging process I call *McDonaldization*, that is

> the process by which the principles of the fast-food restaurant are coming to dominate more and more sectors of American society as well as of the rest of the world.

As we will see throughout the following pages, McDonaldization not only affects the restaurant business, but also education, work, travel, leisure-time activities, dieting, politics, the family, and virtually every other sector of society. McDonaldization has shown every sign of being an inexorable process as it sweeps through seemingly impervious institutions and parts of the world.

The impact of McDonald's, and the process of McDonaldization that it played a central role in spawning, has been manifest in a variety of ways:

Citations may be found at the back of the book, beginning on page 189.

- The success of McDonald's is reflected in the fact that in 1990 its total sales were $6.8 billion and its profits were in excess of $800 million. Many entrepreneurs envy such sales and profits and are seeking to emulate McDonald's success.

- The sheer number of fast-food restaurants has grown astronomically. For example, McDonald's, which first began franchising in 1955, opened its 12,000th outlet on March 22, 1991. By the end of 1991, McDonald's had 12,418 restaurants. The leading 100 restaurant chains operate more than 110,000 outlets in the United States alone. There is, therefore, 1 chain restaurant for every 2,250 Americans.

- The McDonald's model has not only been adopted by other hamburger franchises but also by a wide array of other fast-food businesses, including those selling fried chicken and various ethnic foods (for example, Pizza Hut, Sbarro's, Taco Bell, Popeye's, and Charley Chan's).

- The McDonald's model has also been extended to more "up-scale" foods and restaurants (for example, the Sizzler chain that sells steaks, Fuddrucker's and its "gourmet" burgers, and Red Lobster which purveys . . . you guessed it).

- As a result of the expansion of the fast-food business, Americans eat an increasingly large proportion of their meals at McDonald's and its clones.

- This American institution is making increasing inroads around the world as evidenced by the opening of American fast-food restaurants throughout Europe. (Not too many years ago scholars wrote about European resistance to fast-food restaurants.) Fast food has become a global phenomenon; consider the booming business at the brand-new McDonald's in Moscow where, as I write, almost 30,000 hamburgers a day are being sold by a staff of 1,200 young people working two to a cash register. There are plans to open 20 more McDonald's in the remnants of the Soviet Union in the next few years, and a vast new territory in Eastern Europe is now laid bare to an invasion of fast-food restaurants.

  Already possessing a huge Kentucky Fried Chicken outlet, Beijing, China, witnessed the opening of the world's largest McDonald's, with 700 seats, 29 cash registers, and nearly 1,000

employees, in April 1992. On its first day of business, it set a new
one-day record for McDonald's by serving about 40,000 customers. In 1991, for the first time, McDonald's opened more
restaurants abroad (427) than in the United States (188). The
top 10 McDonald's outlets in terms of sales and profits are already
overseas. By 1994, it is expected that more than 50 percent of
McDonald's profits will come from its overseas operations. It has
been announced that starting in 1992, McDonald's will start serving food on the Swiss railroad system. One presumes that the
menu will include Big Macs and not cheese fondue.

- ◆ Other nations have developed their own variants of this American
institution, as is best exemplified by the now-large number of fast-
food *croissanteries* in Paris, a city whose love for fine cuisine might
have led one to think that it would prove immune to the fast-food
restaurant. Perhaps the most unlikely spot for an indigenous fast-
food restaurant was then-war-ravaged Beirut, Lebanon; but in 1984
Juicy Burger opened there (with a rainbow instead of golden arches
and J.B. the clown replacing Ronald McDonald) with its owners
hoping that it would become the "McDonald's of the Arab world."

- ◆ Other countries not only now have their own McDonaldized institutions, but they have also begun to export them to the United
States. For example, the Body Shop is an ecologically sensitive
British cosmetics chain with 620 shops in 39 countries; 66 of
those shops are in the United States. Furthermore, American
firms are now opening copies of this British chain, such as the
Limited, Inc.'s, Bath and Body Works.

- ◆ As will be shown throughout this book, an ever-expanding number
of other types of business have adapted the principles of the fast-
food restaurant to their needs. Said the vice chairman of one of
these chains, Toys R Us, "We want to be thought of as a sort of
McDonald's of toys." The founder of Kidsports Fun and Fitness
Club echoed this desire: "I want to be the McDonald's of the kids'
fun and fitness business." Other chains with similar ambitions in
other arenas include Jiffy-Lube, AAMCO Transmissions, Midas
Muffler & Brake Shops, Hair Plus, H&R Block, Pearle Vision
Centers, Kampgrounds of America (KOA), Kinder Care (dubbed
"Kentucky Fried Children"), Nutri/System, and Wal-Mart.

McDonald's as "Americana," Sacred "Icon," and at 35,000 Feet

McDonald's as well as its many clones have become ubiquitous and immediately recognizable symbols throughout the United States as well as much of the rest of the world. For example, when plans were afoot to raze Ray Kroc's first McDonald's outlet, hundreds of letters poured into McDonald's headquarters, including the following:

> Please don't tear it down! . . . Your company's name is a household word, not only in the United States of America, but all over the world. To destroy this major artifact of contemporary culture would, indeed, destroy part of the faith the people of the world have in your company.

In the end, the outlet was not torn down, but rather turned into a museum! Said a McDonald's executive, explaining the move, "McDonald's . . . is really a part of Americana." Similarly, when Pizza Hut opened in Moscow in 1990, a Russian student said, "It's a piece of America."

In fact, McDonald's is such a powerful symbol that we have come to give many businesses nicknames beginning with *Mc* in order to indicate that they follow the McDonald's model. Examples include "*Mc*Dentists" and "*Mc*Doctors" (for drive-in clinics designed to deal quickly and efficiently with minor dental and medical problems), "*Mc*Child" Care Centers (for child care centers like Kinder-Care), "*Mc*Stables" (for the nationwide racehorse training operation of Wayne Lucas), and "*Mc*Paper" (for the newspaper *USA TODAY* and its short news articles often called "News *Mc*Nuggets"). When *USA TODAY* began an aborted television program modeled after the newspaper, some began to call it "News *Mc*Rather."

McDonald's has come to occupy a central place in popular culture. It can be a big event when a new McDonald's opens in a small town. Said one Maryland high school student at such an event, "Nothing this exciting ever happens in Dale City." Newspapers cover fast-food business developments; the opening of the McDonald's in Beijing was big news. McDonald's is spoofed or treated with reverence on television programs and in the movies. A skit on the television show *Saturday Night Live* makes fun of the specialization of such businesses by detailing the trials and tribulations of a franchise that sells nothing but Scotch tape. The movie *Coming to America* casts Eddie

Murphy as an African prince whose introduction to America includes a job at "McDowell's," a thinly disguised McDonald's. In *Moscow on the Hudson*, Robin Williams, newly arrived from Russia, obtains a job at McDonald's. H.G. Wells, a central character in the movie *Time After Time*, finds himself transported to the modern world of McDonald's, where he tries to order the tea he was accustomed to drinking in Victorian England. In *Sleeper*, Woody Allen awakens in the future only to encounter a McDonald's. Finally, *Tin Men*, which shows the passage from the era of the Cadillac to that of the Volkswagen, ends with the heroes driving off into a future represented by a huge golden arch looming in the distance.

Many people identify strongly with McDonald's; in fact to some it has become a sacred institution. On the opening of the McDonald's in Moscow, one journalist described it as the "ultimate icon of Americana," while a worker spoke of it "as if it were the Cathedral in Chartres . . . a place to experience 'celestial joy.'" Kowinski argues that shopping malls—which we will show to be crucial to McDonaldization—are the modern "cathedrals of consumption" to which we go to practice our "consumer religion." Similarly, a visit to what we shall see is another central element of our McDonaldized society, Walt Disney World, has been described as "the middle-class haj, the compulsory visit to the sunbaked holy city."

McDonald's has achieved its exalted position as a result of the fact that virtually all Americans, and many of those from other countries, have passed through its golden arches, often on innumerable occasions. Furthermore, we have all been bombarded by commercials extolling McDonald's virtues. These commercials have been tailored to different audiences. Some are aimed at young children watching Saturday morning cartoons. Others point toward young adults watching prime-time programs. Still others are oriented toward grandparents who might be coaxed into taking their grandchildren to McDonald's. In addition, McDonald's commercials change as the chain introduces new foods (such as breakfast burritos), creates new contests, and ties its products to things such as new motion pictures. These ever-present commercials, combined with the fact that we cannot drive very far without having a McDonald's pop into view, have served to embed McDonald's deep into our consciousness. In a survey taken in 1986, 96 percent of the schoolchildren polled were able to identify Ronald McDonald, making him second only to Santa Claus in name recognition.

Over the years McDonald's has appealed to us on a variety of different grounds. The restaurants themselves are depicted as spick-and-span, the food is said to be fresh and nutritious, the employees are shown to be young and eager, the managers appear gentle and caring, and the dining experience itself seems to be fun-filled. We are even led to believe that we contribute, at least indirectly, to charities by supporting the company that supports Ronald McDonald homes for sick children.

McDonald's has continually extended its reach, within American society and beyond. It began as a suburban and medium-sized-town phenomenon, but in recent years it has moved into big cities not only in the United States, but also in many other parts of the world. Fast-food outlets can now be found in New York's Times Square as well as on the Champs Élysées in Paris. They have also now migrated into smaller towns that supposedly could not support such a restaurant. At first, McDonald's and its fast-food clones settled on specific strips of road, such as Route 161 in Columbus, Ohio. Said one local resident, "You want something for the stomach? . . . Drive that car down Route 161 and you'll see more eating than you ever saw in your life." Although such strips continue to flourish, fast-food restaurants are now far more geographically dispersed.

Another significant expansion has occurred more recently as fast-food restaurants have moved onto college campuses, instead of being content, as they have in the past, merely to dominate the strips that surround many campuses. Installed on college campuses with the seeming approval of college administrations, McDonald's is in a position to further influence the lifestyle of the younger generation.

Another, even more recent, incursion has occurred: Fast-food restaurants are taking over the restaurant business on the nation's highways. Now we no longer need to leave the road to dine in our favorite fast-food restaurant. We can stop for fast food and then proceed with our trip, which is likely to end in another community that has about the same density and mix of fast-food restaurants as the locale we left behind. Also in the travel realm, fast-food restaurants are more and more apt to be found in railway stations and airports and even on the tray tables of inflight meals. The following advertisement appeared on September 17, 1991, in the *Washington Post* (and *The New York Times*): "Where else at 35,000 feet can you get a McDonald's meal like this for your kids? Only on United's Orlando flights." Thus, children can now get McDonald's fare on United Airline's flights to Orlando. How soon before adults can have the same option? How much longer before such meals will be available on all United flights? On all flights everywhere by every carrier?

In other sectors of society, the influence of fast-food restaurants has been more subtle, but no less profound. Few high schools and grade schools have in-house fast-food restaurants, but many have had to alter school cafeteria menus and procedures so that fast food is readily and continually available to children and teenagers. Apples, yogurt, and milk may go straight into the trash can, but hamburgers, fries, and shakes are devoured. Things may be about to change dramatically, however, since Domino's, in conjunction with Marriott, has recently signed an agreement to market Domino's pizza in school cafeterias that are run by Marriott, which presently serves 200 school systems in 20 states and about a 120 million meals a year. The effort to hook schoolchildren on fast food, long a goal of advertisements aimed at this population, reached something of a peak in Illinois where McDonald's outlets operated a program called "A for Cheeseburger." Students who received an A on their report cards were rewarded with a free cheeseburger, thereby linking success in school with McDonald's.

The military has been pressed into offering fast-food menus on its bases and on its ships. Despite the criticisms by physicians and nutritionists, fast-food outlets are increasingly turning up *inside* hospitals. No homes have a McDonald's of their own, but dining within the home has been influenced by the fast-food restaurant. Home-cooked meals often resemble those available in fast-food restaurants. Frozen, microwavable, and preprepared foods, also bearing a striking resemblance to McDonald's meals and increasingly modeled after them, often find their way to the dinner table. Then there is the home delivery of fast foods, especially pizza, as revolutionized by Domino's.

Dunkin' Donuts, "Critter Watch," and "The McDonald's of Sex"

Clearly, McDonald's has not been alone in pressing the fast-food model on American society and the rest of the world. Other fast-food giants, such as Burger King, Wendy's, Hardee's, Arby's, Big-Boy, Dairy Queen, TCBY, Denny's, Sizzler, Kentucky Fried Chicken,

Popeye's, Taco Bell, Chi Chi's, Pizza Hut, Domino's, Long John Silver, Baskin-Robbins, and Dunkin' Donuts, have played a key role, as have the innumerable other businesses built on the principles of the fast-food restaurant.

Even the derivatives of McDonald's are, in turn, having their own influence. For example, the success of *USA TODAY* has led to changes in many newspapers across the nation, for example, shorter stories and color weather maps. As one *USA TODAY* editor put it, "The same newspaper editors who call us McPaper have been stealing our McNuggets." The influence of *USA TODAY* is blatantly manifest in the *Boca Raton News*, a Knight-Ridder newspaper. This newspaper is described as "a sort of smorgasbord of snippets, a newspaper that slices and dices the news into even smaller portions than does *USA TODAY*, spicing it with color graphics and fun facts and cute features like 'Today's Hero' and 'Critter Watch'." As in *USA TODAY*, stories in the *Boca Raton News* usually do not jump from one page to another; they start and finish on the same page. In order to meet this need, long and complex stories often have to be reduced to a few paragraphs. Much of a story's context, and much of what the principals have to say, is severely cut back or omitted entirely. With its emphasis on light and celebrity news, its color maps and graphics, the main function of the newspaper seems to be to entertain.

One issue to be addressed in this book is whether McDonaldization *is* inexorable and will therefore come to insinuate itself into every aspect of our society and our lives. In the movie *Sleeper*, Woody Allen not only created a futuristic world in which McDonald's was an important and highly visible element, but he also envisioned a society in which even sex underwent the process of McDonaldization. The denizens of his future world were able to enter a machine called an "orgasmatron" that allowed them to experience an orgasm without going through the muss and fuss of sexual intercourse.

In fact, sex, like virtually every other sector of society, has undergone a process of McDonaldization. "Dial-a-porn" allows us to have intimate, sexually explicit, even obscene, conversations with people we have never met and probably never will meet. There is great specialization here, and dialing numbers like 555-FOXX will lead to a very different phone message than dialing 555-SEXY. Escort services advertise a wide range of available sex partners. Highly specialized pornographic movies (heterosexual, homosexual, sex with children, sex with animals) can be seen at urban multiplexes and are available at local video stores for viewing in the comfort of our living rooms. Various technologies (vibrators, as an example) enhance the ability of people to have sex on their own without the bother of having to deal with a human partner. In New York City, an official called a three-story pornographic center "the McDonald's of sex" because of its "cookie-cutter cleanliness and compliance with the law." The McDonaldization of sex suggests that no aspect of our lives is safe from it.

The Dimensions of McDonaldization: From Drive-Throughs to Uncomfortable Seats

Even if some domains are able to resist McDonaldization, this book intends to demonstrate that many other aspects of society are being, or will be, McDonaldized. This raises the issue of why the McDonald's model has proven so irresistible. Four basic and alluring dimensions lie at the heart of the success of the McDonald's model and, more generally, of the process of McDonaldization.

First, McDonald's offers *efficiency*. That is, the McDonald's system offers us the optimum method for getting from one point to another. Most generally, this means that McDonald's proffers the best available means of getting us from a state of being hungry to a state of being full. (Similarly, Woody Allen's orgasmatron offered an efficient method for getting us from quiescence to sexual stimulation to sexual gratification.) Other institutions, fashioned on the McDonald's model, offer us similar efficiency in losing weight, lubricating our cars, filling eyeglass prescriptions, or completing income tax forms. In a fast-paced society in which both parents are likely to work, or where there may be only a single parent, efficiently satisfying the hunger and many other needs of people is very attractive. In a highly mobile society in which people are rushing, usually by car, from one spot to another, the efficiency of a fast-food meal, perhaps without leaving one's car while passing by the drive-through window, often proves impossible to resist. The fast-food model offers us, or at least appears to offer us, an efficient method for satisfying many of our needs.

Second, McDonald's offers us food and service that can be easily *quantified* and *calculated*. In effect, McDonald's seems to offer us "more bang for the buck." (One of its recent innovations, in response to the growth of other fast-food franchises, is to proffer "value meals" at discounted prices.) We often feel that we are getting a *lot* of food for a modest amount of money. Quantity has become equivalent to quality; a lot of something means it must be good. As two observers of contemporary American culture put it, "As a culture, we tend to believe—deeply—that in general 'bigger is better.'" Thus, we order the *Quarter Pounder*, the *Big* Mac, the *large* fries. We can quantify all of these things and feel that we are getting a lot of food, and, in return, we appear to be shelling out only a nominal sum of money. This calculus, of course, ignores an important point: the mushrooming of fast-food outlets, and the spread of the model to many other businesses, indicates that our calculation is illusory and it is the owners who are getting the best of the deal.

There is another kind of calculation involved in the success of McDonald's—a calculation involving time. People often, at least implicitly, calculate how much time it will take them to drive to McDonald's, eat their food, and return home and then compare that interval to the amount of time required to prepare the food at home. They often conclude, rightly or wrongly, that it will take less time to go and eat at the fast-food restaurant than to eat at home. This time calculation is a key factor in the success of Domino's and other home-delivery franchises, because to patronize them people do not even need to leave their homes. To take another notable example, Lens Crafters promises us "Glasses fast, glasses in one hour." Some McDonaldized institutions have come to combine the emphases on time and money. Domino's promises pizza delivery in one-half hour, or the pizza is free. Pizza Hut will serve us a personal pan pizza in five minutes, or it, too, will be free.

Third, McDonald's offers us *predictability*. We know that the Egg McMuffin we eat in New York will be, for all intents and purposes, identical to those we have eaten in Chicago and Los Angeles. We also know that the one we order next week or next year will be identical to the one we eat today. There is great comfort in knowing that McDonald's offers no surprises, that the food we eat at one time or in one place will be identical to the food we eat at another time or in another place. We know that the next Egg McMuffin we eat will not be awful, but we also know that it will not be exceptionally delicious. The success of the McDonald's model indicates that many people have come to prefer a world in which there are no surprises.

Fourth and finally, *control*, especially through the *substitution of nonhuman for human technology*, is exerted over the human beings who enter the world of McDonald's. The humans who work in fast-food restaurants are trained to do a very limited number of things in precisely the way they are told to do them. Managers and inspectors make sure that workers toe the line. The human beings who eat in fast-food restaurants are also controlled, albeit (usually) more subtly and indirectly. Lines, limited menus, few options, and uncomfortable seats all lead diners to do what the management wishes them to do— eat quickly and leave. Further, the drive-through (and in some cases walk-through) window leads diners to first leave and then eat rapidly. This attribute has most recently been extended by the Domino's model, according to which customers are expected to *never* come, yet still eat speedily.

McDonald's also controls people by using nonhuman technology to replace human workers. Human workers, no matter how well they are programmed and controlled, can foul up the operation of the system. A slow or indolent worker can make the preparation and delivery of a Big Mac inefficient. A worker who refuses to follow the rules can leave the pickles or special sauce off a hamburger, thereby making for unpredictability. And a distracted worker can put too few fries in the box, making an order of large fries seem awfully skimpy. For these and other reasons, McDonald's is compelled to steadily replace human beings with nonhuman technologies, such as the soft-drink dispenser that shuts itself off when the glass is full, the french-fry machine that rings when the fries are crisp, the preprogrammed cash register that eliminates the need for the cashier to calculate prices and amounts, and, perhaps at some future time, the robot capable of making hamburgers. (Experimental robots of this type already exist.) All of these technologies permit greater control over the human beings involved in the fast-food restaurant. The result is that McDonald's is able to reassure customers about the nature of the employee to be encountered and the nature of the service to be obtained.

In sum, McDonald's (and the McDonald's model) has succeeded because it offers the consumer efficiency and predictability, and because it seems to offer the diner a lot of food for little money and a slight expenditure of effort. It has also flourished because it has been able to exert greater control through nonhuman technologies over both employees and customers, leading them to behave the way the organization wishes them to. The substitution of nonhuman for human technologies has also allowed the fast-food restaurant to deliver its fare increasingly more efficiently and predictably. Thus, there are good, solid reasons why McDonald's has succeeded so phenomenally and why the process of McDonaldization continues unabated.

A Critique of McDonaldization: The Irrationality of Rationality

There is a downside to all of this. We can think of efficiency, predictability, calculability, and control through nonhuman technology as the basic components of a *rational* system. However, as we shall see in later chapters, rational systems often spawn irrationalities. The downside of McDonaldization will be dealt with most systematically under the heading of the *irrationality of rationality*. Another way of saying this is that rational systems serve to deny human reason; rational systems can be unreasonable.

For example, the fast-food restaurant is often a dehumanizing setting in which to eat or work. People lining up for a burger, or waiting in the drive-through line, often feel as if they are dining on an assembly line, and those who prepare the burgers often appear to be working on a burger assembly line. Assembly lines are hardly human settings in which to eat, and they have been shown to be inhuman settings in which to work. As we will see, dehumanization is only one of many ways in which the highly rationalized fast-food restaurant is extremely irrational.

Of course, the criticisms of the irrationality of the fast-food restaurant will be extended to all facets of our McDonaldizing world. This extension has recently been underscored and legitimated at the opening of Euro DisneyLand outside Paris. A French socialist politician acknowledged the link between Disney and McDonald's as well as their common negative effects when he said that Euro Disney will "bombard France with uprooted creations that are to culture what fast food is to gastronomy."

Such critiques lead to a question: Is the headlong rush toward McDonaldization around the world advantageous or not? There are great gains to be made from McDonaldization, some of which will be discussed below. But there are also great costs and enormous risks, which this book will focus on. Ultimately, we must ask whether the creation of these rationalized systems creates an even greater number of irrationalities. At the minimum, we need to be aware of the costs associated with McDonaldization. McDonald's and other purveyors of the fast-food model spend billions of dollars each year outlining the benefits to be derived from their system. However, the critics of the system have few outlets for their ideas. There are no commercials on Saturday morning between cartoons warning children of the dangers associated with fast-food restaurants. Although few children are likely to read this book, it is aimed, at least in part, at their parents (or parents-to-be) in the hope that it will serve as a caution that might be passed on to their children.

A legitimate question may be raised about this analysis: Is this critique of McDonaldization animated by a romanticization of the past and an impossible desire to return to a world that no longer exists? For some critics, this is certainly the case. They remember the time when life was slower, less efficient, had more surprises, when people were freer, and when one was more likely to deal with a human being than a robot or a computer. Although they have a point, these critics have undoubtedly exaggerated the positive aspects of a world before McDonald's, and they have certainly tended to forget the liabilities associated with such a world. More importantly, they do not seem to realize that we are *not* returning to such a world. The increase in the number of people, the acceleration in technological change, the increasing pace of life—all this and more make it impossible to go back to a nonrationalized world, if it ever existed, of home-cooked meals, traditional restaurant dinners, high-quality foods, meals loaded with surprises, and restaurants populated only by workers free to fully express their creativity.

While one basis for a critique of McDonaldization is the past, another is the future. The future in this sense is what people have the potential to be if they are unfettered by the constraints of rational systems. This critique holds that people have the potential to be far more thoughtful, skillful, creative, and well-rounded than they now are, yet are unable to express this potential because of the constraints of a rationalized world. If the world were less rationalized, or even derationalized, people would be better able to live up to their human potential. This critique is based not on what people were like in the past, but on what they could be like in the future, if only the constraints of McDonaldized systems were eliminated, or at least eased substantially. The criticisms to be put forth in this book are animated by the latter, future-oriented perspective rather than by a romanticization of the past and a desire to return to it.

The Advantages of McDonaldization: From the Cajun Bayou to Suburbia

Much of this book will focus on the negative side of McDonald's and McDonaldization. At this point it is important, however, to balance this view by mentioning some of the benefits of these systems and processes. The economic columnist, Robert Samuelson, for example, is a strong supporter of McDonald's and confesses to "openly worship McDonald's." He thinks of it as "the greatest restaurant chain in history." (However, Samuelson does recognize that there are those who "can't stand the food and regard McDonald's as the embodiment of all that is vulgar in American mass culture.")

Let me enumerate some of the advantages of the fast-food restaurant as well as other elements of our McDonaldized society:

- The fast-food restaurant has expanded the alternatives available to consumers. For example, more people now have ready access to Italian, Mexican, Chinese, and Cajun foods. A McDonaldized society is, in this sense, more egalitarian.

- The salad bar, which many fast-food restaurants and supermarkets now offer, enables people to make salads the way they want them.

- Microwave ovens and microwavable foods enable us to have dinner in minutes or even seconds.

- For those with a wide range of shopping needs, supermarkets and shopping malls are very efficient sites. Home shopping networks allow us to shop even more efficiently without ever leaving home.

- Today's high-tech, for-profit hospitals are likely to provide higher quality medical care than their predecessors.

- We can receive almost instantaneous medical attention at our local, drive-in "McDoctors."

- Computerized phone systems (and "voice mail") allow people to do things that were impossible before, such as obtain a bank balance in the middle of the night or hear a report on what went on in their child's class during the day and what home-work assignments were made. Similarly, automated bank teller machines allow people to obtain money any time of the day or night.

- Package tours permit large numbers of people to visit countries that they would otherwise not visit.

- Diet centers like Nutri/System allow people to lose weight in a carefully regulated and controlled system.

- The 24-second clock in professional basketball has enabled outstanding athletes such as Michael Jordan to more fully demonstrate their extraordinary talents.

- Recreational vehicles let the modern camper avoid excessive heat, rain, insects, and the like.

- Suburban tract houses have permitted large numbers of people to afford single-family homes.

Conclusion

The previous list gives the reader a sense not only of the advantages of McDonaldization but also of the range of phenomena that will be discussed under that heading throughout this book. In fact, such a wide range of phenomena will be discussed under the heading of McDonaldization that one is led to wonder: What isn't McDonaldized? Is McDonaldization the equivalent of modernity? Is everything contemporary McDonaldized?

While much of the world has been McDonaldized, it is possible to identify at least three aspects of contemporary society that have largely escaped McDonaldization. First, there are phenomena traceable to an earlier, "premodern" age that continue to exist within the modern world. A good example is the Mom and Pop grocery store. Second, there are recent creations that have come into existence, at least in part, as a reaction against McDonaldization. A good example is the boom in bed and breakfasts (B&Bs), which offer rooms in private homes with personalized attention and a homemade breakfast from the proprietor. People who are fed up with McDonaldized motel rooms in Holiday Inn or Motel 6 can instead stay in so-called B&Bs. Finally, some analysts believe that we have moved into a new, "postmodern" society and that aspects of that society are less rational than their predecessors. Thus, for example, in a postmodern society we witness the destruction of "modern" high-rise housing projects and their replacement with smaller, more livable communities. Thus, although it is ubiquitous, McDonaldization is *not* simply another term for contemporary society. There *is* more to the contemporary world than McDonaldization.

In discussing McDonaldization, we are *not* dealing with an all-or-nothing process. Things are not either McDonaldized or not McDonaldized. There are degrees of McDonaldization; it is a continuum. Some phenomena have been heavily McDonaldized, others moderately McDonaldized, and some only slightly McDonaldized. There are some phenomena that may have escaped McDonaldization completely. Fast-food restaurants, for example, have been heavily McDonaldized, universities moderately McDonaldized, and the Mom and Pop grocers mentioned earlier only slightly McDonaldized. It is difficult to think of social phenomena that have escaped McDonaldization totally, but I suppose there is local enterprise in Fiji that has been untouched by this process. In this context, McDonaldization thus represents a process—a process by which more and more social phenomena are being McDonaldized to an increasing degree.

Overall, the central thesis is that McDonald's represents a monumentally important development and the process that it has helped spawn, McDonaldization, is engulfing more and more sectors of society and areas of the world. It has yielded a number of benefits to society, but it also entails a considerable number of costs and risks.

Although the focus is on McDonald's and McDonaldization, it is important to realize that this system has important precursors in our recent history, as will be discussed in greater detail in the next chapter. That is, McDonaldization is not something completely new, but rather its success has been based on its ability to bring together a series of earlier innovations. Among the most important precursors to McDonaldization are bureaucracy, scientific management, the assembly line, and the original McDonald brothers' hamburger stand.

Because this is a work in the social sciences, broadly defined, it is not enough to assert that McDonaldization is spreading at an alarming rate throughout society. This text must present *evidence* for that assertion. After a discussion of the precursors to McDonaldization in Chapter Two, the next four chapters provide that evidence in the context of a discussion of the four basic dimensions of rationalization—efficiency, calculability, predictability, and greater control through the replacement of human by nonhuman technology. Numerous examples are presented in each chapter of the degree to which McDonaldization has penetrated society and how that process continues at, if anything, an accelerating rate. In Chapter Seven, we turn to the fifth and paradoxical element of rationalization—the irrationality of rationality.

Though much of the book is critical of McDonaldization, it is in this chapter that we make the critique most clearly and directly. This chapter discusses a variety of irrationalities, the most important of which is the dehumanization associated with progressive rationalization.

In Chapter Eight we discuss whether we are faced inevitably with an increasingly extensive and coercive process of McDonaldization. Although the answer depends partly on how one feels about McDonaldization, the fact is that at a structural level we are likely, at least in this author's opinion, to face such a future. Given this conclusion, in the final chapter, we discuss some practical steps that can be taken to allow those who are bothered, if not enraged, by rationalization to survive in a McDonaldized world. We will see that these measures can be at least partially successful. We can, for example, force McDonald's to eliminate its worst excesses, and we can create and find nonrational niches for ourselves in an otherwise rational world. However, in the end, such measures, while making life more palatable, offer little genuine hope of overcoming the liabilities of McDonaldization or of halting its spread throughout the world.

2

McDonaldization and Its Precursors
From the Iron Cage to the Fast-Food Factory

McDonaldization did not emerge in a vacuum; it was preceded by a series of developments that not only anticipated it but also gave McDonald's many of the basic characteristics touched on in Chapter One. In other words, rationalization predates the birth of Ray Kroc's McDonald's franchises in 1955. In this chapter we look briefly at a few of them—first at the notion of bureaucracy and Max Weber's theories about it as well as the larger process of rationalization. We then look at scientific management as it was invented at the turn of the century by F.W. Taylor, Henry Ford's assembly line, the mass-produced suburban houses of Levittown, the shopping mall, and the original McDonald's founded by the McDonald brothers. These are not only of historical interest; in most cases they continue to be important to this day. Thus, in the body of this book we will return to them on numerous occasions. (The precursors to be discussed in this chapter do not exhaust the rationalized institutions that predated McDonald's. However, these precursors are the most important, at least to the understanding of McDonald's and McDonaldization.)

Bureaucratization and Rationalization: Into the Iron Cage

The roots of modern thinking on bureaucracy lie in the work of the turn-of-the-century German sociologist Max Weber. His ideas on bureaucracy were embedded in his broader theory of the rationalization process and the idea of the iron cage of rationality that emerged from it. In fact, the contemporary phenomenon that is here labeled *McDonaldization* is an extension of the Weberian theory of rationalization. To Weber, the paradigm case of the rationalization process was bureaucracy. In the modern world, while bureaucracies continue to exist and to be of great importance, it is my view that the fast-food restaurant has become the model of rationality. Weber fretted over the emerging iron cage of rationality, while I see the likelihood of a similar iron cage being created by the increasing ubiquity of the fast-food model. Weber was particularly upset by the irrationality of rationality, a concern that also lies at the heart of this book. Thus, the themes developed in this book can be seen as an effort to bring Weber's theory, developed at the turn of the twentieth century, to bear on developments that are accelerating as we approach the twenty-first century.

Weber believed (and demonstrated in his research) that the modern Western world had produced a distinctive kind of rationality that was unknown not only in its own history, but also in the history and current reality of every other part of the world. Rationality of one type or another had existed in all societies at one time or another, but none had produced the type of rationality distinctive to the modern West—what Weber called *formal rationality*. When I discuss McDonaldization, or more generally the rationalization process, it is the advance of formal rationality that I have in mind.

What is formal rationality? To Weber, *formal rationality* means that the search by people for the optimum means to a given end is shaped by rules, regulations, and larger social structures. Thus, individuals are not left to their own devices in searching for the best means of attaining a given objective. Rather, there exist rules, regulations, and structures that either predetermine or help them discover the optimum methods. Weber identified this as a major development in the history of the world: Previously, people had to discover such mechanisms on their own or with vague and general guidance from larger value systems. After the development of formal rationality, they could use rules and regulations to help them decide what to do, or, more strongly, people existed in structures that dictated what they should do. In effect, people no longer had to discover for themselves the optimum means to an end; rather, optimum means had already been discovered and were institutionalized in rules, regulations, and structures. People simply had to follow the rules, regulations, and dictates of the structure. An important aspect of rationality was that it allowed less room for individual variation in choice of means to ends. Since the choice of means was guided or even determined, virtually everyone could make the same, optimal choice.

It is in this context that Weber's focal concern with the bureau-cracy makes sense. The bureaucracy is a formally rationalized struc-ture. It (or more accurately, its top officials) develops rules and regula-tions that lead those employed in the bureaucracy to make the best choices of means to arrive at their ends. The rules and regulations are institutionalized in the bureaucracy and are utilized by contempo-raries seeking the attainment of some end.

Further, the bureaucracies themselves are structured in such a way as to guide or even to force people to choose certain optimal means to ends. For example, a given task is broken up into a variety of compo-nents and each office is made responsible for a separate portion of the larger task. Incumbents of each office handle their part of the task (usually following preset rules and regulations), often in a predeter-mined sequence. When all of the incumbents have, in order, handled the required task, the goal is attained. Furthermore, in handling the task in this way, the bureaucracy has utilized what its past history has shown to be the optimum means to the desired end.

The bureaucracy, and the formal rationality it represents so well, was a creation of the modern Western world. For Weber, it was the height of formal rationality. Weber praised bureaucracies, and more generally formal rationality, for its many advantages over other mechanisms for discovering and implementing optimum means to ends. Weber saw the same advantages (for example, speed and effi-ciency) for bureaucracies that we have outlined in Chapter One for fast-food restaurants. At the same time, Weber (like this author) was painfully aware of the problems associated with bureaucracies and for-mal rationality; in other words, he knew of the irrationalities of formally rationalized systems. Thus, Weber described bureaucracies as dehu-manizing, in much the same way and with many of the same concerns as this book describes fast-food restaurants.

Weber defined formal rationality using terms similar to those used throughout this book to describe the fast-food restaurant: efficiency, predictability, quantification, and control through the substitution of nonhuman for human technology. He also saw the irrationality of rationality as a result of the rush toward formal rationalization.

Weber viewed the bureaucracy as the paradigm case of formal rationality; as such, he saw the bureaucracy as employing the four ele-ments of formal rationality. It is the most *efficient* structure for han-dling large numbers of tasks requiring a great deal of paper work. No other structure could handle a massive quantity of work as efficiently as a bureaucracy. Weber might have used as an example the highly bureaucratized Internal Revenue Service, for no other structure could handle millions of tax returns as well.

Because of their well-entrenched rules and regulations, bureaucracies operate in a highly *predictable* manner. Incumbents of a given office know with great assurance how the incumbents of other offices will behave. They know what they will be provided with and when they will receive it. Outsiders who receive the services the bureaucracies dispense know with a high degree of confidence what they will receive and when they will receive it. Again, to use an example Weber might have used, the millions of recipients of checks from the Social Security Administration know precisely when they will receive their checks and exactly how much money they will receive.

Bureaucracies seek to *quantify* as many things as can possibly be quantified (*calculability*). The performance of the incumbents of positions within the bureaucracies is reduced to a series of quantifiable tasks. Thus, for example, let's say an IRS agent is expected to process a certain number of tax returns each day. Satisfactory performance is regarded to be the actual handling of the required number of cases. Handling less than that number is unsatisfactory; handling more is viewed as excellence. There is a problem in this kind of quantitative approach: There is little or no concern for the actual quality of the handling of each case. The employee is expected to finish the task, and little attention is paid to how well each case is handled. Thus, an IRS agent may manage large numbers of cases and, as a result, receive positive evaluations from his superiors. Yet he may actually handle the cases poorly, costing the government thousands, or even millions, of dollars in uncollected revenue. Or, the agent may handle them so quickly that the taxpayers the agent works with may be angered by the way the agent treats them.

Bureaucracies emphasize *control* over people through the replacement of human with nonhuman technology. Indeed, the bureaucracy itself may be seen as one huge nonhuman technology. Its nearly automatic functioning may be seen as an effort to replace human judgment with the dictates of rules, regulations, and structures. Employees are controlled by the division of labor, which allocates to each office a limited number of well-defined tasks. Incumbents must do those tasks, and they are not permitted to do others. Incumbents must do the tasks in the manner prescribed by the organization; they may not, in most cases, come up with idiosyncratic ways of doing those tasks. Furthermore, the idea is to reduce people to human robots or computers that make few, if any, judgments. Having reduced people to this status, it is then possible to think about actually replacing human beings with machines. This has already occurred to some extent: In many settings, computers have taken over bureaucratic tasks once performed by humans. One can imagine that once the technology has been developed and priced reasonably, robots will begin replacing humans in the office.

Similarly, the bureaucracy's clients are also controlled. They may receive only certain services and not others from the organization. (For example, the Internal Revenue Service can offer us advice on our tax returns, but not on our married lives.) They may receive those services in a certain way and not others. (For example, welfare payments are made by check; the individual cannot receive cash.)

Thus, the bureaucracy, as is the case with the fast-food restaurant, is well-defined by the four basic components of formal rationality—efficiency, predictability, quantification, and control through the substitution of nonhuman for human technology. It also suffers, as we have briefly mentioned, from the *irrationality of rationality*. The bureaucracy, like the fast-food restaurant, is a dehumanizing place in which to work and by which to be serviced. As Ronald Takaki put it, these rationalized settings are places in which "the self was placed in confinement, its emotions controlled, and its spirit subdued." In other words, they are settings in which people cannot behave as human beings, where people are dehumanized.

But the irrationalities of bureaucracies (as well as fast-food restaurants) hardly stop there. Instead of remaining efficient, bureaucracies can degenerate into inefficiency as a result of "red tape" and the other pathologies we usually associate with them. Bureaucracies often become unpredictable as employees grow unclear about what they are supposed to do and clients do not get the services they expect. The emphasis on quantification often leads to large amounts of poor-quality work. Because of these and other inadequacies, bureaucracies begin to lose control over those who work within and are served by them. Anger at the nonhuman technologies that are replacing them often lead people to undercut or sabotage the operation of these technologies. All in all, what were designed to be highly rational operations often end up growing quite irrational.

Although Weber was concerned about the irrationalities of formally rationalized systems like bureaucracies, he was even more animated by what he called the "iron cage of rationality." As mentioned earlier, these are cages in the sense that people are trapped in them and their basic humanity is denied by them. What Weber feared most was that these systems would grow more and more rational and that an accelerating number of sectors of society would come to be dominated by rational principles. Weber anticipated a society in which people would be locked into a series of rational structures, and their only mobility would be to move from one rational system to another. Thus, people would move from rationalized educational institutions to rationalized workplaces and from rationalized recreational settings to rationalized homes. There would, in effect, be no escape from rationality; society would become nothing more than a seamless web of rationalized structures.

A good example of what Weber feared is found in the contemporary rationalization of recreational activities. Recreation can be thought of as an effort to escape the rationalization of our daily lives. The nonrationalized world of recreation is an escape route from the rationalized world in which we all live. The only problem with this is that over the years the escape routes have been rationalized and have come to embody the same principles as bureaucracies and fast-food restaurants. Recreation has become yet another domain for rationalization, not an escape from it.

There are innumerable examples of the rationalization of recreational escape routes. Perhaps the best is the rationalization of today's vacations. Typically, a vacation involves an effort to flee the rationalized routines of our work lives. For those Americans who wish to escape to less rationalized European society, there is the package tour that rationalizes the process. People can efficiently see, in a rigidly controlled manner, many sights while traveling in conveyances, staying in hotels, and eating in fast-food restaurants that are predictably like those they are accustomed to at home. For those who wish to escape to the Caribbean, there are resorts such as Club Med that offer a large number of routinized activities and where one can stay in predictable settings without ever venturing out into the unpredictability of native life on a Caribbean island. For those who wish to flee back to nature within the United States, there are rationalized campgrounds where one can have little or no contact with the unpredictabilities of nature. One can even remain within one's camper and "enjoy" all of the rationalized forms of recreation available at home—TV, VCR, Nintendo, CD player. The examples are legion, but the point is that the escape routes from rationality have been rationalized. There is no way out; we do live to a large extent in what Weber called the iron cage of rationality.

Returning to bureaucracy as the model of the rationalization process, there is little question that it has spread further, and become even more firmly entrenched, than it was in Weber's day. The fast-food restaurant is part of a bureaucratic system; in fact, huge conglomerates now own many of the fast-food chains. Further, the fast-food restaurant has employed the rational principles pioneered by the bureaucracy. McDonald's has utilized bureaucratic principles, and others have been combined with them to help create the process of McDonaldization.

Scientific Management: There *Is* One Best Way

A second turn-of-the-century development that is an important precursor to McDonaldization is scientific management. (In fact, Weber at times mentions scientific management in his discussion of the rationalization process.) Scientific management was created by Frederick W. Taylor, and his ideas played a key role in shaping the work world throughout the twentieth century. Taylor developed a series of principles designed to rationalize work and was hired by a number of large organizations (for example, Bethlehem Steel) to implement those ideas. Taylor was animated by the lack of efficiency in the work world, and his principles were designed to make work more efficient. He did studies (called *time-and-motion* studies) of workers he regarded as already reasonably efficient in order to discover the best way to do a job. He broke tasks down into minute components and attempted to discover the "one best way" of doing each of them. When he felt he had discovered the best way to do a job, he selected workers and taught them to perform the work in exactly the way he prescribed.

Overall, scientific management produced a *nonhuman technology* that exerted great *control* over workers. Employers found that when workers followed Taylor's methods, they worked much more *efficiently*, everyone performed the same steps (that is, their work exhibited *predictability*), and they produced a great deal more while their pay had to be increased only slightly (*calculability*). Thus, Taylorism meant increased profits to those enterprises that adopted them.

Like all rational systems, scientific management had its *irrationalities*. Above all, it was a dehumanizing system in which people were treated like animals or mechanical robots. Furthermore, workers were required to do only one or a few things with the result that most of their skills and abilities were not used. Eventually, this had disastrous consequences as American industry was outstripped by Japanese industry, which found a way not only to be formally rational, but also to use the capabilities of its workers more fully.

Although one no longer hears about Taylor and Taylorism, his ideas have shaped the way that work, especially manual work, is performed. The fast-food restaurant has, at least implicitly, utilized Taylorism in organizing the way in which its employees work. Labor in the fast-food restaurant is highly rationalized, and the goal is the discovery of the best, the most efficient way of grilling a hamburger, frying chicken, or serving a meal. McDonald's did not invent these ideas, but rather brought them together with the principles of the bureaucracy (discussed earlier) and of the assembly line to contribute to the creation of McDonaldization.

The Assembly Line: Producing Robot-Like Workers

Like the modern bureaucracy and scientific management, the assembly line was "invented" at the dawn of the twentieth century. It was pioneered in the bureaucratized automobile industry, and the ideas of scientific management helped shape it. Henry Ford generally receives credit for its invention, although it had precursors in other industries, (such as meatpacking), and the automobile assembly line was more a product of Ford engineers (as will be discussed in Chapter Three). It was in the automobile industry, though, that the assembly line found its best-known manifestation. The assembly line represented a remarkable step forward in the rationalization of manufacturing and was employed in a large number of different types of manufacturing operations. Like bureaucracy and the fast-food restaurant, the automobile assembly line beautifully illustrates the basic elements of formal rationality.

It is an *efficient* system for manufacturing an automobile. It is far more efficient to put a large number of highly specialized, unskilled workers along a moving conveyor belt than it is to put a number of craftsmen in a room and ask them to build a car.

What each worker on the line does (for example, putting a hubcap on each passing car) is highly *predictable*, and the end product is identical to all others. The assembly line permits the *quantification* of many elements of the production process and maximizes the number of cars produced.

The assembly line permits maximum *control* over workers. Workers must do the tasks that are required of them when they are necessary. It is immediately obvious when a worker fails to perform the required task on time. (There would, for example, be a missing hubcap as the car moves down the line.) The limited time allotted for each job makes it necessary that the task be done as required. There is little or no room for innovative ways of doing a specific task. Assembly lines are nonhuman technologies that allow fewer, less-skilled people to produce cars. Furthermore, the specialization of each task permits the replacement of human workers with robots. The routine repetitive tasks required on the line are just the kind of work that robots were created to handle. Once tasks have been simplified so that they can be handled by "human robots," the stage is set for the replacement of human by nonhuman robots. We are beginning to see more and more assembly-line tasks being handled by mechanical robots.

As has been well-detailed by many observers, the assembly line carries with it much irrationality. It is clearly a dehumanizing setting in which to work. Human beings, equipped with a wide array of skills and abilities, are asked to perform a limited number of highly simplified tasks over and over. Instead of expressing their human abilities on the job, people are forced to deny their humanity and act in a robot-like manner. People do not express themselves in their work, but rather deny themselves. This is but one of many ways in which the seemingly rationalized assembly line operates in an irrational manner.

Despite its irrationalities, the assembly line had a profound influence on the development of the fast-food restaurant. The most obvious example of this is the conveyor belt used by Burger King to cook its hamburgers. Less obvious is the fact that much of the work in the fast-food restaurant is performed in assembly-line fashion with the tasks broken down into, for example, grilling the burgers, putting them on the rolls, smearing on the "special sauce," laying on the lettuce and tomato, and wrapping the fully dressed burgers. Even customers are placed on a kind of assembly line; the drive-through window is the most obvious example of this. As one observer notes, "The basic elements of the factory have obviously been introduced to the fast-food phenomenon . . . [with] the advent of the feeding machine."

It is worth noting here that the automobile assembly line made possible the mass-production of affordable automobiles. And the fact that so many people had ready access to automobiles laid the groundwork for the fast-food restaurant and McDonaldization in general. The mass availability of automobiles led to the immense expansion of the highway system and the tourist industry that grew up alongside it. Restaurants, hotels, campgrounds, gas stations, and the like arose and served as the precursors to many of the franchises that lie at the base of the McDonaldized society. The most notable predecessors were the Best Western motel chain, which was founded in 1946, Holiday Inn, which had its start in 1952, and the development of the Howard Johnson's chain in the 1920s and 1930s. By the late 1950s, there were about 500 standardized Howard Johnson's restaurants scattered around the United States, many of which had similarly standardized motels attached to them.

While Ford pioneered the rationalized assembly line, it was General Motors, especially Alfred Sloan, which further rationalized the automobile industry's bureaucratic structure. Sloan is famous for GM's multidivisional system in which long-range decisions were handled by the central office while day-to-day decisions were made by the divisions. This innovation proved so successful that it was picked up by the other automobile companies as well as by many other corporations.

Levittown: "Houses Go Up Boom, Boom, Boom"

The availability of the automobile not only helped make possible the fast-food restaurant, but also the development of suburbia, especially the highly rationalized, mass-produced houses that were pioneered by Levitt & Sons, founded by William Levitt. Between 1947 and 1951, this company built 17,447 homes on former New York potato fields, thereby creating Levittown, Long Island, and an instant community of 75,000 people. In the early 1950s, the Levitts created Levittown, Pennsylvania. In addition to highly rationalized homes, this Levittown, unlike its predecessor on Long Island, was a planned community from inception to completion. The expansion of such rationalized suburban communities provided the population base for the development of the fast-food restaurant. In fact, the denizens of these communities, as well as of the legion of more contemporary suburban developments, with their need for and access to automobiles, were and *are* a natural constituency for the fast-food restaurant.

Levitt & Sons thought of their building sites as large factories. Instead of having the product move, as on the automobile assembly line, the Levitts' product, the emerging house, was stationary, and it was the workers who moved around the building site. The workers performed specialized tasks, much like their compatriots on the automobile assembly line. Said Alfred Levitt, one of the sons, "The same man does the same thing every day, despite the psychologists. It is boring; it is bad; but the reward of the green stuff seems to alleviate the boredom of the work." Thus, the Levitts rationalized the work of the construction laborer much like Ford had done with the automobile worker, and with much the same attitude toward the worker. That is, it was recognized that rationalized work was alienating, but the worker was seen as being interested only in increased income possibilities.

In addition to the work being rationalized, the housing site was as well. In and around the locale, the Levitts constructed warehouses, woodworking shops, plumbing shops, and a sand, gravel, and cement plant. Thus, instead of buying these services and their resulting products from others and then shipping them to the construction site, the products and services existed at the site and were controlled by the Levitts. Where possible, the Levitts also used prefabricated products. However, the use of an entirely prefabricated house was deemed to be less efficient than the construction of the house at the site using some prefabricated components.

The actual construction of each house followed a series of rigidly defined and rationalized steps. For example, in constructing the wall framework, the workers did no measuring or cutting; each piece was cut to fit. A wall siding consisted of $73\frac{1}{2}$ large sheets of Colorbestos, replacing the former requirement of 570 small shingles. All houses were painted under high pressure, using the same two-tone paint—green on ivory. As a result, another of the Levitts said: "Once the groundwork is down, houses go up boom, boom, boom." The result, of course, was a large number of nearly identical houses produced quickly and at low cost.

The emphasis on quantitative factors went beyond the physical elements that went into the construction of the house. For example, when it came to selling the houses, instead of emphasizing the total cost of the house, real estate agents focused their pitches on the size of the down payment and of the monthly payments. The agents believed that the kinds of buyers attracted to Levittown were far more interested in such immediate numbers than the apparently more remote issue of the asking price for the house. Advertisements for Levittown houses stressed "the size and value of the house." In other words, Levittown, like its many successors in the march toward increasing rationalization, emphasized that the consumer was getting the most house for the least money. Similarly, today's fast-food restaurants often tell us, explicitly and implicitly, that they are offering us the most meal at the lowest cost.

There have been many critics of life in identical houses in highly rationalized communities. An early critique renamed suburbia "Disturbia," and described the suburban home as a "split level trap." However, it is possible to look more positively upon suburban rationalization. For example, many residents of Levittown have customized their homes so that they no longer look as homogenous as they once did. Other observers have found much of merit in suburbia in general and Levittown in particular. Herbert Gans, for example, concluded his study of a third Levittown built in New Jersey by arguing that "whatever its imperfections, Levittown is a good place to live." Whether or not it is a "good" place to live, Levittown is certainly a rationalized place in which to live.

Shopping Centers: "The Malling of America"

Another aspect of the rationalized society whose development was fueled by the rise of the automobile, as well as of suburban housing, was the fully enclosed shopping mall. The modern mall had precursors in the Galleria Vittorio Emanuele in Milan, Italy (completed in 1877), and the first planned outdoor shopping center in the United States built in 1916. The original fully enclosed shopping mall, however, was Southdale Center in Edina, Minnesota, which opened in 1956, not long after the opening of Kroc's first McDonald's. Today, there are almost 37,000 malls in the United States visited by about 175 million shoppers per month. The United States's largest shopping mall to date is due to open in mid-1992 down the road from Edina in Bloomington, Minnesota. It will include 4 department stores, 400 specialty shops (many of them parts of chains), and an amusement park.

As is pointed out throughout this book, shopping malls exhibit all of the basic characteristics of McDonaldization. What needs to be noted at this point, however, is that shopping malls and McDonaldized chains complement one another beautifully. On the one hand, the malls provide a predictable, uniform, *and* profitable venue for such chains. When a new mall is built, the chains line up to gain entry. On the other hand, most malls would have much unrented space and not be able to exist were it not for the chains. Thus, the malls and the chains need one another. Simultaneous products of our fast-moving automobile age, the malls and the chains feed off of one another and in the process serve to further the process of McDonaldization.

William Kowinski argues that the mall "was the culmination of all the American dreams, both decent and demented; the fulfillment, the model of the postwar paradise." One could give priority to the mall, as Kowinski does, and discuss the "malling of America." However, in my view, the fast-food restaurant is a far more powerful and influential force. Like the mall, however, McDonaldization can be seen as, in Kowinski's words, both "decent and demented."

Ray Kroc and the McDonald Brothers: Creating the "Fast-Food Factory"

Ray Kroc was the creator of the McDonald's empire and he is usually credited with developing its rational principles, but the basic McDonald's approach was created by two brothers, Mac and Dick McDonald. The McDonald brothers opened their first restaurant in Pasadena, California, in 1937. They based the restaurant on the quantifiable principles of speed, volume, and low price. In order to avoid chaos, customers were offered a highly circumscribed menu. Instead of personalized service and time-worn cooking techniques, the McDonald brothers utilized assembly-line procedures for cooking and serving food. In place of trained cooks, the brothers' "limited menu allowed them to break down food preparation into simple, repetitive tasks that could be learned quickly even by those stepping into a commercial kitchen for the first time." They pioneered the use of specialized restaurant workers such as "grill men," "shake men," "fry men," and "dressers" (those who put the "extras" on burgers and who wrapped them). They developed rules and regulations dictating what workers should do and even what they should say. In these and other ways the McDonald brothers took the lead in the development of the rationalized "fast-food factory."

Kroc did not invent the McDonald's principles, nor did he create the idea of a franchise. Franchising was pioneered by the Singer Sewing Machine company after the Civil War and was being utilized by automobile manufacturers and soft-drink companies by the turn of the twentieth century. By the 1930s, it had found its way into retail industries like Western Auto, Rexall Pharmacy, and the IGA chain of food markets.

Furthermore, there were many efforts to franchise food service before Kroc arrived on the scene in the early 1950s. The first food-service franchises were the A&W Root Beer stands, which debuted in 1924. The first Dairy Queen opened in 1944; as a result of efforts to franchise it nationally, the chain had about 2,500 outlets by 1948. Other well-known food franchises predated McDonald's. Big Boy developed in the late 1930s, and Burger King (then InstaBurger) and Kentucky Fried Chicken began in 1954. Thus, Kroc's first McDonald's, which opened on April 15, 1955, was a relative latecomer to the franchising business in general, and the food-franchise business in particular. But we are getting a bit ahead of the story.

In 1954, when Roy Kroc first visited it, McDonald's was but a single hamburger stand now in San Bernardino, California. The basic menu, approach, and even some of the techniques that McDonald's is famous for today had been created by the McDonald brothers. It was by that time a local sensation, but the McDonald brothers were content (in spite of a few halting efforts at expansion) to keep it that way; they were doing very well and had few grand ambitions (although they had taken some tentative steps toward franchising). It was Kroc who had such ambitions, and it was he who built the McDonald's empire of franchises, thereby helping to give impetus to the process of McDonaldization. At first, Kroc worked in partnership with the McDonald brothers, but he later bought them out and was then free to build the business as he wished.

It is important to reiterate that Kroc invented little that was new. Basically, he took the specific products and techniques of the McDonald brothers and combined them with the principles of other franchises (including other food-service franchises), bureaucracies, scientific management, and the assembly line. Kroc's genius was in bringing all of these well-known ideas and techniques to bear on the fast-food business and adding his ambition to turn it, through franchising, into a national, and international, business. *McDonald's and McDonaldization, then, do not represent something new, but rather the culmination of a series of rationalization processes that had been occurring throughout the twentieth century.*

Kroc's major innovation lay in the way he franchised McDonald's. For one thing, he did not permit regional franchises whereby a single franchisee was granted control over all of the outlets to be opened in a given area. Other franchisers had foundered because regional franchisees had grown too powerful and subverted the basic principles of the company. Kroc maximized central control, and thereby uniformity throughout the system, by granting franchises one at a time and rarely granting more than one franchise to a specific individual. Another of Kroc's innovations was to set the fee for a franchise at a rock-bottom $950. Other franchisers had set very high initial fees and made most of their money from them. As a result, they tended to lose interest in the continued viability of the franchisees. At McDonald's, profits did not come from high initial fees, but from the 1.9 percent of store sales that it demanded of its franchisees. Thus, the success of Kroc and his organization depended on the prosperity of the franchisees. It was this mutuality of interest that was Kroc's greatest contribution to the franchise business and a key factor in the success of McDonald's and a large number of its franchisees, many of whom became millionaires in their own right.

McDonald's was able to achieve a balance between centralized control and the independence of franchisees. Kroc was able to impose and enforce a uniform system, but the franchisees were encouraged to come up with innovations that could enhance not only their operations but also those of the system as a whole. Take the case of product innovations. Kroc himself was not a great product innovator. One of his most notorious flops was the Hulaburger, a slice of grilled pineapple surrounded by two pieces of cheese on a toasted bun. New creations, such as the fish sandwich, the Egg McMuffin, and, more generally, McDonald's breakfast meals, came from franchisees.

While not a major innovator, Kroc spearheaded a series of developments that further rationalized the fast-food business. For one thing, he (unwittingly) served as preacher and cheerleader for the principles of rationalization as he lectured "about uniformity, about a standardized menu, one size portions, same prices, same quality in every store." This uniformity allowed McDonald's to differentiate itself from its competitors, whose food was typically inconsistent. Other developments of which McDonald's was in the forefront was the imposition of a limited menu (at first ten items), tough standards on the fat content of hamburgers, the conversion to the use of frozen hamburgers and french fries, the use of inspectors to check on uniformity and conformity, the formation in 1961 of the first full-time training center in the business called Hamburger University (which offered a "degree" in "Hamburgerology"), and the publication in 1958 of an operations manual designed to spell out in detail how a franchise is to be run. That first manual laid down many of the rational principles for operating a fast-food restaurant:

> It told operators *exactly* how to draw milk shakes, grill hamburgers, and fry potatoes. It specified *precise* cooking times for all products and temperature settings for all equipment. It fixed *standard* portions on every food item, down to the *quarter ounce* of onions placed on each hamburger patty and the *thirty-two slices per pound* of cheese. It specified that french fries be cut at *nine thirty-seconds of an inch* thick. And it defined quality *controls* that were unique to food service, including the disposal of meat and potato products that were held more than *ten minutes* in a serving bin.
>
> . . . Grill men . . . were *instructed* to put hamburgers down on the grill moving from left to right, creating *six rows* of *six patties* each. And because the first two rows were farthest from the heating element, they were *instructed* (and still are) to flip the third row first, then the fourth, fifth, and sixth before flipping the first two. (Italics added.)

Conclusion

McDonald's and the process of McDonaldization did not occur in a historical vacuum; it had important precursors, predecessors that remain important to this day. These precursors provided the principles (of the assembly line, scientific management, and bureaucracy) on which the chains of fast-food restaurants were built. Furthermore, they contributed some of the structural bases needed for chains of fast-food restaurants to thrive—large numbers of factory workers and bureaucrats working great distances from their suburban dwellings, possessing automobiles to transport them not only to and from work but also to and from the fast-food restaurants they increasingly needed and desired, and visiting the shopping malls that were destined to house many of the fast-food restaurants and their rationalized derivatives.

Although the fast-food restaurant adopts elements of its predecessors, it also represents a quantum leap in the process of rationalization. While McDonaldization is a logical extension of the idea of rationalization, it is also sufficiently more extreme to legitimize the use of it as a label to describe the most contemporary aspects of this process.

Given this historical backdrop, we turn in the next five chapters to a discussion of the basic dimensions of McDonaldization—efficiency, calculability (or quantification), predictability, increased control through substitution of nonhuman for human technology, as well as the seemingly inevitable byproduct of rational systems—the irrationality of rationality. The goal of these chapters is to both define these dimensions and to illustrate, through the use of many examples, the way each is manifest not only in fast-food restaurants, but also in a wide and increasing array of social settings in the United States and throughout the world. The examples marshaled throughout the next five chapters represent the "evidence" to support the assertion that McDonaldization is sweeping through society.

3

Efficiency
Driving Through the Magic Kingdom
Munching on Finger Food

McDonald's has sought to construct highly efficient systems, and *McDonaldization* implies the search for maximum efficiency in increasingly numerous and diverse social settings. *Efficiency* means the choice of the optimum means to a given end, but this definition requires some clarification. First, although we use the term *optimum*, it is rare that the truly optimum means to an end is ever found. Rather, there is a striving to find and to use the *best possible* means. Following the economist Herbert Simon, we believe that people and organizations rarely maximize. However, the drive for efficiency implies the search for a far better means to an end than would be employed under ordinary circumstances. Second, the generality of the terms *means* and *ends* makes it clear that efficiency can be applied to innumerable means and ends. In other words, there can be a search for optimum means within settings that involve a large number of disparate ends. This means that the drive for efficiency can and does occur within a wide variety of social settings.

In a McDonaldized society, people rarely search for the best means to an end on their own. Rather, the previously discovered best possible means to innumerable ends have been institutionalized in a variety of social settings. Thus, the best means may be part of a technology, written into an organization's rules and regulations, or taught to employees in an occupational socialization process. It would be inefficient for people to be required to continually rediscover the optimum means to ends.

Although the fast-food restaurant did not create the yearning for efficiency, it has helped turn it into a near-universal desire. Many sectors of society have had to change or develop in order to operate in the efficient manner demanded by those accustomed to life in the fast lane of the fast-food restaurant. Let us look at manifestations of efficiency in an array of social institutions, bearing in mind that many of these instances cannot be traced directly to the influence of the fast-food restaurant (some of them even predate and helped shape the fast-food restaurant), but they are part of the mania for efficiency that McDonald's has played a key role in fueling.

Wireless Keyboards and Self-Service Slurpees

The emphasis of McDonaldization on efficiency implies that contrasting, nonrational systems are less-efficient, or even inefficient. The fast-food restaurant grew as a result of its greater efficiency in comparison to alternative methods of obtaining a meal. In the early 1950s, at the dawning of the era of the fast-food restaurant, the major alternative was the home-cooked meal made largely from ingredients previously purchased at various markets. This clearly was more efficient than earlier steps in obtaining a meal, such as hunting game and gathering fruits and vegetables before one could even begin to cook. By the 1950s, few Americans still foraged in the wild for the ingredients for their meals; local stores and the burgeoning supermarket were more efficient sites for obtaining food.

Of course, a series of intervening developments had increased the efficiency of home cooking. The refrigerator, freezer, and gas or electric stove were welcome technological advances. The coming of the cookbook made a major contribution to more efficient home cooking. Instead of creating a dish anew each time it was prepared, the cook could follow the recipe each time and more efficiently produce the dish.

But the home-cooked meal was, and still is, a relatively inefficient way of obtaining a meal. The restaurant has long been a more efficient alternative. But restaurants can be inefficient in that it may take several hours to go to the restaurant, consume a meal, and then return home. The desire for more efficient restaurants led to the rise of some of the ancestors of the fast-food restaurant—diners, cafeterias, and early drive-through or drive-in restaurants. The modern fast-food restaurant can be seen as being built on the latter models and as a further step in the direction of more efficient food consumption. Indeed, as we saw in Chapter Two, it was on the basis of the McDonald brothers' restaurant that Ray Kroc revolutionized the franchising of the fast-food restaurant.

Above all else, it was the efficiency of the McDonald brothers' operation that impressed Kroc, as well as the enormous profit potential of such a system if it was applied in a large number of sites. Here is how Kroc described his initial reactions to the McDonald's system:

I was fascinated by the simplicity and effectiveness of the system.
. . . Each step in producing the limited menu was stripped down to its
essence and accomplished with a minimum of effort. They sold hamburgers and cheeseburgers only. The burgers were . . . all fried the
same way.

But Kroc's obsession with efficiency predated his discovery of
McDonald's and was manifest during his earlier career, which involved
the sale of blenders to restaurants. What disturbed him in many of these
restaurants was their lack of efficiency:

There was inefficiency, waste, and temperamental cooks, sloppy service and food whose [sic] quality was never consistent. What was
needed was a simple product that moved from start to completion in a
streamlined path.

Kroc toyed with other alternatives for increasing the efficiency of
the restaurant meal before settling on the McDonald's hamburger as
a model of efficiency:

He had contemplated hot dogs, then rejected the idea. There were
too many kinds of hot dogs—hot dogs with cereal and flour, the all-
meat hot dog which is all kinds of meat, the all-beef hot dog, the
kosher hot dog. And along with the different varieties, there were all
sorts of different ways of cooking hot dogs. They could be boiled,
broiled, rotisseried, charcoaled, and on and on. Hamburgers, on the
other hand, were simplicity itself. The condiments were added to the
hamburger, not built in. And there was only one way to prepare the
hamburger—to grill it.

Kroc and his associates looked at each component of the hamburger
in order to increase the efficiency with which it could be produced
and served. For example, they started with only partially sliced buns
that were attached to one another. However, it was found that buns
could be used more efficiently if they were sliced all the way through
and separated from one another. At first, the buns arrived in cardboard
boxes and the griddle workers had to spend time opening the boxes,
separating the buns, slicing them, and discarding the left-over
paper and cardboard. In addition to separating and preslicing them,
buns were made efficient to use by having them shipped in reusable

boxes. Similar attention was devoted to the meat patty. For example, the paper between the patties had to have just the right amount of wax so that the patties would readily slide off the paper and on to the grill.

Kroc makes it clear that the goal of these kinds of refinements was greater efficiency:

> The purpose of all these refinements, and we never lost sight of it, was to make our griddle man's job easier to do quickly and well. And the other considerations of cost cutting, inventory control, and so forth were important to be sure, but they were secondary to the critical detail of what happened there at the smoking griddle. This was the vital passage of our *assembly-line*, and the product had to flow through it smoothly or the whole plant would falter. (Italics added.)

Kroc saw his entire operation as one huge assembly line and, as we have already discussed (and will discuss further below), the assembly line as it was conceived and implemented by Henry Ford was highly oriented toward improving efficiency.

The fast-food restaurant, as it eventually evolved based on the McDonald's model, is efficient from the point of view of both the diner (although, as we will see later, there are also profound inefficiencies for the consumer) and the franchise owner. Let us begin with the diners who are seeking a means to satisfy the end of filling their stomachs. Several means are available—preparing a home-cooked meal, going to a traditional restaurant, or driving to McDonald's or other fast-food restaurants. In comparing these three alternatives, it would appear that dining at McDonald's is the most efficient available means for satisfying peoples' hunger. A home-cooked meal requires a trip to the supermarket, preparation of the ingredients, cooking the food, eating it, and cleaning up afterward. A restaurant meal may be more efficient than a home-cooked meal, but it is likely that it would consume an hour or more. Dining at a fast-food restaurant eliminates all of the steps involved in a home-cooked meal *and* it takes only a fraction of the time required to eat in a traditional restaurant.

Once diners enter the fast-food restaurant, the process continues to appear to be efficient. Parking lots are adjacent to the restaurant and parking spots are readily available. It's a short walk to the counter, and although there is sometimes a line, food is usually quickly ordered, obtained, and paid for. The highly limited menu makes the choice of a meal's components quite easy. This contrasts to the many choices available in many of the alternatives to the fast-food restaurant. With the food obtained, it is but a few steps to a table and the beginning of the "dining experience." The fare almost always involves an array of finger foods (for example, Chicken McNuggets and french fries) that can be popped into the diner's mouth with the result that the entire meal is ordinarily consumed in a few minutes. Because there is little inducement to linger, the diners generally gather the leftover paper, styrofoam, and plastic, discard them in a nearby trash receptacle, and are back in their car and on their way to the next (often McDonaldized) activity.

Not too many years ago, those in charge of fast-food restaurants discovered that there was a way—the drive-through window—to make this whole process far more efficient for both themselves and the consumer. Instead of the "laborious" and "inefficient" process of parking the car, walking to the counter, waiting in line, ordering, paying, carrying the food to the table, eating, and disposing of the remnants, the drive-through window offered diners the choice of driving to the window (perhaps waiting in a line of cars), ordering, paying, and driving off with the meal. It was even possible to engage in the highly efficient act of eating while driving, thereby eliminating the need to devote a separate time period to dining. The drive-through window is also efficient from the perspective of the fast-food restaurant. As more and more people use the drive-through window, fewer parking spaces, tables, and employees are needed. Further, consumers take their debris with them as they drive away, thereby eliminating the need for additional trash receptacles and employees to periodically empty those receptacles.

Modern technology is bringing with it further advances in efficiency in the fast-food restaurant. Here is a description of some of the recent progress in efficiency offered by Taco Bell in one of its California outlets:

> Inside, diners in a hurry for tacos and burritos can punch up their own orders on a touch-screen computer.
>
> Outside, drive-through customers see a video monitor flash back a list of their orders to avoid mistakes. They then can pay using a pneumatic-tube like those many banks employ for drive-up transactions. Their food, and their change, is waiting for them when they pull forward to the pickup window. And if the line of cars grows too long, a Taco Bell worker will wade in with a wireless keyboard to take orders.

Another efficient aspect of the fast-food restaurant is the nature of the food served. As was pointed out above, fast-food restaurants serve finger food, food that can be held in one's hand and eaten without utensils. Hamburgers, french fries, fried chicken, slices of pizza, tacos—the staples of the fast-food business—are all finger foods. What is interesting here are the innovations over the years that have greatly increased the number and types of finger foods available to the consumer of fast foods. The Egg McMuffin is basically an entire breakfast—egg, Canadian bacon, English muffin—combined into one handy sandwich that can be eaten quickly, easily, and without utensils. It is far more efficient to devour such a sandwich than to sit down with knife and fork and eat a plate full of eggs, bacon, and toast. The Chicken McNugget is perhaps the ultimate finger food, and its creation reflects the fact that the chicken is pretty inefficient as far as McDonald's is concerned. The bones, gristle, and skin of the chicken are barriers to efficient consumption, and all have been eliminated in the Chicken McNugget. (Were they able to, the mass purveyors of chicken, for example, Perdue, would breed a more efficiently consumed chicken free of bones, gristle, and skin. They already have McDonaldized the process of breeding, raising, and slaughtering chickens [see Chapter Six].) The customer is presented with several bite-size morsels of fried chicken that can be readily popped into one's mouth using one hand while the other hand can be used to steer the car in the direction of the next stop on the day's itinerary. McDonald's also offers an apple pie which, because it is completely encased in dough, can be munched like a sandwich.

From the point of view of the fast-food restaurant, efficiency is also built into the preparation and delivery of foods. The limited number of menu items allows for highly efficient ordering of supplies and food delivery. Food is often prepared on a kind of assembly line involving a number of people in specialized operations (for example, the burger "dresser").

The ultimate application of the assembly line to the fast-food process is Burger King's conveyor belt: A raw, frozen hamburger is placed on one end, it is moved slowly by the conveyor under a flame, and emerges in about 94 seconds on the other end fully cooked. (Henry Ford would be proud to know the ways in which his assembly line has been utilized.) Similar techniques are employed to prepare and serve food at Dunkin' Donuts, Kentucky Fried Chicken (if you want spicy

Cajun fried chicken you must wheel on down the road to Popeye's), Taco Bell, and Pizza Hut. A newer and even more specialized fast-food outlet is Cinnabon, which has perfected the techniques needed to mass produce and serve cinnamon buns.

It needs to be said, however, that what is efficient from the perspective of the fast-food restaurant is often inefficient from the viewpoint of the consumer. For example, it is efficient for the fast-food restaurant to set up a system whereby the consumer, either on foot or in a car, waits in line, but waiting in line is inefficient from the consumer's perspective. For another, it is efficient as far as the fast-food restaurant is concerned to have the diner do much of the work that is done by employees in a traditional restaurant, but is this efficient given the consumer's interest? Is it efficient to order one's own food rather than having a waiter do it? Or to bus one's own paper, plastic, and styrofoam rather than having it done by a busperson?

Some fast-food restaurants have also pioneered the movement toward handing the consumer little more than the basics of the meal. In a number of fast-food restaurants, including Hardee's, the consumer is expected to take the naked burger to the "fixin' bar" and there turn it into the desired sandwich by adding such things as lettuce, tomatoes, and onions. In such cases, we are expected to log a few minutes a week as sandwich makers. In a more recent innovation in Burger King and some other franchises, we are handed an empty cup and expected to go to the fountain and fill our glasses with ice and a soft drink, thereby spending a few moments as what used to be called a "soda jerk." As we saw in the case of Taco Bell, in some ultramodern fast-food restaurants, people are met by computer screens when they enter, and they must punch in their own orders. In these and other ways, the fast-food restaurant has grown more efficient at the expense of imposing inefficiency on the consumer.

The salad bar is a classic example of putting the consumer to work. The customer "buys" an empty plate and then ambles on over to the salad bar to load up on the array of vegetables (and other foods) available that day. Quickly seeing the merit in this, many supermarkets have now instituted their own salad bars with a more elaborate array of alternative foods available to the consumer. The salad lover can now work as a salad chef at lunch hour in the fast-food restaurant and then do it all over again in the evening at the supermarket in making the salad for the evening meal. All of this is very efficient from the perspective of the fast-food restaurant and the supermarket, since only a very small number of employees are needed to keep the various compartments well-stocked.

Of course, the fast-food restaurant did not create the idea of imposing work on the consumer, causing the consumer to be what is, in effect, an unpaid employee, but it institutionalized and expedited this development. There are many other examples of the process of imposing work on the consumer. The old-time grocery store, where the grocer retrieved the needed items, has been replaced by the supermarket, where the shopper may put in several hours a week "working" as a grocery clerk seeking out wanted (and unwanted) items during lengthy treks down seemingly interminable aisles. Having obtained the groceries, the shopper then unloads the food at the checkout counter and, in some cases, even bags the groceries. This is all efficient from the point of view of the supermarket, but it is clearly inefficient from the perspective of the shopper.

Virtually gone are gas station attendants who filled gas tanks, checked the oil, and cleaned windows; we all now put in a few minutes a week as unpaid gas station attendants. Furthermore, instead of having a readily available attendant to pay for the gasoline we buy, we must trek into the station, or up to the kiosk, to pay for our gas. Indeed, in many stations we must pay first, return to pump our gas, and if we haven't pumped as much gas as we expected, trek back to the kiosk to get our change. In the latest "advance" in this realm, customers put their credit cards into a slot and pump the gas; their account is automatically charged the correct amount (they hope) for the gas pumped, and, finally, the receipt and the card are retrieved with no contact with, or work done by, anyone working in the gas station.

The latter development was pioneered in the banking industry with the advent of the automated teller machine, which allows us all to work, for at least a few moments, as unpaid bank tellers (and often pay fees for the privilege). The phone companies now make us put in a few minutes a day as operators. Instead of asking a long-distance operator to make our calls, we are urged to dial such calls ourselves, thereby requiring us to keep lengthy lists of phone numbers and area codes. Another such effort by the phone companies involves having us look up numbers in the phone book rather than calling an operator for information. For those who do still use the operator for such information, there is now likely to be a fairly hefty charge for the service. In some doctors' offices, we are now being asked to weigh ourselves and take our own temperatures. Instead of being interviewed by the government census taker, we are now likely to receive a questionnaire in the mail that we are expected to fill out on our own.

In calling many businesses these days, instead of dealing with a human operator who makes the desired connection for us, we must deal with "voice mail" and follow a series of instructions from a computer voice by pushing a bewildering array of numbers and codes before we get, one hopes, to the desired extension. Here is the way one humorist describes such a "conversation" and the work involved for the caller:

> The party you are trying to reach—Thomas Watson—is unavailable at this time. To leave a message, please wait for the beep. To review your message, press 7. To change your message after reviewing it, press 4. To add to your message, press 5. To reach another party, press the star sign and enter the four-digit extension. To listen to Muzak, press 23. To transfer out of phone mail in what I promise you will be a futile effort to reach a human, press 0—because we treat you like one.

The postal service has us do some of its work by pressing us to know and use increasingly lengthy zip codes. The post office is also relying on more and more automated technologies to sort mail. However, the technology breaks down when an address is not clearly written on the envelope. Thus, the postal service is now asking people to do more than just write clearly; it is now asking us to type addresses on envelopes.

Many of these examples of institutions putting the customer to work may seem trivial, and in many cases they are. Clearly, it is not highly burdensome to write a zip code on an envelope or to look up a telephone number. But when one considers the totality of these various activities, one realizes that a wide-ranging development is taking place. The modern consumer is spending a not insignificant, and increasing, amount of time and energy doing unpaid labor in and for a number of different organizations.

Another positive aspect of efficiency from the point of view of the fast-food restaurant that often operates to the detriment of the diner is the limited number of available choices and options. McDonald's does not serve pizza and Taco Bell does not offer fried chicken. Fast-food restaurants (in spite of what they tell us) are far from not only full-serve restaurants but also the old cafeterias that offered a vast array of different types of foods.

Once in the fast-food restaurant, pity the consumer who has a special request. The fast-food advertisement that used to say "we do it your way" reminds one of Henry Ford's famous statement: "Any customer can have a car painted any color that he wants so long as it is black." The last thing that fast-food restaurants want to do is to do it your way. In fact, much of their efficiency stems from the fact that they virtually always do it one way—*their* way! The typical hamburger is usually so thin that it can only be cooked one way—well done. Bigger burgers (the McDonald's Quarter-Pounder, for example) can be prepared rare, but the fast-food restaurant prefers, for the sake of efficiency, that they all be cooked one way. Customers with the temerity to ask for a rare burger, well-browned fries, or a soft drink without ice, are likely to cool their heels for a long time waiting for such "exotica." Few customers are willing to do this because it defeats one of the main purposes of going to a fast-food restaurant—efficiency.

Many other businesses have adopted the idea of offering the consumer a limited number of choices and options. AAMCO Transmissions works mainly on transmissions and Midas Muffler largely restricts itself to the installation of mufflers. H&R Block does simple tax returns and is undoubtedly not the best place to have complicated tax returns completed. Nor does it offer the full array of tax and financial services available from a CPA. "McDentists" may be relied on for simple dental procedures, but one would be ill-advised to have root canal work done there. Pearle Vision Centers offer eye examinations, but one should go to an eye doctor with any major vision problem.

Of course, the employment of consumers as unpaid workers and the offering of highly limited options are far from the only aspects of the fast-food model adopted by other sectors of society. Banks, for example, have instituted the drive-through window as a way of increasing the efficiency of banking from both the consumer's and the banker's perspectives. Photo processors have often been reduced to drive-by kiosks that merely receive the film and then send it off to a central location for development.

Seven-Eleven and its clones have become drive-up, if not drive-through, mini-supermarkets. For those in need of only a few items, it is far more efficient (albeit much more costly) to pull up to a Seven-Eleven and make the needed purchases. No need to park in a large lot, obtain a cart, wheel through myriad extraneous aisles in search of needed items, wait in lines at the check-out counter, and then tote one's purchases back to a sometimes distant car. At Seven-Eleven, the consumer can park right in front and quickly find an array—albeit thin and over-priced—of goods. Not only can one purchase a loaf of bread and a quart of milk, but also hot coffee ("efficiently" poured and prepared by the consumers themselves), a hot lunch (usually a hot dog or a [self-] microwaved sandwich), a cold soda (with consumers serving themselves), a Slurpee (now also self-serve), aspirin, cigarettes, a newspaper, even a video. While the fast-food restaurant moved in the direction of offering a highly circumscribed menu, Seven-Eleven has sought to cram its little shops with a wide array of commonly wanted and needed food and other goods. From the point of view of Seven-Eleven, efficiency stems from the fact that ordinarily only one brand of each item is offered for sale and many items are unobtainable. For greater selection or unstocked goods the consumer must go to the comparatively inefficient supermarket.

Thus, there is more than one way to make operations efficient, but efficiency remains the common theme that unifies the various components of the McDonaldized world. As we will see, in other rationalized settings (for example, a supermarket or a shopping mall) efficiency involves a large number of options.

"Home-Made" Fast Food and the StairMaster

Given the efficiency of the fast-food restaurant, the home kitchen has had to grow more efficient or it might have faced total extinction. Had the kitchen not grown more efficient, a comedian could have envisioned a time when the kitchen would have been replaced by a large, comfortable telephone lounge used for calling Domino's for pizza delivery. The key to the salvation of the kitchen was the development and widespread adoption of the microwave oven. The microwave is simply a far more efficient means than its major alternative, the convection oven, for preparing a meal. It is usually faster than the old oven and one can prepare a wider array of foods in it than the old-fashioned oven. Perhaps most importantly from the point of view of this chapter, it spawned the development of a number of microwavable foods (including soup, pizza, hamburgers, fried chicken, french fries, and popcorn) that permit the efficient preparation of the fare one usually finds in fast-food restaurants. For example, one of the first microwavable foods produced by Hormel was an array of biscuit-based breakfast sandwiches "popularized in recent years by many of the fast-food chains," most notably

McDonald's and its Egg McMuffin. Banquet rushed to market with microwavable chicken breast nuggets. In fact, many food companies now employ people who continually scout fast-food restaurants for new ideas for foods that can be marketed for the home. As one executive put it, "Instead of having a breakfast sandwich at McDonald's, you can pick one up from the freezer of your grocery store." As a result, one can now, in effect, enjoy fast foods at home without venturing out to the fast-food restaurant. Indeed, the efficiency of "home-made" fast foods would, at least in some ways, *seem* to be greater than that afforded by the fast-food restaurant. Instead of getting into one's car, driving to (and perhaps through) the restaurant, and then returning home, one need only pop the desired foods in the microwave. On the other side, the efficiency of the home-microwaved meal suffers because it requires a prior trip to the market to purchase the microwavable foods.

This leads to the point that people ordinarily do not employ a precise calculation in deciding which things are more or less efficient than others. A general perception develops that some things are efficient (for example, a fast-food restaurant, a microwave dinner) and others are not (such as a multi-course dinner at a traditional restaurant or a home-cooked meal using an old-fashioned oven). People in a McDonaldized society tend toward activities in the efficient category and away from those that are deemed inefficient. Little differentiation is made among those things thought to be efficient. This helps to account for the fact that in spite of its greater efficiency, the home-cooked microwave meal has not cut appreciably into the business done by fast-food restaurants. (In fact, it could be argued that such meals have contributed to the overall attraction of the efficiency of fast-food restaurants and the kinds of food they serve. That is because microwaved meals are part of the process of McDonaldization and contribute to its spread.)

Another factor in the continued success of the fast-food restaurant is that it has many advantages over the "home-cooked" microwave dinner. For example, a trip to the fast-food restaurant offers people a dinner out rather than just another meal at home. For another, as Stan Luxenberg has pointed out in *Roadside Empires*, McDonald's offers more than an efficient meal, it offers fun—brightly lit, colorful, and attractive settings, garish packaging, special inducements to children, give-aways, contests—in short, it offers a kind of carnival-like atmosphere in which to buy and consume fast food. Thus, faced with the choice of an efficient meal at home or one in a fast-food restaurant, many people are still likely to choose the fast-food restaurant because it not only offers efficiency but a range of other rewards.

The microwave oven (as well as the range of products it spawned) is but one of many contributors to the increasing efficiency of home cooking. Among other obvious technological advances are the replacement of the hand beater by the electric beater; slicers, dicers, and even knives by the Cuisinart; and the presence of either stand-alone freezers or those that are an integral part of the refrigerator.

The large freezer has permitted a range of efficiencies, such as a few trips to the market for enormous purchases rather than many trips for small purchases. It has permitted the storage of a wide range of ingredients that can be readily extracted when needed for food preparation. It has allowed for the cooking of large portions which can then be divided up, frozen, and defrosted periodically for dinner. The widespread availability of the home freezer led to the expansion of the production of frozen foods of all types. The most notable frozen food from the point of view of efficiency is the "TV dinner." People can stock their freezers with an array of such dinners (for example, Chinese, Italian, and Mexican dinners as well a wide variety of "American" cooking) and quite readily bring them out and pop them into the oven, sometimes even the microwave. (More recently this has become comparatively inefficient with the advent of microwavable meals that can be stored on the shelves of one's pantry.)

Still another recent competitor for the most efficient meal at home is the fully-cooked meal consumers may now buy at the supermarket. One may merely stop at the market on the way home and purchase all of the courses for a meal. A meal is "prepared" by unwrapping the packages; no cooking is required at all.

Supermarkets have long been loaded with other kinds of products that increase efficiency for those who want to continue to "cook" at home. Instead of starting from "scratch," the cook can utilize prepackaged mixes to make an array of "home-made" foods—cakes, pies, pancakes, and waffles. No need to endlessly stir hot cereal; it can be made by simply pouring boiling water over the contents of a premeasured packet. We no longer need to cook pudding from scratch, or even use the more efficient instant mixes; we can now purchase already made pudding in the dairy case of our supermarket.

The McDonaldization of food preparation and consumption has been extended to the booming diet industry. Diet books promising all sorts of efficient short cuts to weight loss are often at the top of the best-seller lists. Losing weight is normally difficult and time-consuming, hence the lure of various diet books that promise to make weight loss easier and quicker, that is, more efficient.

For those on a diet, and many people are on more or less perpetual diets, the preparation of low-calorie food has been made more efficient. Instead of needing to cook diet foods from scratch, they may now purchase an array of prepared diet foods in frozen and/or microwavable form. For those who do not wish to go through the inefficient process of eating these diet meals, there are the diet shakes, like Slim•Fast, that can be mixed and consumed in a matter of seconds.

A fairly recent development is the growth of diet centers like Nutri/System and Jenny Craig. Nutri/System sells dieters, at substantial cost, prepackaged freeze-dried food. All the dieter need do is add water when it is time for the next meal. Freeze-dried foods are not only efficient for the dieter but also for Nutri/System, because they can be efficiently packaged, transported, and stored. Furthermore, the dieter's periodic visit to a Nutri/System center is efficiently organized. A counselor is allotted ten minutes with each client. During that brief time the counselor takes the client's weight, blood pressure, and measurements, asks routine questions, fills out a chart, and devotes some time to "problem-solving." If the session extends beyond the allotted ten minutes and other clients are waiting, the receptionist will buzz the counselor's room. Counselors learn their techniques at Nutri/System University where, after a week of training (no inefficient years of matriculation here), they earn certification and an NSU diploma.

There is a strong emphasis on efficiency in modern health clubs, including such chains as Holiday Spas. These clubs often offer, under one roof, virtually everything needed to lose weight and stay in shape, including a wide array of exercise machines, as well as a running track and a swimming pool. The exercise machines are highly specialized so that one may efficiently increase fitness in specific areas of the body. Thus, working out on running machines and the StairMaster—one kind of exercise machine—increases cardiovascular fitness, whereas using various weightlifting machines increases strength and muscularity in targeted areas of the body. Another efficiency associated with many of these machines is that one can do other things while exercising. Thus, many clubs have television sets throughout the gym allowing people to both watch television and exercise. The exerciser can also read, listen to music, or even listen to a book-on-tape while working out. The exercise machines also offer a high degree of calculability, with many of them registering miles run, level of difficulty, and calories burned. All of this in the kind of clean, sterile environment we have come to associate with McDonaldization.

"Selling Machines" and L.L. Bean

Shopping has also grown more efficient. The department store obviously is a more efficient place in which to shop than a series of specialty shops dispersed throughout the city or suburbs. The shopping mall increases efficiency by bringing a wide range of department stores and specialty shops under one roof. Kowinski describes the mall as "an extremely efficient and effective selling machine." It is cost-efficient for retailers because it is the collection of shops and department stores ("mall synergy") that brings in throngs of people. And it is efficient for consumers because in one stop they can visit numerous shops, have lunch at a "food court" (likely populated by many fast-food chains), see a movie, have a drink, and go to an exercise or diet center.

The drive for shopping efficiency did not end with the malls. In recent years, there has been a great increase in catalogue sales (via L.L. Bean, Land's End, and other mail-order companies), which enables people to shop while never leaving the comfort of their homes. Still more efficient, although it may require many hours in front of the tube, is home television shopping. A range of products are paraded in front of viewers who may simply phone each time a product catches their eye and conveniently charge their purchases to their credit card accounts. The latest advance in home shopping is the "scanfone," an at-home phone machine that includes "a pen-sized bar-code scanner, a credit card magnetic-strip reader, and a key pad." The customer merely "scans items from a bar-coded catalogue and also scans delivery dates and payment methods. The orders are then electronically relayed to the various stores, businesses, and banks involved." Some mall operators fear that they will ultimately be put out of business because of the greater efficiency of shopping at home.

Video Rentals, Package Tours, "The Magic Kingdom," and Domed Stadiums

With the advent of video tapes and video-rental stores, many people no longer deem it efficient to drive to their local theater to see a movie. Movies can now be viewed, often more than one at a sitting, in one's own den. For those who wish even greater efficiency, viewers can buy one of the new television sets that enables viewers to see a movie while also watching a favorite television program on an inset on the television screen.

The largest video rental franchise in the United States is Blockbuster, which, predictably, "considers itself the McDonald's of the video business." Blockbuster has more than 2,000 outlets, and its growth is reflected in the fact that its profits rose 36 percent in 1991. However, there may already be signs that Blockbuster is in danger of being replaced by even more efficient alternatives. One is pay-per-view movies offered by many cable companies. Instead of trekking to the video store, all one need do is turn to the proper channel and phone the cable company. Another, experimental alternative is an effort by GTE to deliver movies to one's home through fiber-optic cables. Just as the video store replaced many movie theaters, video stores themselves may soon be displaced by even more efficient alternatives.

As was briefly mentioned in Chapter Two, travel to exotic foreign locales has also grown more efficient. The best example of this is the package tour. Let us take, for example, a 30-day tour of Europe. To make these efficient, only the major locales in Europe are visited. Within each of these locales, the tourist is directed toward the major sights. (In Paris, the tour would definitely stop at the Louvre, but perhaps not at the Rodin Museum.) Because the goal is to see as many of the major sights as possible in a short period of time, the emphasis is on the efficient transportation of people to, through, and from each of them. Buses hurtle to and through the city, allowing the tourist to glimpse the maximum number of sights in the time allowed. At particularly interesting or important sights, the bus may slow down or even stop to permit some picture-taking. At the most important locales, a brief stopover is planned; there the visitor can hurry through the site, take a few pictures, buy a souvenir, and then hop back on the bus to head to the next attraction.

There is no question that this is a highly efficient way of seeing the major tourist attractions of Europe. Indeed, the package tour can be seen as a vast people-moving mechanism that permits the efficient transport of people from one locale to another. If tourists attempted to see the major sights of Europe on their own, it would take more time to see the same things and the expense would be greater. There are, of course, costs associated with the package tour (for example, does the tourist ever really have time to experience Europe?), as there are with every other highly rational system, but we will reserve a discussion of them for later in the book.

The idea of efficient people-moving mechanisms is clearly tied to the fast-food restaurant, which has pioneered efforts to maximize the flow of people to, through, and out of the restaurant. New heights in people-moving have been reached by modern amusement parks, particularly Disneyland and Walt Disney World. At Disney World and Epcot Center in Florida, for example, a vast highway and road system funnels many thousands of cars each day into the appropriate parking lots. Once the driver has been led to a parking spot (often with the help of information broadcast over the car radio), jitneys are waiting, or soon will arrive, to whisk family members to the gates of the park. Once in the park, visitors find themselves on what is, in effect, a vast (albeit not self-propelled) conveyor belt which leads them from one ride or attraction to another. One may get off the larger "conveyor system" to enter one of the local systems that move people to a particular attraction. Once the attractions themselves are reached, the visitors find themselves on one conveyance or another (cars, boats, submarines, planes, rocket ships, or moving walkways) that moves them through and out of the attractions as rapidly as possible. The speed with which one moves through each attraction enhances the experience and reduces the likelihood that one will question the "reality" of what one sees. In fact, one is often not quite sure what one has witnessed, although it "seems" exciting. The entire system is set up to move large numbers of people through the entire park as efficiently as possible. Of course, Disney World has been victimized by its own success, and even its highly efficient systems cannot handle the hordes that descend on the park each day. Thus, visitors still must face long lines at many of the most popular attractions. The waits would be far longer were it not for the efficiency with which Disney World processes people.

People are not the only thing that Disney World must process efficiently. Let us note just one other example of this efficiency—trash disposal. The throngs that frequent such amusement parks eat a great deal (mostly fast finger foods) and, as a result, generate an enormous amount of trash. Snack bars and restaurants are dispersed throughout the park and virtually everything they dispense is wrapped in some kind of disposable paper, foil, or plastic wrap. If Disney World relied simply on trash receptacles that were emptied at the end of each day, the barrels would quickly overflow and the ground would be littered with debris. To prevent this (and it must be prevented since cleanliness is a key component of the McDonaldized world in general and Disney World in particular), hordes of employees constantly sweep, collect, and empty trash. Advanced technology has also been employed to efficiently dispose of the mountains of garbage. Disney World employs an elaborate system of underground tubes. Receptacles are emptied and the garbage is fed into this tube system, where it is whisked away at about 60 miles per hour to a central trash disposal plant far from the view of visitors. The trash magically disappears; Disney World is a magic kingdom in more ways than one.

Thus, in various ways, the modern amusement park is a highly efficient place, especially in comparison to its ancestors, such as county fairs and Coney Island. Here is the way one observer describes another of the modern, highly rational amusement parks—Busch Gardens:

> Gone is the dusty midway, the cold seduction of a carnie's voice, the garish, gaudy excitement and all the harsh promise evoked by a thousand yellow lights winking in darkness. In its place is a vast, self-contained environment, as complex as a small city and endowed with the kind of *efficiency* beyond the reach of most cities of any size. (Italics added.)

The new athletic stadiums that have been built in the United States in recent years have also focused on the efficient movement of people. The new stadiums tend to be built with easy access to and from highways. Huge parking lots are adjacent to the stadiums. Elaborate systems of ramps and escalators move people in and out of them. But people-moving is not the only form of efficiency found in modern stadiums. In baseball, a rain-out is a highly inefficient (to say nothing of costly) event; a game that may have been begun must be played over again. To eliminate inefficient rain-outs, some stadiums have been built with domes, while in some nondomed stadiums, rain-outs have been reduced by the replacement of grass (which when rain-soaked could become unplayable) with artificial turf, which drains far more readily.

Assembly-Line Medicine and "McDoctors"

An institution that one might assume to be immune to this drive for efficiency, and rationalization more generally, is modern medicine. However, we have seen considerable movement in the direction of greater efficiency and rationality in medicine. In fact, in a few instances we now can find instances of what may be termed "assembly-line medicine." One example is Dr. Denton Cooley (his "fetish is efficiency") who performs delicate open-heart surgery in a "heart surgery factory" that operates "with the precision of an assembly-line." Even more striking is the following description of the Moscow Research Institute of Eye Microsurgery:

> In many ways the scene resembles any modern factory. A conveyor glides silently past five work stations, periodically stopping, then starting again. Each station is staffed by an attendant in a sterile mask and smock. The workers have just three minutes to complete their tasks before the conveyor moves on; they turn out 20 finished pieces in an hour.
>
> Nearly everything else about the assembly line, however, is highly unusual: the workers are eye surgeons, and the conveyor carries human beings on stretchers. This is . . . where the production methods of Henry Ford are applied to the practice of medicine . . . a "medical factory for the production of people with good eyesight."

Such assembly lines are not yet the norm in medicine in the United States (or Russia), yet one can imagine that they will grow increasingly common in the coming years.

A variety of factors are impelling the medical profession in the direction of becoming more efficient, or more systematically finding the optimum means to the end of providing medical services. One key factor in increasing efficiency within medicine is the rise of investor-owned corporations (for example, Humana Inc. and Hospital Corporation of America) that are interested in medicine as a profit-making venture. In their efforts to maximize profits, these institutions and their professional managers seek to make operations as efficient as possible. Because of the need to be competitive, the emphasis on efficiency in for-profit organizations is likely to carry over into nonprofit medical organizations.

Pressure from the federal government and third-party payers such as insurance companies (for example, Blue Cross-Blue Shield) to reduce costs is forcing medicine to streamline its activities. There is great pressure to do fewer things (for example, to eliminate unnecessary tests and surgical procedures) and to speed up those things that are done. In addition, more procedures are being done on an outpatient basis. Thus, instead of hospitalizing a patient for a day or two for a few tests or a minor surgical procedure, increasingly, tests or procedures are being performed during brief day trips to the hospital. The federal government, through Medicare, has implemented the prospective payment and DRG (Diagnostic Related Groups) programs, in which a set amount is reimbursed to hospitals for a given medical diagnosis, no matter how long the patient is hospitalized. This replaces the system wherein the government paid whatever "reasonable" amount it was billed. The result is that instead of a leisurely stay in a hospital and a lengthy course of treatment, medical personnel are being pushed to streamline their operations. Because the amounts paid are fixed, it behooves medical personnel to get patients in and out of hospitals as efficiently as possible.

Another factor in introducing efficiencies to medicine is the increase in competition. This was given impetus by a 1975 Supreme Court decision, which declared that physicians are subject to the Sherman Antitrust Act, and a succeeding series of successful antitrust suits filed by the Federal Trade Commission against the medical profession's anti-competitive practices. The American Medical Association (AMA) had long sought to restrict competition through its code of ethics. The successful antitrust suits have led to a reduction in these restrictions, an increase in competition, and, as a result, pressure on physicians to seek ways of becoming more efficient in order to compete successfully within the medical marketplace. Also contributing to this change were the procompetitive policies of the Reagan administration in the 1980s. Still another factor fueling increased competition, and therefore greater efficiency, in medicine is the increasing number of physicians. The substantial growth in the medical profession was encouraged, at least in part, by the Health Professions Educational Assistance Act of 1963.

Still another factor is the expansion of medical bureaucracies with their inherent interest in efficiency. Hospitals, medical conglomerates, chains, health maintenance organizations (HMOs), third-party payers, and the government are all, or can be, huge bureaucratic systems. These bureaucracies, indeed all bureaucracies, are constructed for the efficient handling of large quantities of work. Physicians are likely to be pushed in the direction of greater efficiency to the degree that they are employed in, or affected by, these bureaucracies.

Beyond bureaucracies, many modern medical technologies have served to make the practice of medicine more efficient. Just to take one of many examples, laser technology has greatly increased the efficiency of performing highly delicate eye operations.

Perhaps the best example of the increasing efficiency of medical practice in the United States *and* of the pervasive influence of McDonaldization is the growth of walk-in/walk-out surgical or emergency centers. These so-called "McDoctors" or "Docs-in-the-Box" are designed for patients who want medical problems handled with maximum efficiency. Each center handles only a limited number of minor problems, but those that are dealt with are done with great dispatch. Although the patient with a laceration cannot be stitched as efficiently as a customer in search of a hamburger can be served, many of the same principles can be applied to the two operations. In any case, it is more efficient for the patient to be able to walk in without an appointment than it is to make an appointment with a regular physician and then wait until that time arrives. If one has a minor emergency (for example, a minor laceration), it is more efficient to walk through a "McDoctors" than it is to work one's way through the labyrinth of the emergency room of a large hospital. (Hospitals, after all, are set up to handle much more serious problems for which efficiency is not [yet] the norm [although there is movement in that direction with the employment of specialized emergency-room physicians and teams of medical personnel].)

From the organization's point of view, a "McDoctors" can be run more efficiently than a hospital emergency room. "Docs-in-the-Box" also can be more efficient than private doctor's offices because, for one thing, they are not structured to permit the kind of personal (and therefore inefficient) attention patients expect from their private physicians.

Customized Textbooks, Books-on-Tape, "News McNuggets," and Drive-In Churches

Turning to the educational system, specifically the university, one manifestation of the pressure for greater efficiency is the machine-graded, multiple-choice examination. In a much earlier era, students were examined on a one-to-one basis by their professors. This may have been a very good way of finding out what students knew, but it was (and is) highly labor-intensive and inefficient. Later, the essay examination became very popular. While grading a set of essays was more efficient from the professor's perspective than giving individual oral examinations, it was still relatively inefficient and time-consuming. Enter the multiple-choice examination, the grading of which was a snap in comparison to giving oral tests or reading essays. In fact, the grading could be passed on to graduate assistants, an act that was very efficient for the professor. Now we have computer-graded examinations that maximize efficiency of evaluation for both professors and graduate assistants.

The multiple-choice examination still left the professor saddled with the inefficient task of composing the necessary sets of questions. Furthermore, at least some of the questions had to be changed each semester because new students were likely to gain possession of old exams. The solution: Textbook companies provided professors with books (free of charge) full of multiple-choice questions to go along with the textbooks required for use in large classes. Professors no longer had to make up their own questions; they could use those provided by the publisher. However, the professor still had to retype the questions or to have them retyped by the office staff. Recently, however, publishers have been kind enough to provide their sets of questions on computer disks. Now all the professor needs to do is select the desired questions and let the printer do the rest. With these great advances in efficiency, professors now have very little to do with the entire examination process, from question composition to grading.

Publishers have provided other services to make teaching more efficient for those professors who adopt their textbooks. With the adoption of a textbook, a professor may receive many materials with which to fill class hours—lecture outlines, computer simulations, discussion questions, video tapes, movies, even ideas for guest lecturers and student projects. With luck, professors can use all of these devices and do little or nothing on their own for their classes. Needless to say, this is a highly efficient means of teaching from a professor's perspective, and it frees up valuable time for the much more valued activities (by professors, but not students) of writing and research.

Most colleges and universities, and especially primary and secondary schools, are highly bureaucratized. In Chapter Two, we saw that bureaucracy was the model of rationalization in general, and efficiency in particular. Although bureaucracy has in our view been replaced by McDonald's as the model of rationalization, it remains a structure designed to efficiently handle large amounts of work. While the amusement park can be seen as a people-moving machine, bureaucracy can be viewed as a mechanism for the efficient movement of paper and, more recently, computer-generated information. This is the case in educational bureaucracies, but it is also true of bureaucracies in a wide array of social institutions.

In the realm of publishing, this author has been involved in an excellent example of modern efficiency—custom publishing. In a customized textbook, the publisher recruits a wide range of authors to write chapters on specific topics. The professor who is interested in adopting the book for class use is provided with a list of the available chapters. The professor may choose any subset of the chapters, which can be put together in the order that the professor wishes. A customized book is produced, and the number required for the professor's class is printed. This development has been made possible by the advent of new computer technology as well as ultra high-speed printers.

Customized textbooks are more efficient than their predecessors in at least two senses. First, it is far more efficient to have a wide range of experts write single chapters than to have a single author write them all. A book can be put together in a matter of months rather than the years it would require one person to write all the chapters. Second, it is far more efficient for both professors and students, since only those chapters that will actually be used will appear in the book. (It is often the case that when traditional textbooks are adopted, several of the chapters are not assigned to students.)

Another example of efficiency in publishing is the advent of books-on-tape. There are a number of companies that now rent or sell books recorded on audio tape. The availability of such tapes permits greater efficiency in "reading" books. Instead of doing nothing but reading, one can now engage in other activities (driving, walking, jogging, watching TV with the sound off) while listening to a book. Greater efficiency is also provided by many of these books-on-tape being made available in abridged form so that they can be devoured far more quickly. Gone are the "wasted" hours listening to "insignificant" parts of novels. With liberal cutting, a book such as *War and Peace* can now be listened to in a sitting.

Most "serious," nontabloid newspapers (for example, *The New York Times* and *The Washington Post*) are relatively inefficient to read. This is especially true of stories that begin on page one and then carry over to one or more additional pages. Stories that carry over to additional pages are said to have "jumped," and many readers are resistant to "jumping" with the stories. *USA TODAY* eliminated this inefficient way of presenting and reading stories by starting and finishing most of them on the same page, in other words, by offering "News McNuggets." This was accomplished by ruthlessly editing stories so that narrative was dramatically reduced (and no words wasted), leaving a series of relatively bare facts.

In this, *USA TODAY* was anticipated by the various digests, most notably the still-popular *Reader's Digest*. The basic principle of *Reader's Digest* was that "magazine articles could be written to please the reader, to give him the nub of the matter in the new fast-moving world of the 1920s, instead of being written at length and with literary embellishments to please the author or the editor." Other precursors to *USA TODAY* are magazines such as *Time*, *Newsweek*, and *Business Week*. The efficiency of the latter in comparison to the *Wall Street Journal* was stressed by two observers: "The message is that busy executives don't have time to read in depth so don't waste time reading the *Wall Street Journal* every day when one quick bite of *Business Week* once a week is sufficient to give you a step ahead of the competition."

In the realm of religion, McDonaldization is manifest, among other places, in drive-in churches. Another is the widespread development of televised religious programs whereby people can get their religion in the comfort of their living rooms. A particularly noteworthy example of such religious rationalization occurred in 1985 when the Vatican announced that Catholics could receive indulgences through the Pope's annual Christmas benediction on TV or radio. ("Indulgences are a release by way of devotional practices from certain forms of punishment resulting from sin.") Before this development Catholics had to engage in the far less efficient activity of going to Rome for the Christmas benediction and manifesting the "proper intention and attitude" in order to receive their indulgences in person.

Henry Ford, "Just-in-Time," and "Efficiency Experts"

Turning to the automobile industry, one of Henry Ford's prime motivations in "inventing" the automobile assembly line was his desire to save time, energy, and money (that is, to be more efficient) in the production of automobiles in order to increase car sales and the profitability of the Ford Motor Company. As mentioned earlier, Ford got the idea for the automobile assembly line from the overhead trolley system then being used by Chicago meatpackers to butcher cattle. As the steer was propelled along on the trolley system, a line of highly specialized butchers performed specific tasks, and by the end of the line the steer had been completely butchered. This system was clearly more efficient than having a single meat cutter handle all of the tasks involved in butchering a steer.

On the basis of this experience and his knowledge of the automobile business, Ford developed a set of principles for the construction of an automobile assembly line, principles that to this day stand as models of efficiency:

- Workers are not to take any unnecessary steps; work-related movements are reduced to an absolute minimum.

- Parts needed in the assembly process are to travel the least possible distance.

- Mechanical (rather than human) means are to be used to move the car (and parts) from one step in the assembly process to the next. At first, gravity was used, but later electrical conveyor belts were employed.

- Complex sets of movements are eliminated and the worker does "as nearly as possible only one thing with one movement."

The introduction of the assembly line allowed for a massive increase in the efficiency of automobile manufacture. As a result of its pioneering efforts, the Ford Motor Company was able in a short period of time to increase productivity, lower costs, and, as a result, increase its sales and profitability. Other automobile companies quickly adopted the assembly line, and many other industries adopted the model in whole or in part. As we have already pointed out, the influence of the assembly line is felt throughout the fast-food business and other aspects of our McDonaldized society.

Today, the assembly line continues to dominate the automobile industry, but its most efficient manifestations are now found not in and around Detroit, but in Japan. The Japanese adopted American assembly-line technology after World War II, and they have continued to refine it and make it more efficient. But the Japanese have also made their own distinctive contributions to heightened efficiency.

A good example of this is the Japanese "just-in-time" system, which replaced the American "just-in-case" system. Both of these systems refer to the supply of needed parts to a manufacturing, in particular an assembly-line, operation. In the American "just-in-case" system, parts are stored in the plant until, or in case, they are needed. This leads to inefficiencies, especially the purchasing and storage (at great cost) of

parts that will not be needed for quite some time. To counter these inefficiencies, the Japanese developed the "just-in-time" system: needed parts
arrive at the assembly line just as they are to be placed in the car or
whatever object is being manufactured. This eliminates the inefficiencies associated with the "just-in-case" system. It does so by, in effect,
organizing all of the Japanese company's suppliers into one, huge
assembly-line process.

Let us close this chapter with one final historic, work-related example of the emphasis on efficiency, Taylor's "scientific management."
It is relevant to touch on this again because the followers of Taylor and
scientific management came to be known as "efficiency experts."

Taylor was animated by the belief that the United States was suffering from "inefficiency in almost all our daily acts" and that there
was a need for "greater national efficiency." We will encounter more
details of Taylor's approach in later chapters, but from the point of
view of efficiency, the key lies in the "time and motion" studies done
by his efficiency experts. These studies were designed to replace what
Taylor called the inefficient "rule of thumb" methods that dominated
work in his day with what he thought of as the "one best way"—that
is, the optimum means to the end—of doing a job.

Taylor outlined a series of steps to be followed in time and motion
studies:

1. Find a number of workers, preferably in diverse work settings, who
   are particularly skillful at the work in question.
2. Make a careful study of the elementary movements (as well as the
   tools and implements) employed by these people in their work.
3. Time each of these elementary steps carefully with the aim of discovering the most efficient way of accomplishing each step.
4. Make the work efficient by eliminating inefficient steps such as "all
   false movements, slow movements, and useless movements."
5. Finally, after all unnecessary movements have been eliminated,
   combine the most efficient movements (and tools) to create the
   famous (or infamous) "one best way" of doing a job.

Although one hears little these days of Taylor, efficiency experts, and
time and motion studies, their impact is strongly felt in a McDonaldized
society. The goal in the fast-food restaurant (as well as its many derivatives) is to discover and implement the one best way (that is, the most
efficient method) to grill hamburgers, cook french fries, prepare shakes,

process customers, and the rest. The most efficient ways of handling a variety of tasks have been written in training manuals and taught to managers who, in turn, teach them to new employees. The design of the fast-food restaurant, and its various technologies, have been put in place to aid in the attainment of the most efficient means to the end of feeding large numbers of people.

Conclusion

This chapter has focused on efficiency, or the search for the optimum means to an end, within a McDonaldizing society. We began with food and diet and dealt with such efficiencies as the drive-through windows at fast-food restaurants, finger food, the development of home-made fast food, and the increasing use of such specialized conditioning machines as the StairMaster. In the area of shopping, we discussed the efficiencies associated with shopping malls and the still greater efficiencies of catalogue shopping and TV shopping networks. In the entertainment realm, video rental stores, package tours, amusement parks, and contemporary sports arenas were discussed in terms of their efficiencies. Modern medicine was shown to be growing increasingly efficient with the advent of assembly-line medicine and "McDoctors." Books and newspapers have grown more efficient as exemplified by the development of customized textbooks, the increasing popularity of books-on-tape, and the "news McNuggets" found in newspapers such as *USA TODAY.* Finally, the work world was made more efficient by Henry Ford's assembly line and F.W. Taylor's "efficiency experts." Thus, efficiency is not just the norm in the fast-food industry, but is found throughout our McDonaldizing society.

4

Calculability
Big Macs and Little Chips

McDonaldization involves an emphasis on things that can be calculated, counted, quantified. It means a tendency to use quantity as a measure of quality. This leads to a sense that quality is equal to certain, usually (but not always) large, quantities of things.

Whoppers, Whalers, and Weight Watchers

McDonald's has been conscious of quantification from the beginning and it has emphasized it in various ways. For many years, the most visible symbols (although they have now largely disappeared) of this emphasis on bigness were the large signs (usually beneath the even larger golden arches) touting the millions, and later billions, of hamburgers sold by the McDonald's chain of restaurants. This was a rather heavy-handed way of letting everyone know about McDonald's great success. (With the wide-scale recognition of that success in recent years, there is less need for McDonald's to be so brazen; hence the disappearance of such signs and the decrease in size of the golden arches. In addition, as we will see in Chapter Nine, protests against these garish signs helped lead to their virtual disappearance.) The potential customer was expected to assume that the ever-mounting number of hamburgers sold indicated not only the success of the chain, but also that such immense sales were the result of the high quality of the burgers. Hence, the link was made, albeit implicitly, between large numbers of sales and quality; quantity equaled quality.

McDonald's carries this emphasis on quantity over into the naming of some of its foods, especially the Big Mac. Here the focus is on the amount of food the consumer receives. A large burger is considered desirable simply because it is large. Furthermore, there is an implicit calculus here. Consumers are led to believe that they are getting a *large* amount of food for a *small* expenditure of money. Calculating consumers come away with the feeling that they are not only getting a good deal, but perhaps they are also getting the best of McDonald's. If they are not getting something for nothing, they at least believe they are getting something for very little.

As in many other aspects of its operation, McDonald's emphasis on quantity is mirrored by many other fast-food restaurants. The most notable is Burger King, which stresses the quantity of the meat in its hamburger called the *Whopper* and of the fish in its sandwich called the *Whaler.* Then there is Wendy's with its various Biggies, including Biggie fries. Similarly, Seven-Eleven offers its customers a hot dog called the *Big Bite* and a large soft drink called the *Big Gulp*, and now, the even larger *Super Big Gulp.* This emphasis on quantity in a McDonaldized society is not restricted to fast-food restaurants. Continuing their emulation of the fast-food business, manufacturers of food products for the home are bringing out products, such as Campbell Soup Company's Big Start home breakfasts. To take a nonfood example, United Airlines boasts that it serves more cities than any other airline.

What is particularly interesting about all this emphasis on quantity is the seeming absence of interest in communicating anything about quality. Thus, United Airlines does not tell us anything about the quality of their numerous flights, for example, the likelihood that their planes will be on time. The result is a growing concern about the decline or even the absence of quality, not only in the fast-food business but also in society as a whole. Were fast-food restaurants interested in emphasizing quality, they might give their products names such as the "Delicious Mac," or the "Mac with Prime Beef," or the "All Beef Frankfurter." (Obviously some Madison Avenue wizard would need to be hired to come up with more clever labels to communicate this emphasis on quality.) But the fact is that typical McDonald's customers know they are *not* getting the highest quality food. Here is one observation on the quality of the McDonald's burger:

> No one, but no one, outside of a few top McDonald's executives, knows exactly what's in those hamburger patties, and, whatever they're made of, they're easy to overlook completely. I once opened up a bun . . . and looked at a McDonald's patty in its naked state. It looked like a Brillo pad and I've never forgotten it.

> Let's face it. Nobody thinks about what's between the bun at McDonald's. You buy, you eat, you toss the trash, and you're out of there like the Lone Ranger.

One observer has argued that we do not go to McDonald's for a delicious, pleasurable meal, but rather we go to "refuel." McDonald's is a place to which we go when we need to fill our stomachs with lots of calories and carbohydrates so that we are able to move on to the next rationally organized activity. It is far more efficient to think of eating as refueling rather than as a dining experience.

The propensity for fast-food restaurants to minimize quality in their search for a great number of rapidly made sales is well-reflected in the sad history of Colonel Harland Sanders, the founder of Kentucky Fried Chicken. The quality of his cooking techniques and his secret seasoning (which his wife originally mixed, packed, and shipped by herself) led to great success and a string of about 400 franchised outlets by 1960. Sanders had a great commitment to quality, especially to his gravy: "To Sanders himself the supreme stuff of his art was his gravy, the blend of herbs and spices that time and patience had taught him. It was his ambition to make a gravy so good that people would simply eat the gravy and throw away 'the durned chicken.'"

In 1964 Sanders sold his business, and he became little more than the spokesperson and symbol for Kentucky Fried Chicken. The new ownership soon made clear its commitment to (quantifiable) speed rather than quality: "The Colonel's gravy was fantastic, they agreed, . . . but it was too complex, too time-consuming, too expensive. It had to be changed. It wasn't fast food." Ray Kroc, who befriended Colonel Sanders, recalls him saying, "That friggin' . . . outfit. . . . They prostituted every goddam thing I had. I had the greatest gravy in the world and those sons of bitches they dragged it out and extended it and watered it down that I'm so goddamn mad."

At best, what customers expect from a fast-food restaurant is only modestly good, but strong-tasting food. Hence, the emphasis is on powerful, simple tastes: salty/sweet french fries, "special" highly seasoned sauces, saccharine shakes. Many fast foods combine both sweet and salty tastes. Given such modest expectations about quality, customers do have greater expectations in terms of quantity. They expect to get a lot of food *and* they expect to pay relatively little for it.

There are those who claim that getting a lot of food for little cost in a fast-food restaurant is more an illusion than reality. There is a

lot of ice in the soft drinks and a big, fluffy (and inexpensive) bun sur-
rounds and enlarges the burger. The size of the portion of french fries
is particularly illusory. Special scoops are used to arrange the fries
in such a way that it looks like a large quantity is being offered to the
customer. The bags and boxes are structured so that they seem to
be bulging at the top, overflowing with french fries. The insides of
the boxes for McDonald's large fries are striped to further the illusion.
In fact, there are, given the price, relatively few fries in each package,
a few pennies worth of potato. Indeed, there is a huge profit margin
in the fries. In fact, Reiter reports that at Burger King, fries are sold
at 400 percent of their cost! Thus, in fact, the consumers' calculus
is wrong; they are *not* getting a lot for a little. This is not only true for
french fries but also the rest of the menu items at a fast-food restaurant.
Drinks at Burger King, for example, involve a 600-percent markup.
Indeed, given the enormous rush of people into this business, and
the huge growth in fast-food outlets, it is clear that there are great
profits to be made, and they are made the old-fashioned way—getting
people to pay comparatively a lot for relatively little.

To be fair, fast-food restaurants probably give more food for
less money than is the case in a traditional restaurant. However, fast-
food restaurants make up for this by doing much more business
than a traditional restaurant. They may earn less profit on each meal,
but they sell many more meals.

The emphasis on the number of sales made and the size of the
products offered are not the only ways in which fast-food restaurants
focus on quantity. Another example is the great emphasis on the speed
with which a meal can be served. In fact, Ray Kroc's first outlet was
named *McDonald's Speedee Service Drive-In.* At one time, McDonald's
sought to be able to serve a hamburger, shake, and french fries in 50
seconds. The restaurant made a great breakthrough in 1959 when it
served a record 36 hamburgers in 110 seconds. Today, Burger King
seeks to serve a customer within 3 minutes of entering the restaurant.

Speed is obviously a quantifiable factor of monumental importance in a *fast*-food restaurant. Speed is another reason why the
drive-through window was embraced by the fast-food business. The
amount of time required to process a customer through the fast-
food restaurant is drastically reduced by the drive-through window.
Speed is of even greater importance in the pizza-delivery business.
Not only are the number of pizzas sold dependent on how quickly
they can be delivered, but also for a pizza to arrive hot and fresh it must

be transported quickly (although special insulated containers keep the pizzas hot longer). As a result of this emphasis on rapid delivery, there have been several scandals where pressure to make fast deliveries led to the young delivery people being involved in serious and sometimes fatal automobile accidents.

Still another aspect of the emphasis on quantity lies in the precision with which every component of the fast-food meal is measured. For example, great care is taken to be sure that each raw McDonald's hamburger weighs 1.6 ounces, no more, no less; there are 10 hamburgers to a pound of meat. The precooked hamburger measures precisely 3.875 inches across. The hamburger bun measures exactly 3.5 inches in diameter. This width permits the grilled hamburger to stick out beyond the bun, giving the illusion of large size. McDonald's invented a technology called the "fatilyzer" and used it to ensure that its hamburger meat (in the regular, pre-McLean burger) had no more than 19-percent fat content. This is important because greater fat content would lead to greater shrinkage during cooking and lessen the ability to appear to offer a hamburger that is so big that it cannot be contained by the bun. In addition to giving the illusion that there are a lot of fries in each package, the french-fry scoop also helps to make sure that each package has about the same number of fries. The new automatic drink dispensers ensure that each cup gets the correct amount of soft drink with nothing lost to spillage.

Arby's has reduced the cooking and serving of roast beef to a series of exact measures. All roasts weigh 10 pounds at the start. They are then roasted at 200 degrees fahrenheit for 3.5 hours until the internal temperature is 135 degrees. They are then allowed to cook in their own heat for 20 minutes more until the internal temperature is 140 degrees. By following these steps and making these measurements, Arby's doesn't need a skilled chef; virtually anyone who can read and count can cook an Arby's roast beef. When the roasts are done, each weighs between 9 pounds, 4 ounces, and 9 pounds, 7 ounces. Every roast beef sandwich has 3 ounces of meat. This allows Arby's to get 47 sandwiches (give or take one) from each roast.

Burger King has reduced the issue of the quality control of its products to a series of quantities. Hamburgers must be served within 10 minutes of being cooked. French fries may be allowed to stand under the heat lamp for no more than 7 minutes. A manager is allowed to throw away 0.3 percent of all food.

The franchised frozen yogurt businesses that have sprung up in recent years have adopted this emphasis with a vengeance. Rather than simply filling a container to the brim as was traditionally done in ice cream parlors, each container is weighed to be sure it includes the correct quantity of frozen yogurt.

Of course, the fast-food restaurant and its derivatives are not the only examples of great emphasis being placed on precise quantification. Take the cookbook. In the original (1896) *The Boston Cooking School Cook Book*, Fannie Farmer (yes, she was a real person) emphasized precise measurement and in the process helped to rationalize home-cooking:

> Before her death she had changed American kitchen terminology from "a pinch" and "a dash" and "a heaping spoonful"—all vague terms which she detested—to her own *precise*, standardized, scientific terms, presenting a model of cooking that was easy, reliable, and could be followed even by inexperienced cooks. To Fannie Farmer, "the mother of level measurement," we can attribute the popularity of such *precise* everyday kitchen terms as level teaspoon, $1/2$ teaspoon, measuring cup, oven thermometer, and "bake at 350 degrees for 40 minutes."

Calculability is not only an integral part of eating, but also of dieting. The diet industry is huge and growing. It encompasses diet drugs, diet books, exercise video tapes, diet meals, diet drinks, weight loss clinics, and "fat farms." Given its very nature, the diet industry is obsessed with things that can be quantified. Weight, weight loss (or gain), and time periods are measured precisely. Food intake is carefully measured and monitored. The packages of diet foods carefully detail the number of ounces of food, the number of calories, and many other things as well.

Organizations like Weight Watchers and Nutri/System are obsessed with calculability. Not surprising are their efforts to carefully measure caloric intake per day, number of calories in each food product, and weight lost per week. What is striking is their increasing desire to provide foods that can be prepared rapidly. For example, Nutri/System boasts that most of its freeze-dried dinner entrees "can be ready in under five minutes. So you don't have to spend a lot of time in the kitchen." But in its endless search to further reduce the amount of time devoted to food preparation, Nutri/System is now offering "an increasing number of microwavable entrees that can be on your plate, ready to eat, 90 seconds after you take them from your cupboard."

Mona Lisa, *thirtysomething*, and Michael Jordan

The package tour represents a clear emphasis on the quantity of sights visited rather than the quality of those visits. It is obviously impossible to get any real sense of what Paris has to offer in a day or two, or do much more in the Louvre (an enormous museum) in a brief visit than rush to the Mona Lisa, glance at the masterpiece, and rush back to the bus. One sees *lots* of sights (often through bus windows) in *many* different countries, but the quality of the sight-seeing is very superficial. When tourists return from such a trip, they can crow about the large number of countries and sights visited, slides taken, and video tapes filled. (They can even bore their friends for hours with interminable slide or video shows of their trip.) However, given the nature of such trips, devotees of packaged tours are hard-pressed to tell their friends very much about the countries they visited or the sights they saw.

What we see on television is heavily, if not almost exclusively, determined by quantitative rather than qualitative factors. It is not the high quality of a program that determines whether it will be broadcast, but rather the size of its ratings and, as a result, the amount of advertising revenue it is likely to generate. A vice president of programming for ABC made this emphasis on quantity rather than quality quite clear: "Commercial television programming is designed to attract audiences to the advertisers' messages which surround the programming. . . . Inherent creative aesthetic values [that is, quality!] are important, but always secondary." (Bracketed words added.)

Potential programs are tested on sample audiences in an effort to predict which shows will achieve high ratings. Pilots for new shows are broadcast, and those that achieve high ratings, or demonstrate the potential for such ratings, are the ones selected for regular broadcast. Ratings services such as Nielsen determine the fate of television programs. In fact, it is argued that "Nielsen is television." Said one ABC executive, "The thing we've always had has been this set of numbers. . . . It's the foundation upon which program decisions are made." Sophisticated measuring devices are placed in the homes of a sample of American television viewers. The current technology requires that the selected viewers push remote control buttons to indicate when television viewing begins and ends. Periodically the meter flashes indicating that it wants to know whether anyone is still watching. To respond, the viewer must press the OK button. We are likely to see soon a new, improved passive audience meter, which will measure viewing habits without requiring that the viewers do anything.

Ratings are derived from the number of Nielsen-selected homes that tune into a particular program. Those programs with high ratings will generate high revenues and thus enjoy a long life on television. Low-rated programs are unlikely to survive very long. Of course, ratings tell us nothing about the quality of the programs. Indeed, it is likely that very high-quality programs will receive low ratings. This is the reason for the existence of public broadcasting (PBS) which, because of its public funding and its fund raisers, is far more interested in the quality of a program than in its rating potential.

Television stations in Europe are far more likely to be run by the government than to be owned privately. As a result, they are less responsive to the wishes of commercial sponsors for high ratings and far more interested in the quality of programs. Hence, one sees much more quality programming on European than American television. However, it should be noted that even these government-run stations do program a number of the most popular American shows. Further, the advent of various kinds of private European cable and satellite television networks is likely to mean that the quality of European television in the future will move further in the direction of that now available on American television.

Over the years, television ratings systems have grown more sophisticated. Instead of relying solely on absolute numbers, some programs succeed or fail on the basis of their ratings within specific demographic groups. Advertisers who sell primarily to a particular demographic group will support a program with relatively low overall ratings as long as its ratings within the targeted demographic group are high. Thus, for example, a program such as the highly acclaimed *thirtysomething*, with modest overall ratings, remained on the air because of high ratings among consumption-oriented so-called Yuppies. Though this may involve greater statistical sophistication, it still involves a focus on things that can be quantified. Although we could debate the quality of a program such as *thirtysomething*, it remained on the air as long as it did because of its high ratings within a specific demographic group.

The quality of various sports has been altered and, in the view of some, sacrificed in the name of quantifiable dimensions. To continue with television for a moment, the nature of sporting events has been changed by the need for television contracts and the enormous revenues derived from such contracts. (Sports are not alone in this; in politics, the Democratic party is considering shortening and streamlining its convention to accommodate the needs and demands of television.) Teams in many sports earn a comparatively large proportion of their revenue from television contracts, and thus they are willing to sacrifice the interests of in-person spectators, and even the games themselves, in order to increase their television income.

A good example of this is the so-called TV time-out. In the old days, TV commercials occurred during natural breaks in a game, for example, during a time-out called by one of the teams, at half-time, or between innings. But this meant that commercials appeared too intermittently and too infrequently to bring in the increasingly large fees that advertisers were willing to pay. This led to the appearance of regular TV time-outs in sports such as football and basketball. The owners of sports franchises may be maximizing their incomes from advertising, but many observers feel that they have sacrificed the quality of the sport. For example, the momentum of a team may be lost because of an inopportune TV time-out. Thus, these time-outs do alter the nature of some sports, and they may, on occasion, even affect the outcome of a game. There are also adverse consequences for the fans who pay to watch these sporting events in person. From their point of view, these time-outs interrupt the flow of the game. The fans at home can at least watch the commercials; the spectators at the games are left with nothing to watch until the commercial ends and the game resumes. But team owners consider such negative effects on the quality of the game insignificant in comparison to the economic gain from increased advertising.

Turning to sports themselves, it is clear that by their very nature they place a premium on the quality of individual (for example, the acrobatics of basketball star Michael Jordan) and team (for example, the teamwork of the Boston Celtics) performance. At the same time, quantitative factors have always been enormously important in sports. In many cases quality is directly related to quantity—the better the performance, the more the points, and the greater the number of victories. Thus, there has always been a strong link between quantity and quality in sports.

However, over the years there has been increasing emphasis on attributes of sports that can be quantified. Here is the way one observer describes this trend:

> Modern sports are characterized by the almost inevitable tendency to transform *every* athletic feat into one that can be quantified and measured. The accumulation of statistics on every conceivable aspect of the game is a hallmark of football, baseball, hockey, and of track and field too, where the accuracy of quantification has, thanks to an increasingly precise technology, reached a degree that makes the stopwatch seem positively primitive.

Not only has the emphasis on quantification increased, but some sports have been altered to allow for quantification: "How can one rationalize and quantify a competition in gymnastics, in aesthetics? The answer now seems obvious. Set up an interval scale and a panel of judges and then take the arithmetic mean of the subjective evaluations. . . . Nadia Comeneci scored exactly 79.275 points in Montreal, neither more nor less. The ingenuity of *Homo Mensor* must not be underestimated."

The growing emphasis on quantity can sometimes adversely affect the quality of play in a sport. For example, the basketball star who is motivated by a need to stand out individually and score as many points as possible may have a negative impact on his teammates and the overall performance of the team. But this is not the most basic problem in this area. That difficulty stems from the attempts to McDonaldize sports by seeking to maximize things like points scored to the detriment of the quality of play.

In basketball this has taken the form of the 24-second clock for professionals and the 45-second clock for college athletes. This means that the offensive team must attempt a shot within 24 or 45 seconds. Not long ago, basketball was a more leisurely game. A team brought the ball down the court and took as long as necessary to get a player into position to take a good shot. Basketball fans of that era enjoyed the strategy and maneuvers involved in this process. Toward the end of the game, a team holding a slim lead could attempt to "freeze" the ball, that is, not risk taking and missing a shot thereby giving their opponents a chance to take possession of the ball and narrow, or even take, the lead.

In the past few decades, the leadership of collegiate and professional basketball decided that fans raised in the McDonald's era wanted to see faster games and many more points scored. In other words, fans wanted from basketball what they got from their fast-food restaurants—great speed and large quantities. It was believed, apparently correctly, that faster and higher scoring games would mean greater attendance and higher profits. Hence, the appearance of the 24- and 45-second time clocks led to a more fast-paced and higher scoring game in which many more shots are attempted and made. But many basketball aficionados feel that the "run and shoot" style of play generated by the time clocks has adversely affected the quality of play. Gone are many of the individual and team maneuvers and strategies that made the game so interesting to purists. But a "run and shoot" style of basketball fits well in the McDonaldized "eat and move" world of dinners purchased at drive-through windows and consumed on the run.

Baseball's ownership decided long ago that baseball fans preferred to see high-scoring games with lots of hits, home runs, and runs scored rather than pitcher's duels in which the final score might be 1-0. Thus, a number of steps have been taken to increase the number of runs scored. Livelier baseballs are used that can travel farther than old-fashioned baseballs. In some baseball parks, outfield fences have been brought closer to home plate so that it is easier to hit home runs. The artificial turf used on many fields in place of natural grass makes routine ground balls roll faster and therefore more likely to skip by the infielders for base hits.

The most notable effort to increase offensive production, found in the American League but not in the more traditional National League, is the use of the so-called designated hitter. Instead of the generally weak-hitting pitcher taking his turn at bat, in the American League he is replaced in the line-up by someone whose main (and sometimes only) skill is hitting. Designated hitters will get more hits, hit more home runs, and help produce more runs than pitchers who are allowed to bat.

Although the designated hitter in American League baseball has undoubtedly increased the number of runs scored, it has also affected, some feel adversely, the quality of the game. For example, when pitchers bat in certain situations they often employ a sacrifice bunt, a very artful practice. But a designated hitter rarely sacrifices an at-bat in order to advance a runner by bunting. Pinch hitters have less of a role where the designated hitter is employed because there is far less need to pinch hit when a skillful designated hitter replaces a weak-hitting pitcher in the line-up. Finally, because there is less need to pinch hit for them, starting pitchers can remain in games longer and this reduces the need to use relief pitchers. (However, specialization in baseball has more than compensated for this and it is undoubtedly the case that we now see more rather than less use of relief pitchers. Indeed, we now have very specialized relief roles—the "long reliever" who comes in early in the game, the "closer" who finishes off a game in which his team is ahead, and relievers who specialize in getting out left- or right-handed batters.) In these and other ways, baseball is a different game when a designated hitter is employed. In other words, the quality of the game has changed, some would say for the worse, because of the emphasis on quantity.

Junk-Food Journalism, GPAs, Sound Bites, and Throw Weight

An interesting example of the emphasis on quantity rather than quality is the newspaper *USA TODAY*, which is noted for its "junk-food journalism," that is, the lack of substance in its stories. Instead of offering detailed stories, *USA TODAY* offers a large number of short, easily and quickly read stories. It is the kind of newspaper that can be read in about the time it takes one to consume a meal at a fast-food restaurant. Said one executive, "*USA TODAY* must sell news/info at a fast, hard pace." One observer underscored the newspaper's corresponding lack of concern for quality and, in the process, its relationship to the fast-food restaurant: "Like parents who take their children to a different fast-food joint every night and keep the refrigerator stocked with ice cream, *USA TODAY* gives its readers only what they want. No spinach, no bran, no liver."

Education is another institution in which there has been an increasing emphasis on quantifiable phenomena. Throughout the educational system there is a preoccupation with grades and the grade point average (GPA), and far less attention is paid to the quality of what is learned and of the educational experience. The entire high school or college experience can be summed up in a single number, the GPA. Armed with their GPAs, students can then take quantified examinations like the PSAT, SAT, and GRE. Graduate and professional schools can look at three or four numbers and decide whether or not to admit a student. For their part, students may decide on whether or not to attend a university on the basis of its rating. Is it one of the top 10 universities in the country? Is its physics department in the top 10? Are its sports teams usually top-ranked? Potential employers may decide whether or not to hire graduates on the basis of their various scores, their class ranking, as well as the ranking of the university from which they graduated. In order to increase their job prospects, students may seek to amass a number of different degrees and credentials with the hope that prospective employers will believe that the longer the list of degrees, the higher the quality of the job candidate. Personal references may be important, but these now often take the form of quantifiable ratings (for example, "top 5 percent of the class," "ranks 5th in class of 25").

The number of credentials one possesses plays a role in situations other than obtaining a job. For example, people in various occupations are increasingly using long lists of initials after their names to convince prospective clients of their competence. (My BA, MBA, and PhD are supposed to persuade the reader that I am competent to write this book.) Said one insurance appraiser with ASA, FSVA, FAS, CRA, and CRE after his name, "the more [initials] you tend to put after your name, the more impressed they [potential clients] become." However, the sheer number of credentials tells us little about the competence of the person sporting them. Furthermore, this emphasis on quantity of credentials has led people to simply concoct letters to put after their names. For example, one camp director put the letters ABD after his name in order to impress parents of prospective campers. While these letters may appear impressive to a layperson, all academics know that this is an informal, and largely negative, label—"All But Dissertation"—for people who have completed their graduate courses and exams, but who have not written their dissertations. Also noteworthy here is the development of organizations whose sole reason for existence is to supply meaningless credentials, often through the mail.

The emphasis on quantifiable factors is even common among college professors. For example, more and more colleges and universities use student ratings forms and systems. Each course is evaluated by the students on a variety of dimensions with each dimension involving, for example, a one to five range with one being low and five being high. At the end of the semester, the professor receives what is in effect a report card with an overall teaching rating as well as scores on the various dimensions related to teaching. There is little or no room for students to offer qualitative evaluations of their teachers. While student ratings are desirable in a number of ways, they also have some unfortunate consequences. For example, they tend to favor the professor who is a performer, who has a sense of humor, and who is not too demanding of students. The serious professor who places great demands on students is not likely to do well in such ratings systems, even though the quality of what is being taught (for example, number and depth of ideas) may be far greater than that communicated by the performer.

Quantitative factors are not only important in teaching, but also in research and publication. The "publish or perish" pressure on academicians in many colleges and universities tends to lead to great attention to the quantity of one's publications. A resumé with a long list of articles and books is generally preferred to one with a shorter list. This quantitative emphasis has some unfortunate consequences, such as causing a professor to publish less than high-quality works, to rush to publication before a work is fully developed, and to publish the same idea or finding several times with only minor variations in the mode of presentation.

Another quantitative factor is the ranking of the place in which a work is published. In the hard sciences, articles in professional journals receive high marks while books are less valued. Books are of much higher value in the humanities than in the hard sciences, and sometimes more prestigious than journal articles. Among those fields that emphasize books, being published by some publishers (for example, university presses such as the University of Chicago Press) gets higher ratings than being published by some others (commercial publishers, or so-called "vanity presses" that publish books if the professor pays at least part of the cost).

There is an even more elaborate ratings system for professional journals. In sociology, for example, a formal ratings system has been developed with certain professional journals receiving high ratings, others moderate ratings, and still others low ratings. Thus, a publication in the prestigious *American Sociological Review* would receive 10 points (the maximum) in this system, and one in the far less prestigious (and in order not to hurt anyone's feelings, fictional) *Antarctic Journal of Sociology* would receive only 1 point. With such a system, it is possible to give all sociologists in the world point scores for their journal publications. By this system, the professor whose journal publications yield 340 points is supposed to be twice as "good" as one who earns only 170 points.

However, as is usually the case, such an emphasis on quantity has a number of adverse effects on quality. For one thing, it is highly unlikely that the quality of a professor's life work can be reduced to a single number. In fact, it seems impossible to quantify the quality of an idea, theory, or research finding. Second, this system deals with quality only indirectly. That is, the rating is based on the quality of the journal in which an article was published, not the quality of the article itself. No effort is made to evaluate the quality of the article or its contribution to the field. The rating of a journal can be a very poor substitute for an evaluation of an individual article. Some very poor articles appear in the highest-ranking journals, and some excellent ones can be found in low-ranking journals. Third, the academician who writes only a few, high-quality papers might not do well in this ratings system. In contrast, someone who produces a lot of mediocre work could well receive a far higher score. Thus, this kind of system tends to reward a lot of published work whether or not it is really any good. It can lead ambitious sociologists (and those in most other academic fields) to conclude that they cannot afford to spend years honing a single work because it will not pay off much in their point score. A great deal of mediocre work is what is called for by a system that places so much emphasis on quantity of publications.

The sciences have come up with another quantifiable measure in an effort to evaluate the quality of work. That measure is the number of times a person's work is cited in the work of other people. The assumption is that high-quality, important, and influential work is likely to be used and cited by other scholars. It supposedly follows, then, that the more times a scholar's work is cited by others, the higher the quality of that work. A variety of citation indexes are published each year. These indexes can be used to come up with a single number of citations for the year in question for every scholar (whose work has been cited by others) in the world. We might find that the work of one sociologist has been cited 140 times while that of another is cited only 70 times. Again, the conclusion seems to follow that the work of the first sociologist is twice as "good" as that of the second.

However, once again we run into the problem of truly evaluating quality when we emphasize quantity. Can the influence of a person's academic work be reduced to a single number? It may be that a few centrally important uses of one scholar's ideas are far more important than many trivial citations of another scholar's work. Furthermore, the mere fact that a work is cited tells us nothing about *how* the work was used by other people. A worthless piece of work could be attacked by many people, thereby being cited in their work and leading to a large number of citations for its creator. Conversely, a truly important piece of work may, for one reason or another (for example, it may be ahead of its time and too sophisticated to be truly understood by other academicians), be ignored by other scholars, leading to a minuscule number of citations for the author. As always, quantity does not necessarily translate easily into quality and may even indicate poor rather than high quality.

Recently, the president (now departed) of Stanford University, Donald Kennedy, announced a change in that university's emphasis on the quantity of publications in the decision to hire, promote, or grant tenure to faculty members. He was disturbed by a report indicating "that nearly half of faculty members believe that their scholarly writings are merely counted—and not evaluated—when personnel decisions are made." Said Kennedy:

> First, I hope we can agree that the quantitative use of research output as a criterion for appointment or promotion is a bankrupt idea. . . . The overproduction of routine scholarship is one of the most egregious aspects of contemporary academic life: It tends to conceal really important work by sheer volume; it wastes time and valuable resources.

To deal with this problem, Kennedy proposed to limit the number of publications used in making personnel decisions. He hoped that the proposed limits would "reverse the appalling belief that counting and weighing are the important means of evaluating faculty research." It remains to be seen whether Stanford, to say nothing of the rest of American academia, will be able to limit the emphasis on quantity rather than quality.

The political sector offers a number of interesting examples of the emphasis on that which can be quantified. Political candidates are obsessed by their ratings in political polls and often adjust the nature of their positions, or the actions they take, on the basis of what the pollsters tell them is likely to increase their ratings and rankings in the polls. Even those who hold office are highly attuned to the polls. The impact on the ratings of taking a specific political position can become more important than the qualities of that position and whether the politician genuinely believes in those qualities.

Earlier, we dealt with the impact of television on sports. Television has also affected politics in various ways, including its effect on political speechmaking. On television, it is the visual images, not the words, that matter. Thus, by the 1984 presidential campaign, only about 15 seconds of a speech was likely to find its way onto a national news program. Four years later, speaking time on such reports had been reduced still further to only 9 seconds (called "sound bites"). Because political campaign speeches are tailored to television coverage and not the immediate audience, they have grown shorter, less than 20 minutes on the average, including time for applause. The focus in candidates' speeches is on the limited, 10- or 15-second portion that is apt to be picked up by the national television networks. All of this emphasis on the length of the political speech has clearly reduced the quality of speeches, to say nothing of the quality of public discourse on important political issues.

In addition to the decline of televised reports of speeches, televised speeches themselves have undergone a similar decline. Prior to the advent of television, political speeches on radio were at first usually an hour in length; by the 1940s the norm had dropped to 30 minutes. In the early years of television, speeches were that same length, but they rapidly decreased to 5 minutes. By the 1970s the speech itself had been largely replaced by the 60-second advertisement. Similarly, in today's televised presidential debates, candidates have a minute or two to offer their position on a given issue. By contrast, according to one observer, "In each of their seven senatorial debates of 1858, Lincoln and Douglas spoke for ninety minutes each on a single topic: the future of slavery in the territories."

In foreign policy, one area in which we see an absolute mania for numbers is nuclear deterrence. Although this is a less important and less publicly visible issue now that the Cold War appears to have ended, there are no signs that either the United States or Russia plan to give up their ability to deter the other from launching a nuclear attack. Both sides possess nuclear arsenals large enough to destroy each other many times over; nevertheless, their efforts to negotiate treaties reducing nuclear weapons have often become bogged down in trying to accurately assess "the relative throw weight" of their respective nuclear arms. While accurate measures are undoubtedly important in trying to achieve parity as both sides draw down their nuclear arsenals, there is a tendency on both sides to get lost in the minutia of the numbers and to lose sight of the qualitative fact that both sides could eliminate most of their nuclear weapons and still have the ability to destroy the other side, even the world as a whole.

Patients, Money, and Profits

In profit-making medical organizations (for example, Humana), pressure is put on physicians, along with all other employees, to contribute to the profitability of the corporation. Derivatively, efforts are made to quantify various aspects of medical practice (for example, time spent with each patient and number of patients seen). This allows the corporation to reduce costs and increase profits by limiting time with each patient and maximizing the number of patients seen in a day. All of this emphasis on quantity can easily threaten the quality of medical care. Profits can be increased by pushing doctors to spend less time with patients, to see more patients, to abandon long-shot diagnostic techniques and treatments, not to see patients who do not have strong prospects of being able to pay the bills, and to see only patients who have the kinds of diseases that are likely to yield large profits.

Profit-making medical organizations are not the only ones pushing medicine in the direction of greater calculability; all medical bureaucracies are moving in that direction. Even nonprofit medical organizations (for example, nonprofit hospitals and health maintenance organizations [HMOs]) are experiencing the external pressures, employing professional managers, and instituting the sophisticated accounting systems that will lead to heightened levels of calculability. Of relevance here is the 25-day strike in 1986 in Washington, D.C., by the Capital Alliance of Physicians (a 160-member union) against its HMO employer, the Group Health Association. The strike centered around quantified productivity issues such as required number of visits, number of patients seen, and an incentive system tying physician salaries to productivity.

Third-party payers, that is, health insurance companies, and the federal government through its prospective payment and DRG (diagnostic related groups) programs are also pushing medicine in the direction of greater calculability. Outside agencies have grown increasingly concerned about spiraling medical costs and have sought to deal with the problem by limiting what they will pay for as well as how much they will pay for it. Thus, a third-party payer may have policies of not paying for certain procedures, not allowing hospitalization for certain procedures, or paying only a given amount for a procedure. All of this leads in the direction of concentrating on quantities of money, time, and so on, and can lead away from an emphasis on quality of patient care. As one physician union leader put it (albeit with a somewhat romantic and unrealistic view of the medical profession), doctors are "the only ones who think of patients as individuals . . . not as dollar signs."

Increased Work Productivity and "First-Class Men"

Turning to the work world, Taylor's scientific management was heavily oriented to transforming everything work-related into quantifiable dimensions. Instead of relying on the imprecise "rule of thumb" of the worker, scientific management sought to develop precise measurements of how much work was to be done by each and every motion of the worker. Everything that could be reduced to numbers was, and all these numbers were then analyzed using mathematical formulas.

Quantification was clearly an aim of Taylor's early work, in which he sought to increase the amount of pig iron a worker could load in a day. As Taylor put it: "We found that this gang were loading on the average about $12^1/_2$ long tons per man per day. We were surprised to find, after studying the matter, that a first-class pig iron handler ought to handle between 47 and 48 long tons per day, instead of $12^1/_2$ tons." To accomplish the goal of almost quadrupling the workload, Taylor set about studying the way the most productive workers (what Taylor called "first-class men") did their work. Their work was divided into its basic elements and each step was timed with a stop watch down to hundredths of a minute.

On the basis of this careful study, Taylor and his associates developed the one best way to carry pig iron. They then sought a worker who could be motivated to work in this way. They did this by locating an able, ambitious, and money-hungry worker named Schmidt. (A co-worker of Schmidt's said, "A penny looks about the size of a cart-wheel to him.") Schmidt was asked if he wanted to be a "high-priced man." Taylor, predictably, used a precise economic incentive, offering Schmidt $1.85 per day (rather than the usual $1.15 per day) if he agreed to work in exactly the way Taylor told him to. After careful training and supervision, Schmidt succeeded at working at the faster pace (and earning the higher pay); other workers were then selected and trained to work in the same way.

Schmidt and his successors were being asked to do about 3.6 times the normal amount of work for an approximately 60-percent increase in pay. Taylor defended this exploitation in various ways. For example, he argued that it would be unfair to workers in other areas who were working up to their capabilities to have pig-handlers earn 3.6 times as much as they did. For another, Taylor argued that he and his associates had decided (without, of course, consulting the workers themselves) that a greater share of the profits would not be in the workers' interests. For Taylor, "the pig iron handler with his 60-percent increase in wages is not an object for pity but rather a subject for congratulations."

Silicon Chips and Plastic Money

We cannot close this chapter without mentioning the impact of the computer on the emphasis on quantification. The tendency to quantify virtually everything has obviously been expedited by the development and now widespread use of the computer. The first computer was constructed in 1946. It weighed 30 tons, employed 19,000 vacuum tubes (that were constantly blowing out), filled an entire room, and had very limited capacity. Now, of course, we have far more compact computers with infinitely greater capacity, to say nothing of the small computers that litter virtually every office and exist in many homes. The massive expansion of the number and capacity of computers, as well as the ability to make them significantly smaller, was made possible by the invention of the silicon chip in the 1970s. The chip is a slice from a crystal of silicon about one-half the size of a fingernail. It replaced the much larger transistor, which had in turn replaced the still-larger vacuum tube. The silicon chip provides the necessary electronic circuitry in microscopic form, with the result that computers are being made ever smaller (laptops and notebook computers, for example), more powerful, cheaper, and (most importantly from the point of view of this chapter) able to do more and more calculations with increasing speed.

Many aspects of today's quantity-oriented society could not exist, or would need to be greatly modified, were it not for the computer. Examples include:

- The registration of masses of students at large state universities, the processing of all their grades, and the constant recalculation of grade point averages.

- Extensive medical testing in which a patient takes a battery of blood and urine tests, and the results are returned in the form of a series of numbers on a variety of factors as well as the normal ranges for each of them. This permits efficient diagnosis of medical problems and allows the patient to be a kind of do-it-yourself physician.

- The development and widespread use of the credit card. ("Plastic money" is more efficient than cash; it is a better means to the end of spending money.) The credit card was made possible by the computer, and it, in turn, made possible a massive increase in consumer spending and business sales.

- The ability of the television networks to give us almost instantaneous election results.

- Virtually continuous political polling and TV ratings.

Although we undoubtedly would, as a society, have moved in the direction of increasing quantification, that movement has been greatly expedited and extended by continuing advances in computer technology.

Conclusion

Calculability, or the emphasis on quantity, often to the detriment of quality, is the second dimension of McDonaldization. There is great emphasis on calculability in the fast-food restaurant, with the most notable example being the Big Mac. A variety of forms of amusement are characterized more by quantity than quality, such as the package tour, decisions on what programs remain on television, and the use of the 24-second clock in professional basketball. A range of disparate areas are also characterized by an emphasis on quantity, such as the focal importance of GPAs in colleges and universities, on "sound bites" of a few seconds in duration in political speeches, and on "throw weight" in the efforts at nuclear disarmament. In medicine there is increasing emphasis on numbers of patients seen, money generated, and profits earned. In the work world, Taylorism helped lead to the focus on the amount of work produced for given amounts of money. Finally, computers have helped make possible the recent dramatic increase in the emphasis on things that can be counted—on quantity rather than quality.

5

Predictability
It Never Rains on Those Little Houses on the Hillside

Rationalization involves the increasing effort to ensure predictability from one time or place to another. In a rational society people prefer to know what to expect in all settings and at all times. They neither want nor expect surprises. They want to know that when they order their Big Mac today it is going to be identical to the one they ate yesterday and the one they will eat tomorrow. People would be upset if the special sauce was used one day, but not the next, or tasted differently from one day to the next. They want to know that the McDonald's franchise they visit in Des Moines, Los Angeles, or Paris is going to be set up in much the same way as their local McDonald's. In order to ensure predictability over time and place, a rational society emphasizes such things as discipline, order, systematization, formalization, routine, consistency, and methodical operation.

Holiday Inn and Those "Magic Fingers"

Instead of starting, as we have in the previous chapters, with the fast-food restaurant, let us begin with other pioneers of the rationalization process—motel chains such as Holiday Inn and Quality Inn. Before the development of these franchises, motels were highly unpredictable places. Run by myriad local owners, every motel was different from every other motel. One motel might be quite comfortable, even luxurious, while another might well be a hovel. One could never be sure whether various amenities were going to be present—soap, shampoo, telephones, radio (and later television), air conditioning, and let us not forget the much-loved "Magic Fingers" massage system. Checking into a motel was an adventure; a traveler never knew what to expect.

The first Holiday Inn opened in 1952 at the dawning of the massive expansion of highways and highway travel. It and other motel chains took pains in their hiring practices to be sure that unpredictable people were not allowed to manage them. One could predict that a motel equipped with the familiar orange and green Holiday Inn sign (now gone the way of McDonald's oversized golden arches) would have most, if not all, of the amenities that one could reasonably expect in a moderately priced motel. Faced with the choice between a local, no-name motel that might or might not be better than the Holiday Inn, many travelers preferred the predictable Holiday Inn even if it had certain liabilities and might not be as good as a locally run motel down the road. The success of Holiday Inn led to many imitators, such as Ramada Inn, Rodeway Inn, as well as the more recent, more price-conscious chains—Days Inn, Econo-Lodge, and Motel 6.

"Howdy Partner," Hamburger University, and TV Dinners

Many other aspects of a rationalized society have followed the basic model of predictability that was pioneered by Holiday Inn and the motel chains. McDonald's and many other franchises picked up the familiar, large, and garish sign. If they had little else in common to proffer, franchises could at least offer a predictable structure that looked the same from one locale to another. This was certainly the case in the fast-food restaurants. McDonald's logo can be linked to predictability: "Replicated color and symbol, mile after mile, city after city, act as a tacit promise of *predictability* and stability between McDonald's and its millions of customers, year after year, meal after meal." (Italics added.) This predictability of structure is now not only the case throughout the United States but also in many other parts of the world as well. Thus American tourists prone to missing the familiar aspects of their home town can now tour far-off countries taking comfort in the knowledge that they are likely to run into those familiar golden arches soon.

Virtually all that some of the more recent entrants into the McDonaldization process have in common is a sign and a physical structure. For example, hair-cutting franchises such as Hair-Plus cannot offer a uniform haircut, because every head is slightly different and every barber or hairdresser operates in a slightly idiosyncratic fashion. To reassure the anxious customer longing for predictability,

Hair-Plus and other hair-cutting franchises offer only a few signs, similar shop set-up, and perhaps a few familiar products.

The fact that the fast-food restaurants could render the dining experience predictable helped make them the center of the process of McDonaldization. In fact, much of what is said and done in fast-food restaurants by both employees and customers is quite ritualized. It is these familiar and comfortable rituals that make fast-food restaurants attractive to legions of people. For example, because interaction between customer and counterperson was of brief duration, it could be routinized. Thus, the Roy Rogers chain used to have its employees, carrying on a Wild West theme and dressed in cowboy and cowgirl uniforms, say "howdy pardner" to every customer about to order food. After paying for the food, people were sent on their way with "happy trails." The repetition of these familiar salutations visit after visit was a source of great satisfaction to regulars at Roy Rogers. Many people (including this author) felt a deep personal loss when Roy Rogers ceased this practice. In a McDonaldized society, such pseudo-interactions are increasingly the norm and one comes to look forward to them. Indeed, we are likely to look back on them longingly when all we have on our visits to fast-food restaurants are interactions with our favorite robot (see Chapter Six).

The fake friendliness of the "cowboys" and "cowgirls" at Roy Rogers reflects the generally false and insincere camaraderie that is characteristic of not only fast-food restaurants but also all other elements of our McDonaldized society, a camaraderie that is used to lure customers and to keep them coming back. As a recent example, the TV screens have been saturated with scenes of the owner of Wendy's, Dave Thomas, seeming to extend a personal invitation to join him for a burger at his restaurant. We will have more to say about this aspect of McDonaldization in Chapter Seven.

More important than what is said in a fast-food restaurant is the predictability of the food sold. In order to allow for predictability, the fast-food restaurant offers its highly limited menu of simple foods. Hamburgers, fried chicken, Chicken McNuggets (or a similar chicken product), pizza, tacos, french fries, soft drinks, shakes, and the like are all relatively easy to prepare and serve in a uniform fashion. Predictability in such end-products is made possible by the use of uniform raw ingredients, identical technologies for food preparation and cooking, similarity in the way the food is served, and identical packaging. The latter is a very important component of predictability in the fast-food restaurant. Because in the end it is food that is being prepared, the fast-food restaurants' best efforts to make food uniform may not be enough and some unpredictabilities may creep in—the food might not be hot enough, the chicken might be gristly or tough, or there may be too few pieces of pepperoni on a particular slice of pizza. Whatever the (slight) unpredictabilities in the food, the packaging—the styrofoam containers (now being phased out by many franchises as we discuss in Chapter Seven) for the burgers, the bags for the small fries, the cardboard box with the Pizza Hut logo on it—can always be the same.

Predictable food requires predictable ingredients. McDonald's has stringent guidelines on the nature (quality, size, shape, and so on) of the meat, chicken, fish, potatoes, and other ingredients that are purchased by each franchisee. We have already discussed, for example, how the precooked McDonald's hamburger must weigh 1.6 ounces, be 3.75 inches in diameter, and have no more than 19-percent fat (the new, lean burgers have a less, but similarly calculable and predictable, amount of fat) so that after it is cooked it just manages to jut out from the bun. The buns are made of the kind of highly predictable white bread that many Americans prefer (and which gives American bread such a bad name throughout much of the rest of the world. Said one wit about Wonder Bread, "I thought they just blew up library paste with gas and sent it to the oven."). To give it this predictability, all of the chewy and nutritious elements of wheat, such as bran and germ, have been milled out. Another threat to predictability are buns that might grow stale or moldy; thus preservatives are added to retard spoilage. In these and innumerable other ways (for example, using precut, uniform frozen french fries rather than fresh potatoes), the serving of predictable foods is made possible by predictable ingredients.

The increasing use of frozen (or freeze-dried) foods in a McDonaldized society also deals with unpredictabilities related to the supply of raw materials. One of the reasons Ray Kroc eventually substituted frozen for fresh potatoes was that for several months a year it was difficult to obtain the desired variety of potato. Freezing potatoes made them readily available on a year-round basis. In addition, the skins left over after potatoes were peeled at each McDonald's outlet often created a stench that was anathema to Kroc and the sanitized and uniform world that he was seeking to create. Frozen, peeled, and precut french fries also eliminated this unpredictability.

Not only are the food, structure, packaging, and logo predictable in fast-food restaurants, but also the people who work there. As a rule, one is generally likely to find well-scrubbed, smiling teenagers behind the counters at these restaurants. (This has changed in recent years as the fast-food industry has been unable to find an adequate supply of teenagers to satisfy its needs [see Chapter Seven].) Thus, you not only know what you are going to get at a fast-food restaurant, but you also know who is likely to serve it to you. It is reassuring to know that you are not going to encounter the kind of surly short-order cooks or gum-chewing waitresses (as much as we may romanticize them now) one encountered in non-McDonaldized "greasy spoons" and diners. Although some of these people might have been quite charming, most diners have come to prefer the predictability of relatively innocent teenage counterpeople.

To use another example from the movies, a classic scene in a Jack Nicholson film, *Five Easy Pieces*, is relevant here. Nicholson's character stops at a diner and encounters a traditional greasy-spoon waitress. Not only does she anger Nicholson, but also the early forms of McDonaldization are represented by the diner's policy that one cannot get an order of toast even though one can order a sandwich made *with* toast. Nicholson's character reacts even more strongly and negatively to the McDonaldization than he does to the surly waitress.

Not only are the counterpeople at fast-food restaurants very predictable, but so are the managers and their assistants. To help ensure predictable managerial behavior, McDonald's has its central Hamburger University as well as a number of local branches. Potential managers are trained in these settings in which they internalize the ethos and the techniques employed by McDonald's. As a result, in look and behavior, McDonald's managers are hard to distinguish from one another. More importantly, it is the managers who have the responsibility to train and oversee counterpeople and to be sure that they behave as they are supposed to. In their efforts to ensure predictability, McDonald's managers are aided by elaborate corporate guidelines that detail how virtually everything is to be done in all restaurants. McDonald's central headquarters periodically sends forth inspectors to be sure that these guidelines are in force. These inspectors also check to be sure that the food meets quality control guidelines, in other words, that it is as predictable as the fast-food consumer has come to expect.

Turning to meals served at home, the predictability of foods has led to a disturbing fact:

Regional and ethnic distinctions are disappearing from American cooking. Food in one neighborhood, city, or state looks and tastes pretty much like food anywhere else. Americans are sitting down to meals largely composed of such items as instant macaroni and cheese, soft white bread, oleomargarine, frozen doughnuts, and Jell-O. Today it is possible to travel from coast to coast, at any time of year, without feeling any need to change your eating habits. . . . Sophisticated processing and storage techniques, fast transport, and a creative variety of formulated convenience-food products have made it possible to ignore regional and seasonal differences in food production.

The frozen TV dinner represented a watershed in the evolution of predictable meals prepared at home. In nicely uniform packaging is a predictable aluminum tray with a comforting set of (usually) four compartments including a main course (for example, a few slices of turkey and a dollop of stuffing), perhaps a helping of peas (presumably including exactly the same [or close to it] number of peas), a mound of mashed potatoes or another starch, and a dessert, such as peach cobbler. Diners may feel a rush of emotion when they peel away the aluminum foil and there before their eyes is that beloved familiar meal. Diners know that it isn't going to be a gourmet meal, but it is going to be just like the TV dinner they had for dinner yesterday (although a few slices of pot roast might have been substituted for the turkey) and the TV dinner they might devour the next night.

Of course, the TV dinner has now been joined and, in some cases, superseded by even more rational meals eaten at home. The microwavable dinner may not be any more predictable than the TV dinner was, but it is more efficient to store (in the closet rather than the freezer) and cook (a few minutes in the microwave rather than a half hour or so in the oven). But make no mistake about it—microwavable foods do offer considerable predictability. And to this list of advances we can also add the freeze-dried foods that blossom into a predictable dish with merely the addition of boiling water.

Norman Bates, RVs, and "McStables"

In his classic thriller *Psycho*, Alfred Hitchcock exploited beautifully the concerns about old-fashioned, unpredictable motels (discussed earlier). The motel in the movie was creepy, but not as creepy as its owner, Norman Bates. Although it offered few amenities, the Bates Motel room did come equipped with a peephole (something most travelers could do without) so that Norman could spy on his victims. Of course, the Bates Motel offered the ultimate in unpredictability—a homicidal maniac and a horrible death to unsuspecting guests. Although few motels were likely to house crazed killers, there were all sorts of unpredictabilities that confronted the traveler.

The movie *Psycho* brings to mind the fact that the movie industry, too, values rationalization in general, and predictability in particular. One manifestation of this is the popularity of sequels to successful movies at the expense of completely new movies based on new concepts, ideas, and characters. *Psycho*, for example, was followed by several sequels, as were other horror films, such as *Halloween* and *Nightmare on Elm Street*. Outside of the horror movie genre, a range of other movies has been succeeded by one or more sequels, including *Star Wars, Raiders of the Lost Ark* (which introduced Indiana Jones), *The Godfather*, and *Back to the Future*.

The routine use of sequels to highly successful movies is a relatively new phenomenon in Hollywood. Its development parallels, and is part of, the McDonaldization of society. The attraction of sequels is their predictability. From the point of view of the studios, the same characters, actors, and basic plot lines can be used over and over. Furthermore, there seems to be a greater likelihood that sequels will be successful at the box office than completely original movies; profit levels are more predictable. From the viewers' perspective, there is great comfort in knowing that they will once again encounter favorite characters played by familiar actors who find themselves in accustomed settings. Thus, in a series of *Vacation* movies, Chevy Chase plays the same character. The only thing that varies is the vacation setting in which he practices his very familiar antics. Moviegoers seem more willing to shell out money for a safe and familiar movie than for a movie that is completely new to them. Like a McDonald's meal, many sequels are not very good, but at least the consumers know what they are getting.

Movie ratings systems also serve to ensure a predictable amount of violence, nudity, and objectionable (to some) language. On the one hand, a G rating means that a parent can be sure that the movie contains no nudity and objectionable language, and only mild forms of violence; on the other hand, an NC-17 rating means that all of these things are likely to be found in the movie and to a high degree. The ratings are quantified by age: A PG rating means that it is okay to take children under 13 years of age, a PG-13 rating indicates that a movie may be inappropriate for children under 13, R supposedly means that parental consent is needed by children under 17, and an NC-17 rating is supposed to ban all children under 17 from seeing the movie.

The package tour is as oriented to predictability as it is to efficiency. That is, a person who signs up for a package tour is looking for a trip that offers no surprises. What this often translates into is an effort to have minimal contact with the people, culture, and institutions of the countries being visited. This creates a paradox: People go to considerable expense and effort to go to foreign countries where they hope to have as little contact as possible with native culture. (An American amusement park, Busch Gardens, offers European attractions, such as a German-style beer hall, without having its clientele leave the predictable confines of the United States and the even more predictable surroundings of the modern amusement park.) The tour group is likely to be made up of like-minded fellow Americans, and the vast majority of one's time is spent with those (highly predictable) people. Further predictability is ensured by the fact that people on such tours often travel with family members and friends. Travel is undertaken, wherever possible, on American carriers. Local transports offer the amenities expected by the American tourist (perhaps even air conditioning, stereo, bathroom). Tour guides are either Americans, people who have spent time in America and with Americans, or at least natives fluent in English and knowledgeable about the needs and interests of Americans. Restaurants visited on the tour are either American (for example, one of the American fast-food chains) or those that in structure and menu cater to the American palate. Hotels are also likely to be either American chains, such as Sheraton and Hilton, or European hotels that have structured themselves to suit American tastes. (On the opening of the Istanbul Hilton, Conrad Hilton said, "Each of our hotels . . . is a 'little America.'") Each day has a firm, often quite tight schedule, so that there is little time available for spontaneous and unpredictable activities. Tourists can take comfort from knowing the day's schedule before the day's outing begins and perhaps even before the trip commences. They can know exactly what they are going to do on a daily, even hourly, basis.

The package tour is also designed to shelter travelers from a variety of the unpredictabilities of travel. People take such tours because they believe they are much less likely to be accosted by beggars or pickpockets, to be humiliated because of their lack of facility with foreign languages, to be made ill by polluted water or bad food, and affected by other vagaries of travel. The tour, the tour guide, and the preselected sites, hotels, and restaurants are all supposed to greatly reduce the possibility of such unpredictable occurrences. Of course, also eliminated in the process are the unanticipated events that can make foreign travel so interesting—meeting a fascinating native, discovering a charming little shop or restaurant, or happening upon an unexpected sight.

A similar process can be seen in camping. At one time people went camping in search of something different: an escape from the predictable routines of their daily lives. City dwellers fled their homes in search of life in nature with little more than a tent and a sleeping bag. There was little or nothing between the camper and the natural environment. This led to some unpredictable events, but that was the whole point. One might see a deer wander close to one's campsite, perhaps even venture into it. Of course, one might also encounter the unexpected thunderstorm, tick bite, or errant snake, but these were accepted as an integral part of escaping one's routine activities. Here is the way one person describes the ups and downs of this kind of camping:

> Of course it began to pour. We had neglected to pack the main tent pole, which is like forgetting the mast on a sailboat. There is no tent without the tent pole. At first we failed to grasp this, so we kept trying to get the tent to stand. The whole structure kept collapsing like some big green bear that had been shot. Just when we were exasperated and began to dream of Holiday Inns [a common fantasy in our rationalized society], a deer appeared not two feet from our son. . . .
>
> "Look!" our child said, enraptured. "Look, my first deer!"

Some people still camp in this manner; many others have sought to eliminate unpredictability from camping. Said the owner of a campground, "All they wanted [in the past] was a space in the woods and an outhouse. . . . But nowadays people aren't exactly roughing it." Instead of simple tents, modern campers might venture forth in a recreational vehicle—or RV—such as the Winnebago, or with a trailer with an elaborate pop-up tent, to protect them from the unexpected. Of course, "camping" in an RV also tends to reduce the likelihood of catching sight of wandering wildlife. Furthermore, the motorized camper carries within it all of the predictable elements that one has at home—refrigerator, stove, television, video recorder, and stereo.

Camping technology has not only made for great predictability, but also changes in the modern campgrounds. Relatively few people now pitch their tents in the unpredictable wilderness; most find their way into rationalized campgrounds. Indeed, we have lately witnessed the development of "county-club campgrounds," spearheaded by such franchises as Kampgrounds of America (KOA). Thus, modern campers can drive their campers or trailers into well-maintained campgrounds. Said one camper relaxing in his air-conditioned 32-foot trailer, "We've got everything right here. . . . It doesn't matter how hard it rains or how the wind blows." Modern campgrounds are likely to be divided into sections—one for tents, the other for RVs, each section broken into neat rows of generally tiny campsites. For those with RVs, hook-ups are provided so that the various technologies encased within them can be operated. After campers have parked and hooked up their RVs (or popped up their tents), they can gaze out and enjoy the sights—other tents, RVs, children on bikes—in other words many of the sights they tried to leave behind in the rationalized cities or suburbs. Campsite owners might also provide campers who are "roughing it" with such amenities as a well-stocked delicatessen, bathrooms and showers, heated swimming pools, a game room loaded with video games, a laundromat, a TV room, a movie theater, and even entertainment such as bands or comedians.

Modern amusement parks, especially when one compares them to their honky-tonk ancestors, are in many ways highly predictable places. For example, Disneyland and Walt Disney World take great pains to be sure that the visitor is not subject to any disorder. We have already seen how the garbage is whisked away so that people do not have to be disturbed by the sight of trash. Peanuts are banned from sale because the shells would make a mess underfoot. There is no chewing gum or cotton candy on the ground to cling to the visitors' feet; they too are banned. The classic middle-American family that visits the Disney parks is not likely to have its day disturbed by the sight of public drunkenness and drunken brawls. Disney offers a world of predictable, almost surreal, orderliness.

A second dimension of the predictability of modern amusement parks, like fast-food restaurants, is the sameness of the people who work there. It takes a lot of people to run these parks, and most of them are clean-cut, well-scrubbed high school and college students. A great effort is made to be sure that these employees all look alike. At Busch Gardens, in Virginia, "a certain amount of energy is devoted to making sure that smiles are kept in place. There are rules about short hair (for the boys) and no eating, drinking, smoking, or straw chewing on duty (for everyone). 'We're just supposed to be perfect, see,' one employee . . . said cheerfully."

Not only do the employees all look alike, but they are also supposed to act alike:

> Controlled environments hinge on the maintenance of the right kind of attitude among the lower echelons.
>
> "It is kind of a rah-rah thing. We emphasize cleanliness, being helpful, being polite."
>
> Consequently, there is a lot of talk at Busch Gardens about All American images and keeping people up and motivated. At the giant, *somewhat* German restaurant, the Festhaus, there are contests to determine who has the most enthusiasm and best attitude. One of the prizes is free trips to King's Dominion, Busch Garden's arch rival up the road. (Italics added.)

Thus the visitors to Busch Gardens and the other parks of this genre can expect to see and deal with highly predictable employees throughout their visit. In addition, few unanticipated things happen on any of the rides or in any of the attractions in such parks.

Various steps have been taken to make sporting events more predictable. We have already discussed how domes and artificial turf make unpredictable rainouts unlikely. Artificial turf also serves to allow the baseball to bounce more truly, making for fewer unpredictable hops caused by a clump of grass or a clod of earth that might be found on traditional grass playing fields. The new, more symmetrical baseball stadiums make balls hit off the walls carom more predictably. They also enable greater consistency from one park to another in the distance and height a baseball must be hit to be a home run. The classic nonrationalized and unpredictable baseball stadium is Fenway Park in Boston. An older stadium, it has a grass playing field and asymmetrical dimensions. Its famous "Green Monster," a close-in but high wall in left field, makes home runs out of relatively short high flies (which would be routine outs in other stadiums), and well-hit but low line drives hit the wall and go for base hits. Then there is Wrigley Field in Chicago where balls sometimes get lost in the ivy that covers the fences. Stadiums like Fenway Park and Wrigley Field and their unpredictabilities are now the exception in major league baseball.

Turning to tennis, a relatively recent development that has made tennis matches more predictable is the advent of the tie breaker. Prior to tie breakers, to win a set, one needed to win 6 games with a 2-game margin over one's opponent. But if the opponent was never more than one game behind, the set could go on and on. Some memorable, interminable tennis matches were played in which the scores of sets were on the order of 12-10. In an era of limitations imposed by television and other mass media, the tennis establishment decided to institute the tie breaker in many tournaments. If a set is deadlocked at 6 games each, a 12-point tie breaker is played. The first player to get 7 points with a 2-point margin is the winner. A tie breaker might go on beyond 12 points (if the players are tied at 6 points each), but it rarely goes on as long as close matches could prior to the advent of the tie breaker.

An interesting example of predictability in a previously highly unpredictable area is the rationalization of the training of racehorses. Trainer Wayne Lukas has set up a string of stables around the United States that have been labeled, predictably, "McStables." In the past, training stables have been independent operations specific to a given track. Thus, there has been great variation from one race track to another, and from one stable to another, in the way in which training is done. Lukas has tried to change that:

> Lukas has thrived by establishing and supervising far-flung divisions of his stable. "I think the absolute key to doing this is quality control," he said. "You cannot ever see a deviation of quality from one division to the other. The barns are the same. The feeding program is the same. . . ."
>
> "This is what makes it easy to ship horses around the country. Most horses, when they ship, have to adjust. There's never an adjustment necessary in our divisions. *It's the McDonald's principle.* We'll give you a franchise, and that franchise is going to be the same wherever you go." (Italics added.)

Multiple-Choice Exams, Newspaper Vending Machines, and "It Never Rains"

Turning to the university, whatever else one says about multiple-choice exams, they are highly predictable. The student who takes such an exam knows that there will be a question followed by four or five possible answers. It is highly likely that at least two of the answers will be outrageous which leaves the savvy student with the need to choose among the three remaining alternatives. Grades will likely come from the computer so there is little of the unpredictability associated with subjective grading by professors or graduate students. The exams and the grading are clearly far more predictable than essay exams in which the nature of the questions and the evaluation of the answers are much more likely to be subject to the whim of the grader.

Part of the success of *USA TODAY* is traceable to its predictability. Since it is a national newspaper, travelers are reassured by the fact that the familiar masthead and contents will be available wherever they go. Also *USA TODAY* vending machines (which look reassuringly like television sets), are identical from one place to another. As one executive put it, "A business traveler in Washington, D.C., can pick up a copy on Monday and have an identical rack smiling at him in Los Angeles on Tuesday." The structure and make-up of the newspaper is highly predictable from one day to another. The stories are all predictably short and easily digestible. There are as few surprises in one's daily *USA TODAY* as in one's nightly Big Mac.

The attraction of the shopping mall can also be credited, at least in part, to its predictability. For example, the unpredictabilities of weather are eliminated: "One kid who works here told me why he likes the mall. . . . It's because no matter what the weather is outside, it's always the same in here. He likes that. He doesn't want to know it's raining—it would depress him." The latter quotation points to another predictable aspect of shopping malls—they are always upbeat. The malls, like fast-food restaurants, are virtually the same from one place or time to another. Finally, those who spend their days wandering through malls are relatively free from the unpredictabilities of crime that might beset them when they wander through city streets.

Hierarchies, Standardization, and Identical Automobiles

Bureaucracies are far more predictable than other organizational forms. For one thing, people occupy offices and each office has attached to it a set of expectations about what an incumbent of that office is supposed to do. Those who occupy an office are expected to live up to those expectations. Thus, a coworker or a client who must deal with an office can expect that it will operate as expected, no matter which individual happens to occupy the office at a given point. Although there is some leeway, occupants of given offices cannot refuse to perform their functions or do them very differently.

For another, there is a clear hierarchy of offices in a bureaucracy and incumbents of offices know who to take orders from and who they may give orders to. This means that bureaucrats do not (usually) operate in a setting in which anyone who wants to can give them orders.

Further, virtually everything in a bureaucracy exists in written form. Thus one who reads the organization's rules and regulations knows what can be expected. There are printed forms for virtually every conceivable matter, and the handling of an issue often involves little more than filling out (in triplicate) the required form. Every issue of a given type is handled through the use of the same form.

Scientific management, as it was developed by Taylor, placed great emphasis on predictability. Clearly, in delineating the one best way to do a job, Taylor was seeking to develop an approach to be used by each and every worker. Taylor dealt with the issue of predictability largely under the heading of what he termed "standardization." Taylor believed that what most managers did was allow workers to choose their own individual tools and methods of doing a job. While this may have given the work some individuality, it led to low productivity and poor quality. Instead, Taylor sought the complete standardization of tools and work processes. In fact, he felt that poor standards were better than no standards at all in that they resulted in at least some improvement in productivity and quality. Of course, Taylor favored the development of clear and detailed standards that ensured that all workers did a job of a given type in exactly the same way. He thought this highly predictable manner of working would produce predictably high-quality work from one employee to another and from one day to the next. Standardized tools and procedures would also permit the production of more standardized products.

The assembly line, too, was a highly predictable structure that enhanced the likelihood of predictable work and predictable products. The alternative to the assembly line was to have a number of highly skilled craftspeople build a car. The problem with this was that the steps that each took would be somewhat unpredictable and would vary from person to person and from one time to another. Similarly, there would be small but significant differences in the finished products—each car would differ in some respects from the next. This, in turn, would lead to unpredictabilities in the operation and quality of the automobile. One car might run better or be less prone to breakdowns than another.

The assembly line eliminated much of this unpredictability. Highly specialized workers did one or a few things in a highly predictable fashion. If they did not perform as expected, it would show up down the line or be caught by quality control inspectors at the end of the line. As a result, the finished automobile was far more predictable than that produced by a small number of skilled craftspeople. All automobiles were virtually identical to each other and their performance and quality was also much more similar.

From Subjectivity to Objectivity in Medicine

Historically, medicine has been anything but predictable. Physicians in private practice operated largely autonomously and each tended to have his or her own method of practicing medicine. When they entered organizations—that is, when they affiliated with hospitals or group practices—they were largely free of the organizational constraints that might have made their actions more predictable.

A variety of forces are pushing medicine in the direction of greater predictability, that is, various medical practices being made essentially the same from one time or place to another. The growing influence of various bureaucracies over physicians, especially for the increasing number who will be employed by them, is leading to much more predictability in medical practice. All of these organizations, like all bureaucracies, are based on a series of rules, regulations, and formalized controls that will constrain physicians and lead them to practice medicine in a more predictable manner. That is, the actions of one physician will not be much different from others; medical decisions made at one time or place will be similar to those made at other times or places. Although all organizations will push medicine in the direction of greater predictability, this is especially the case in for-profit organizations. The goal of such organizations is secure profitability as well as predictable increases in profitability from one year to the next. Such demands will lead them to impose more and more predictability on the actions of the physicians they employ. More predictable actions will lead to surer levels of profitability. The larger the organization, the greater the pressure toward predictability and the trend toward medical conglomerates is clearly fostering this development. Furthermore, "McDoctors," modeled after fast-food restaurants, are based on rules, regulations, and controls so that what physicians do in them will be highly predictable.

Similarly, pressures from third-party payers to control costs will also lead to greater predictability in medicine. Instead of the physician making independent subjective judgments about such things as length of stay or tests required, these are being dictated by the policies of the federal government and private third-party payers.

Another factor leading to greater predictability in medicine is the influx of advanced medical technologies. Basically, there is a tendency for the unpredictable, subjective judgments of the doctor to be replaced by more objective judgments rendered by various high-powered technologies. Thus, a physician need no longer guess from a series of diagnostic clues about whether a coronary artery is clogged; he or she can order an arteriogram that will objectively demonstrate whether such a blockage exists. Says one observer, "Medicine has now evolved to a point where diagnostic judgments based on 'subjective' evidence—the patient's sensations and the physician's own observations of the patient—are being supplanted by judgments based on 'objective' evidence, provided by laboratory procedures and by mechanical and electronic devices."

ET Visits Those "Little Boxes on the Hillside"

We can close this discussion of predictability in a McDonaldized society with the example of modern, suburban housing. As the famous folk song puts it:

> Little boxes on the hillside,
>
> Little boxes made of ticky-tacky,
>
> Little boxes, little boxes, little boxes
>
> Little boxes all the same.

In the post–World War II housing boom, an effort was made to make houses, and the homebuilding process, more predictable. This led to the birth of suburban communities made up of houses whose interiors and exteriors were little different from one another. Indeed, it was possible to wander into someone else's house and not realize for a moment that one was not in one's own home. Though there is some more diversity in more expensive developments, many suburbanites live in houses that are nearly identical to their neighbors'.

Furthermore, the communities themselves look very much alike. Established trees have been bulldozed to allow for the more efficient building of houses. In their place, a number of saplings, held up by posts and wire, have been planted. Similarly, hills may have been bulldozed to flatten the terrain. Streets are laid out in straight, symmetrical patterns. With such predictable landmarks, suburbanites may well enter the wrong suburban community or get lost in their own community.

Many of Steven Spielberg's movies take place in these rationalized and highly predictable suburbs. Spielberg's strategy is to lure the viewer into this highly predictable world and then to have a highly unpredictable event occur. For example, in *ET* the extraterrestrial wanders into a suburban development of tract houses and is discovered by a child who lives in one of those houses and who, up to that point, has lived a highly predictable suburban existence. The unpredictable ET eventually disrupts not only the lives of the child and his family, but also that of the entire community. Similarly, *Poltergeist* takes place in a suburban household and the evil spirits ultimately disrupt its predictable tranquility. (The spirits first manifest themselves through another key element of a McDonaldized society—the television set.) The great success of Spielberg's movies may be traceable to our longing for some unpredictability, even if it is frightening and menacing, in our increasingly predictable lives.

Conclusion

The third dimension of McDonaldization is predictability, or the effort to enable people to know what to expect at all times and in all places. The goal is the production of a world that offers no surprises. Motel chains such as Holiday Inn took the lead in providing the modern consumer with a predictable world, but it was closely followed by the food industry and the predictability of the food, setting, and behavior of the employees. Predictable food entered the home in the form of the frozen TV dinner, now being supplanted by the even more predictable microwavable dinners as well as freeze-dried meals. In the area of entertainment, predictability is found in the increasing reliance on movie sequels, the development of RVs and country-club campgrounds, and even in routinized horse-training stables. In the work world, bureaucratic structures, the standardization produced by Taylorism, and identical automobiles flowing from the assembly lines all reflect and extend predictability.

6

Control

Human and Nonhuman Robots

In this chapter we discuss the fourth dimension of McDonaldization—increased control and the replacement of human with nonhuman technology. In fact, the replacement of human with nonhuman technology is very often motivated by a desire for greater control. The great sources of uncertainty and unpredictability in any rationalizing system are people—either the people who work within those systems or who are served by them. Hence, the efforts to increase control are usually aimed at people.

McDonaldization involves the search for the means to exert increasing control over both employees and customers. Over the years, a variety of technologies designed to control people have been developed and deployed. Furthermore, and more extremely, nonhuman technologies have been steadily replacing the people who work in rationalized settings. After all, technologies like robots and computers are far easier to control than humans (except, perhaps, for fictional computers such as HAL in the movie *2001: A Space Odyssey*).

Technology is treated very broadly here to include not only machines and tools, but also materials, skills, knowledge, rules, regulations, procedures, and techniques. This allows us to conceive as technologies not only obvious things such as robots, computers, and the assembly line, but also bureaucratic rules and regulations and manuals defining accepted procedures and techniques.

The basic idea, historically, is to gradually and progressively gain control over people through the development and deployment of a wide variety of increasingly effective technologies. Once people are controlled, it is possible to begin reducing their actions to a series of machine-like actions. And once people are behaving like human machines, then it is possible to replace them with mechanical machines, most recently and most notably, mechanical robots. With the replacement of humans by machines, we have reached the ultimate stage in control over people—people can cause us no more uncertainty and unpredictability because they are no longer involved, at least directly, in the process.

Before the age of sophisticated nonhuman technologies, people were largely controlled by other people. In the work place, a subordinate was controlled on a direct, face-to-face basis by owners and supervisors. But such direct, personal control is difficult, costly, and likely to engender personal hostility among those being controlled. Subordinates are likely to strike out at an immediate supervisor or an owner who exercises excessively tight control over their activities. However, control that is manifest through a technology is easier, less costly in the long run, and less likely to engender hostility toward supervisors and owners. Thus, over the long term we have seen a shift away from control by people and toward control by technologies.

It is clearly *not* the case that the *only* goal of nonhuman technologies is control. Nonhuman technologies are created and implemented for a wide range of reasons, for example, increased productivity, greater quality, and lower cost. In spite of the lack of a perfect fit between control and increasing reliance on nonhuman technology, the main concern in this chapter is with the ways in which nonhuman technologies have increased control over people as employees and clients in a McDonaldizing society.

Bread Refineries, Sea Farms, and Chicken Factories

Instead of beginning with the production and consumption of food in the fast-food restaurant, let us begin with the production of some of the raw materials required by such restaurants—bread, fish, meat, and eggs.

Technologies designed to control people and reduce the uncertainties caused by them are found throughout the manufacture of food. For example, the manufacture of bread is no longer in the hands of skilled bakers who lavish love and attention on a few loaves of bread at a time. (See Chapter Nine for a discussion of one of the alternatives to a McDonaldized bakery.) Such skilled bakers cannot produce enough bread for our mass-consumption society, and the bread they do produce would suffer from the uncertainties involved in having humans do the work. That is, the bread may be too brown or underbaked. To increase productivity and to eliminate these unpredictabilities, mass producers of bread have developed an automated system in which, as in all automated systems, humans play a minimal role, and, when do they do act, it is rigidly controlled by the technology:

> The most advanced bakeries now resemble oil refineries. Flour, water, a score of additives, and huge amounts of yeast, sugar and water are mixed into a broth that ferments for an hour. More flour is then added, and the dough is extruded into pans, allowed to rise for an hour, then moved through a tunnel oven. The loaves emerge after 18 minutes, to be cooled, sliced, and wrapped.

In one food industry after another, technologies in which humans play little more than a planning and maintenance role have replaced production processes dominated by skilled craftspeople. The warehousing and shipping of food has been similarly automated.

Some rather startling technological developments have occurred in the ways in which we raise fish and animals for food. Here, unpredictabilities stem not only from human workers but also from the fish and animals. Thus, rational techniques have been developed to cope with both types of uncertainty.

In the case of fish there is "aquaculture," currently a $5-billion-a-year business, and growing dramatically as a result of the spiraling desire for seafood in an increasingly cholesterol-conscious population. Instead of a lone angler inefficiently casting a line with unpredictable results, or even huge boats catching tons of fish at a time in huge nets, we are witnessing an increase in the much more predictable and efficient "farming" of seafood. For example, more than 50 percent of the fresh salmon found in restaurants is raised in huge sea cages off the coast of Norway.

Sea farms provide a series of rational benefits. Most generally, aquaculture is a technology that allows humans to exert far greater *control* over the unpredictabilities that beset seafood in their natural habitat. The raising of seafood permits greater predictability of supply. Use of various drugs and chemicals permits increased predictability in the amount and quality of the seafood. Aquaculture also permits greater predictability and efficiency in the harvest since the seafood is confined to a limited space. In addition, geneticists can manipulate the seafood so that it is produced more efficiently. For example, it takes a halibut about ten years to reach market size, but a new dwarf variety can reach the required size in only three years. Sea farms also allow for greater calculability—the greatest number of fish for the least expenditure of time, money, and energy.

In the case of the raising of animals for food, relatively small family-run farms are being rapidly replaced by "factory farms." The first animal to find its way into the factory farm was the chicken. Here is the way one observer describes a chicken "factory":

> A broiler producer today gets a load of 10,000, 50,000, or even more day-old chicks from the hatcheries, and puts them straight into a long, windowless shed. . . . Inside the shed, every aspect of the birds' environment is controlled to make them grow faster on less feed. Food and water are fed automatically from hoppers suspended from the roof. The lighting is adjusted . . . for instance, there may be bright light twenty-four hours a day for the first week or two, to encourage the chicks to gain [weight] quickly. . . .
>
> Toward the end of the eight- or nine-week life of the chicken, there may be as little as half a square foot of space per chicken—or less than the area of a sheet of quarto paper for a three-and-one-half-pound bird.

Among its other advantages, such chicken farms allow one person to manage the raising of over 50,000 chickens. Raising chickens in this way involves a series of predictable steps. This not only allows for greater control over individual "farmers," but also the farmers in turn have far greater control over the chickens. As a result, the chickens' size and weight will be more predictable than that of free-ranging chickens. It is also more efficient to "harvest" chickens confined in this way than it is to catch chickens that are free to roam over large areas.

However, confining chickens in such crowded quarters creates such unpredictabilities as violence and even cannibalism. These irrational "vices" (which are caused by the unnaturally crowded conditions in which the chickens are forced to live) are dealt with in a variety of ways, such as dimming the light as the chickens approach full size and the "debeaking" of chickens so that they cannot harm one another.

Hens have another use—producing eggs. In the modern world of factory farming, hens are viewed as little more than "converting machines"—transforming raw material (feed) into a finished product (eggs). Peter Singer describes the technology employed to rationalize egg production:

The cages are stacked in tiers, with food and water troughs running along the rows, filled automatically from a central supply. They have sloping wire floors. The slope . . . makes it more difficult for the birds to stand comfortably, but it causes the eggs to roll to the front of the cage where they can easily be collected . . . in the more modern plants, carried by conveyor belt to a packing plant. . . . The excrement drops through [the wire floor] and can be allowed to pile up for many months until it is all removed in a single operation.

This obviously imposes great control over the hens and is a very efficient way to produce eggs; it also leads to a more predictable supply and more uniform quality of the eggs.

Other animals—pigs, lambs, steer, and especially young steer, or calves—are raised in similar factory-like settings. Calves produce veal; the most desirable calf is one that has the whitest meat and as little muscle as possible. To prevent their developing muscle, which toughens the meat, veal calves are immediately confined to tiny stalls where they cannot exercise and, as they grow in size, may not even be able to turn around. Being kept in stalls also prevents the calves from eating grass that would cause their meat to lose its pale color. The stalls are kept free of straw, which, if eaten by the calves, would also darken the meat. "They are fed a totally liquid diet, based on nonfat milk powder with added vitamins, minerals, and growth-promoting drugs," says Peter Singer in his book *Animal Liberation*. To make sure that the calves take in the maximum amount of food, they are given no water, thereby forcing them to keep drinking their liquid food. By rigidly controlling the size of the stall and the diet, veal producers are able to maximize two quantifiable objectives—the production of the largest amount of meat in the shortest possible time *and* the creation of the tenderest, whitest, and therefore most desirable veal. Young steer that are permitted to roam the fields produce tougher, less desirable veal.

Thus, the production of chicken, eggs, and meat has witnessed a transition from more human small farms and ranches to nonhuman technologies. These technologies obviously lead to greater control over the animals that produce the meat, thereby increasing the efficiency, calculability, and predictability of meat production. In addition, they exert control over farm workers. For example, left to their own devices, ranchers might feed a young steer the wrong food or too little food or permit them too much exercise. In the rigidly controlled factory ranch, such possibilities are eliminated. In fact, to the degree that such a ranch is highly automated, human ranch-hands (and their unpredictabilities) are virtually eliminated.

Automatic Drink Dispensers and Supermarket Scanners

Turning now to the consumption of food, one of the main sources of uncertainty in a traditional restaurant is the chef or cook. The mood of the cook can lead to great variation in meals. If the cook chose not to show up for work, that would spell disaster for the restaurant. Fast-food restaurants have coped with these problems by doing away with a cook, at least in the conventional sense of the term. The cooking, say the grilling of a hamburger, is so simple that anyone can do it with a bit of training. Furthermore, when a modest amount of cooking is required (as in the case of the Arby's roast beef discussed in Chapter Three), the fast-food restaurant develops a routine technology involving a few simple steps and procedures that almost anyone can follow. The cooking that does occur in the fast-food restaurant is essentially like a game of connect-the-dots or paint-by-the-numbers. Following prescribed steps eliminates most of the uncertainties and unpredictabilities associated with cooking.

Like the military, fast-food restaurants have recruited teenagers, at least until recently, because they adjust more easily than adults to surrendering their autonomy to machines, rules, and procedures. In recent years, the shortage of a sufficient number of teenagers to keep turnover-prone fast-food restaurants adequately stocked with employees has led to a widening of the traditional labor pool of fast-food restaurants. The fast-food restaurant seeks to maximize control even over the work behavior of adults, as we have previously discussed in Chapter Five.

Much of the food prepared at McDonald's arrives at the restaurant preformed, precut, presliced, and preprepared, often by nonhuman technologies. This serves to drastically limit what employees need to do—there is usually no need for them to form the burgers, cut the potatoes, slice the rolls, or prepare the apple pie. All they need to do is, where necessary, cook, or often merely heat, the food and pass it on to the customer. The more that's done by nonhuman technology before the food arrives at the fast-food restaurant, the less workers need to do and the less room they have to exercise their own judgments and skill.

At Taco Bell, workers used to spend hours cooking meat and shredding vegetables. Now, bags of frozen ready-cooked beef arrive and all the workers do is drop the bags in boiling water. Preshredded lettuce has been in use for some time, and now preshredded cheese and prediced tomatoes are beginning to appear. As a result, there is less and less for human workers to do at Taco Bell.

McDonald's has developed a variety of machines to control its employees. When a worker must decide when a glass is full and the soft-drink dispenser needs to be shut off, there is always the risk that the worker may be distracted and allow the glass to overflow. Thus, a sensor has been developed that automatically shuts off the soft-drink dispenser when the glass is full. When an employee must watch over the french-fry machine, there is always the danger that misjudgment may lead to fries that are undercooked, overcooked, or even burned. Ray Kroc fretted over the problem of human judgment in the cooking of french fries: "It was amazing that we got them as uniform as we did, because each kid working the fry vats would have his own interpretation of the proper color and so forth." Kroc's dissatisfaction with the vagaries of human judgment led to its elimination and the development of french-fry machines that ring or buzz when the fries are done, or that shut the machine off and lift the french-fry baskets out of the hot oil. When a worker at the cash register has to look at an item being purchased and then to the price list, there is the possibility that the wrong, perhaps even a lower, amount could be rung up. Computerized cash registers forestall that possibility. All the employee need do is press the picture on the register that matches the item purchased; the machine then calculates the correct price. In all of these ways, work traditionally done by people has been taken away from them and built into machines.

It could be argued that the objective in a fast-food restaurant is to reduce its employees to the level of functioning like human robots. There have even been isolated reports over the years of experiments with mechanical robots that serve the food. For example, the University of Wisconsin at Stout has built such a robot that serves hamburgers at the campus restaurant.

> The robot looks like a flat oven with conveyor belts running through and an arm attached at the end. A red light indicates when a worker should slide in a patty and bun, which bob along in the heat for 1 minute 52 seconds. When they reach the other side of the machine, photo-optic sensors indicate when they can be assembled.

The computer functioning as the robot's brain determines when the buns and patty are where they should be. If the bun is delayed, it slows the patty belt. If the patty is delayed, it slows bun production. It also keeps track of the number of buns and patties in the oven and determines how fast they need to be fed in to keep up speed.

These robots are seen as offering a number of advantages—lower cost, increasing efficiency, fewer workers, no absenteeism, and a solution to the decreasing supply of teenagers needed to work at fast-food restaurants. Said the professor who came up with the idea for such a robot, "Kitchens have not been looked at as factories, which they are. . . . Fast-food restaurants were the first to do that. We're just at the beginning." However, this robot still costs a great deal, can make only hamburgers, is relatively slow, and breaks down a great deal.

Taco Bell is currently in the process of developing "a computer-driven machine the size of a coffee table that . . . can make and seal in a plastic bag a perfect hot taco." Pepsico (which owns Kentucky Fried Chicken, Pizza Hut, and Taco Bell) has a prototype for an automated drink dispenser that produces a soft drink in 15 seconds: "Orders are punched in at the cash register by a clerk. A computer sends the order to the dispenser to drop a cup, fill it with ice and appropriate soda, and place a lid on top. The cup is then moved by conveyor to the customer." We *will* see widespread employment of such mechanical robots in fast-food restaurants when the technology is refined and affordable.

A very similar development has taken place in supermarkets. In the past, prices were marked on food products; the supermarket checker had to read the price and enter it into the cash register. As with all human activities, the process was slow and there was a chance for human error. To counter these problems, in recent years many supermarkets have installed optical scanners. Instead of the human checker reading the price, the mechanical scanner "reads" the code, and the price for a given code number has been entered into the computer that is the heart of the modern cash register. This nonhuman technology has eliminated some of the human uncertainty from the job of supermarket checker. It has also reduced the number, and level of sophistication, of the tasks performed by the checker. The checker no longer needs to read the amount and enter it in the cash register. Left are less skilled tasks like scanning the food and bagging it. In other words, the supermarket checker has undergone "deskilling"—that is, a decline in the amount of skill required on the job.

The next step at supermarket checkout stands is to have the customer do the scanning, thereby eliminating the need for a checkout person. In fact, a suburban Maryland Safeway has just instituted such a system. To make things easier, this Safeway provides its customers with a brochure entitled "Checkout for Yourself Just How Easy It Is." (Of course, one might ask easy for whom?) Here are the three "easy" steps for customers to perform:

1. Pass the item's barcode over the scanner. Wait for beep. Place item on conveyor belt.
2. When you are finished scanning all items, touch END ORDER button on screen.
3. Pick up receipt at the end of the lane. Proceed to the pay station.

Such military-like orders exert great control over the customer, and they allow for the elimination of the checkout person. Self checkout is also part of the process, discussed in Chapter Three, of passing more and more work on to the customer. Indeed, after they are done scanning, the customers must then bag their own groceries. The developer of one of these systems predicted that "within five years, self-service grocery technology could be as pervasive as the automatic cash machines used by bank customers." One customer, obviously a strong believer in McDonaldization, said of the system, "It's quick, easy and efficient. . . . You get in and out in a hurry." The next "advance" will permit the insertion of the customer's credit card in the scanning system, thereby avoiding the need to move on to a human cashier and pay for the food. (Such systems are already in existence, as we saw earlier, in some gasoline stations.)

The supermarket scanners permit other kinds of control over customers. Before the scanner, customers could examine their purchases and see how much each cost; they could also check to be sure that they were not being overcharged at the cash register. In those supermarkets with scanners, prices no longer appear on goods, only bar codes. This change gives the supermarket greater control over customers—in an increasing number of states, it is almost impossible for the consumer to keep tabs on the checkers.

Supermarkets control shoppers in other ways as well. Food placement is crucial to what consumers buy. For example, supermarkets take pains to put foods that are attractive to children in places where they can be readily grabbed by youngsters (for example, low on the shelves). For another, what a market chooses to feature through sale prices and strategic placement in the store has a profound effect on what is purchased. On the latter point, manufacturers and wholesalers battle one another for coveted display positions, such as at the front of the market. Whatever foods are placed in these positions are likely to sell far more than if they are relegated to their usual position.

Fast-food restaurants have, of course, greatly refined the effort to control the customer. Whether customers go into the restaurant or use the drive-through window, they enter a kind of conveyor system that moves them through the restaurant in a manner desired by the management. This is clearest in the case of the drive-through window (the energy for this conveyor comes from one's automobile), but it is also true for those who enter the restaurant. Consumers know that they are supposed to line up, move to the counter, order their food, pay, carry the food to an available table, eat, gather up their debris, deposit it in the trash receptacle, and return to their cars. People are moved along in this system not by a conveyor belt, but by the unwritten, but universally known, rules for eating in a fast-food restaurant.

One way fast-food restaurants have tried to tighten control of their customers is by influencing diners to leave the restaurants quickly. This is motivated by the restaurant's need for tables to be vacated quickly in order to allow other diners to have a place to eat their food. Perhaps today's fast-food restaurant owners are fearful of having happen to their franchises what befell the famous chain of cafeterias, the Automat, which was ruined, at least in part, by the fact that people used to occupy tables for hours on end. It became a kind of social center, leaving less and less room for people looking for tables to eat their meals. The death blow was struck when street people began to monopolize the Automat's tables.

To keep people moving through fast-food restaurants, security people may be employed to prevent diners from lingering at their tables or loitering in or around the restaurant. In the cities, this is designed to keep street people on the move, while in the suburbs it is more oriented to preventing potentially rowdy teenagers from monopolizing the tables or the parking lots. Seven-Eleven has sought to deal with the problem of teenagers loitering outside its stores by playing saccharine tunes like *Some Enchanted Evening*. Said a Seven-Eleven spokesperson, "They won't hang around and tap their feet to Mantovani."

Some fast-food restaurants have even put up signs limiting a customer's stay in the restaurant, say to 20 minutes. More generally, fast-food restaurants have structured themselves so that people do not want to linger over meals. The fact that the meal largely consists of easily and quickly consumed finger food leads people to eat quickly and leave. To be even more sure that people leave quickly, some fast-food restaurants have developed chairs that make customers feel uncomfortable after they sit on them for about 20 minutes.

Soups That Cook Themselves, Talking Automatons, Mall Zombies, and Junk Mail

The replacement of human with nonhuman technology, and the consequent increase in control, is found not only in the fast-food restaurant but also in home cooking. Technologies like the microwave or conventional oven with a temperature probe "decide" when food is done rather than leaving that judgment to the cook. Ovens, coffee makers, and other appliances now are able to turn themselves on and off. The instructions on all kinds of packaged foods dictate precisely how the food is to be prepared and cooked. Premixed products, like Mrs. Dash, combine an array of seasonings, eliminating the need for the cook to come up with creative combinations of seasonings. Even the now old-fashioned cookbook was designed to take creativity away from the cook who would be inclined to flavor to taste and to put it in the hands of the rigid guidelines laid down by the cookbook.

One of the latest advances in this realm is Nissin Foods' new Super Boil soup, the soup that cooks itself! There is a special compartment on the bottom of the can of soup. A turn of a key starts a chemical reaction that eventually boils the soup in the top compartment. Although available only in Japan at the moment, it seems only a matter of time until Super Boil soup will be available in the United States.

The modern amusement park is a technological marvel that controls the people who work there as well as the visitors to the park. Ideally, the young people who work in these parks are to look and act like machines and mechanical robots. Columnist Charles Krauthammer, following a visit to Walt Disney World with his children, describes the "forced cheer" of the workers and comments that he "had the momentary feeling of having wandered into a Chinese reeducation camp where everyone, guards included, was on Thorazine."

An interesting example of this kind of control over employees occurred prior to the opening of the new Euro DisneyLand outside Paris in 1992. New workers were told the following:

Employees are compelled to maintain weight in harmony with their height. Men are forbidden to sport beards, moustaches, long hair or jewelry. Women must not wear short skirts or use mascara. Only one ring per hand and one earring per ear will be allowed, and only appropriate undergarments of a natural . . . color should be worn under a dress.

While prospective employees seemed willing to accept these rules and the control they exerted over their appearance, one of France's leading labor unions took Disney to court for impinging on civil liberties.

In some amusement parks, humans do the performing, but their songs, dances, and speeches are rigidly programmed. Again, once human performance is reduced to this level, then it is but a short step to replacing these human robots with nonhuman robots when the technology is available and makes economic sense. In fact, many exhibits already use life-like, talking automatons. Those who visit the parks are similarly controlled, although again not quite so overtly. Traffic patterns, paths, signs, guides, monorails, and moving conveyances of one kind or another are all nonhuman technologies designed to control what people do and to keep them moving through the park.

The shopping mall also exerts great control over shops and shopkeepers. Before allowing shops to open, mall developers often must approve of their design, logo, colors, and even names. Once open, mall management proliferates innumerable rules and regulations and enforces them on shops. Security people are used to inspect shops and to take note of those that violate the rules (for example, opening or closing a few minutes early or late). Persistent violators may be expelled from the mall. Efforts are made to exclude controversy and controversial groups from the malls.

Malls also exert control over customers, especially children and young adults. Programmed by the mass media to be avid consumers, people enter malls that operate in such a way as to make them lifelong frequenters of mall-based shops. Parents are led to accept this role for the malls because it provides them with a safe and controlled environment. Parents feel that their children are safer in the malls than on the streets and roads of our cities and towns. Malls also lull and manipulate adults so that they may feel like they are little more than what Kowinski calls "zombies" wandering the malls hour after hour, weekend after weekend.

Telemarketing is an increasingly popular sales device. Many of us are called several times a day in efforts to sell us something. Those who work in these telemarketing "factories" are strictly controlled. They are usually given scripts and expected to follow them unerringly. The scripts are designed to handle most foreseeable contingencies. Supervisors often listen in on conversations in order to be sure that the correct procedures are being followed. There are requirements for the number of calls made, and sales completed, in a given time period. If employees fail to meet the quotas, they may be fired summarily.

The people who receive such calls, and do not hang up immediately, are dealing with robot-like humans. Again, following the usual progression, instead of having people solicit us over the phone, some companies are now using computer calls. Computer voices are far more predictable and controllable than even the most rigidly controlled human operator. Indeed, in our increasingly McDonaldized society, I have had some of my most interesting conversations with such computer voices.

Not only do we have computer calls, but we are now seeing computers that respond to the human voice via voice recognition systems. A person receiving a collect call might be asked by the computer voice whether she will accept the charges. The computer voice demands, "Please say yes or no." While efficient and cost-saving, such a system is anonymous and dehumanizing: "The person senses that he cannot use free-flowing speech. He's being constrained. The computer is controlling him. It can be simply frustrating. . . . People adapt to it, but only by filing it away subconsciously as another annoyance of living in our technological world."

In addition, we are daily bombarded by a mountain of computerized letters, or "junk mail." In some cases great pains are taken to make it seem as if a letter has actually been sent to us personally, but in most cases it is fairly obvious that our names appear on some computer-generated list and the computer has mailed us the letter. These letters are full of the kind of false fraternization described earlier in the case of the Roy Rogers' workers. For example, the letters often adopt a friendly, personal tone that is designed to lead us to believe that the leaders of our largest businesses have been fretting over the fact that we haven't shopped in their department store or used their credit card in the past few months. For example, a friend of mine recently received a letter from a franchise, The Lube Center, a few days after he had his car lubricated (note the use of the first name and the "deep" personal concern):

Dear Ken:

We want to THANK YOU for choosing The Lube Center for all of your car's fluid needs. . . .

We strongly recommend that you change your oil on a regular basis . . . we will send you a little reminder card. . . . This *will help remind you* when your car is next due to be serviced. . . .

We spend the time and energy to make sure that our employees are trained properly to give you the service that *you deserve.* . . .

> Sandy Grindstaff/Randall S. Simpson
> The Lube Center Management
> (Italics added.)

Also, recently I was sent the following letter by a Congressman from Long Island even though I live in Maryland. I have never met Congressman Downey and I know nothing about him, but this didn't prevent him from writing me a "personal" letter:

Dear George:

It is hard to believe, but I am running for my NINTH term in Congress! . . .

When I think back over the 8,660 votes I've cast . . . I realize how many battles *we've shared.*

Please let me know that I can count on *you.*

> Sincerely,
>
> *Tom* Downey (Italics added.)

A *Washington Post* correspondent offers the following critique of false friendliness in junk mail: "By dropping in peoples' names and little tidbits gleaned from databases hither and yon in their direct mail pitches, these marketing organizations are trying to create the illusion of intimacy. In reality, these technologies conspire to *corrupt and degrade intimacy.* They cheat, substituting the insertable fact for the genuine insight. These pitches end up with their own synthetic substitutes for the real thing."

The Disappearing Black Bag

As in all rational systems, there is a trend in medicine away from human technologies and toward nonhuman technologies. The two most important examples of this are the growing importance of bureaucratic rules, regulations, and controls, and the growth of modern medical machinery. Instead of a physician making an independent, subjective judgment, we are likely to see those judgments determined by bureaucratic rules and regulations. For example, the prospective payment and DRG (diagnostic related groups) systems—not physicians and their medical judgment—tend to determine how long a patient is to be hospitalized. Similarly, the doctor operating alone out of a black bag with a few primitive tools has virtually become a thing of the past. Instead, doctors are serving as dispatchers, sending patients on to the appropriate machines and specialists. The judgment of the physician is being replaced, at least in part, by technological judgments. We are even beginning to see computer programs that diagnose illnesses. Although it is unlikely that the computer will ever replace the physician, computers may one day be the initial, if not the prime, diagnostic agents. There is also a trend toward do-it-yourself medical testing (for pregnancy, diabetes, high blood pressure, and other conditions) that takes control completely away from the physician and is, as well, another example of putting the client to work.

These developments in modern medicine, and many of those discussed in earlier chapters, are leading to increasing external control over the medical profession. Even in its heyday the medical profession was not free of external control, but the nature of the control is changing and its degree and extent is increasing greatly. More and more of the actions of physicians are coming to be controlled by external organizations, such as third-party payers, employing organizations, for-profit hospitals, health maintenance organizations, the federal government, and "McDoctors"-like organizations. Instead of the more autonomous decision making of the doctor in private practice, we have a variety of such organizations controlling, and in some cases even determining, the decision-making process. All of these organizations have rules and regulations, and the physician is increasingly likely to be controlled by them. Bureaucracies are premised on the notion of control from the top, which means that employed physicians are being controlled by superiors in the organization. These superiors are more and more likely to be professional managers and not fellow MDs. The result is that the much more constraining top-down control is replacing peer control. Bureaucracies are also characterized by formalized and codified technical standards. What the physician does in such organizations is likely to be controlled by these formal codes. Also, the existence of such hugely expensive medical technologies often mandates that they be used by the medical profession. As the machines themselves grow more sophisticated, physicians come to understand them less and are less able to control them. Instead, control shifts to the technologies as well as to the experts who create and handle the technologies.

From the patient's point of view, control is shifting away from the primary care physician and to these various structures and technologies. Minimally this involves a qualitative shift in the nature of control over patients, maximally it means a vast increase in the control of patients by large, impersonal systems.

"Education for Docility," TV Preachers, and Automated Check-In

Schools, especially in the lower grades, have developed a variety of technologies aimed at exerting control over students. Many schools' goals, right from the start, are to have students conform to their rules and regulations. This is even noticeable in kindergarten, which has been described as educational "boot camp." Those who conform to the rules are thought of as good students, while those who don't are labeled bad students. Not only are students taught to be obedient to authority, but also to be receptive to the rationalized procedures of rote learning and objective testing to be sure that they have learned what they should have. More importantly, spontaneity and creativity tend not to be rewarded, and may even be discouraged, leading to what one expert calls "education for docility."

The clock and the lesson plan are technologies used to exert control over students. The "tyranny of the clock" pervades the school system (and many other social systems as well). A class must last until, and end at, the sound of the bell, even though learning does not often conform to the clock. Thus, even if students are just about to comprehend something, the lesson must end and the class must move on to something else. Another example of control in education is the "tyranny of the lesson plan." A class must focus on what the teacher's lesson plan says is the topic of the day, no matter what the class (and perhaps the teacher) may be interested in at a given point. There is the example of a teacher "who sees a cluster of excited children examining a turtle with enormous fascination and intensity. Now children, put away the turtle, the teacher insists. We're going to have our science lesson. The lesson is on crabs." In sum, the emphasis tends to be on producing submissive, malleable students; creative, independent students are often, from the point of view of the educational system, "messy, expensive, and time-consuming."

An even more extreme version of this is found in the child-care variant of the fast-food restaurant, Kinder-Care. Kinder-Care tends to hire short-term employees with little or no training in child care. What these employees do in the "classroom" is largely determined by a uniform "instruction book" that includes a preset, ready-made cur-riculum. Staff members open the manual to the appropriate place where activities are spelled out in detail on a day-to-day basis. Clearly, a skilled, experienced, and creative teacher is not the kind of person "McChild" care centers seek to hire. Rather, relatively untrained em-ployees are more easily controlled by the nonhuman technology of the omnipresent "instruction book."

Another example of this is the franchised Sylvan Learning Center, which has been labeled the "McDonald's of Education." Sylvan learn-ing centers are after-school centers for remedial education. The corpo-ration "trains staff and tailors a McDonald's type uniformity, down to the U-shaped tables at which instructors work with their charges."

The greater control resulting from the substitution of nonhuman for human technology can also be found in religion in the growth of television preachers. Even the Vatican has gotten into the act with its Vatican Television Center. Instead of interacting with a human preach-er, millions of worshippers now interact with an image on the televi-sion screen. Television permits preachers to reach far more people than could be reached in a conventional church and thereby to exert, or so they hope, greater control over what people believe and do. TV preachers utilize the full panoply of techniques developed by media experts to control their viewers. Thus, some TV preachers use a for-mat much like that used on entertainment talk shows hosted by Johnny Carson or David Letterman. Jokes, orchestras, singers, and guests— all are employed to entertain the viewer in order to better communicate the preacher's message and, not insignificantly, to extract enormous con-tributions. However, the major impact from the point of view of this chapter is the greater control exerted over people. Here is the way one observer describes Vatican television: "The big advantage to the Vatican of having its own television operation . . . is that they can put their own spin on anything they produce. If you give them the cameras and give them access, they are in control."

Politics has also been dramatically affected by nonhuman technologies. Again, the most obvious example is the use of television to manipulate voters. Indeed, most people never see a politician unless it is on the TV screen. And when politicians are seen on the screen it is most likely in a firmly controlled format designed to communicate just the message and image desired by the politicians and their media advisers. President Ronald Reagan raised this to an art form in the 1980s. On many occasions, visits were set up and TV images arranged so that the viewers and potential voters got precisely the visual message intended by Reagan's media advisers. Most of Reagan's TV appearances were carefully managed to be sure that the right message was communicated. Conversely, less controlled press conferences were held to a minimum because the questions that were asked of the president, and many of the answers he gave, could not be determined in advance.

A new development in hotels is automated check-in. Instead of dealing with a human desk clerk, the guest can deal with a computer screen and automatically receive a key and a receipt. The guest is able to choose the type and price of the room. The machine even politely welcomes the guest, something some desk clerks have been known to forget to do. In the end, of course, the machine limits and controls the guest. Requests that can be made of desk clerks are made impossible by automated check-in systems.

Bureaucratic Constraints, the One Best Way, and Repetitive Labor

Bureaucracies can, in effect, be seen as large-scale, nonhuman technologies. These are huge nonhuman structures with innumerable rules, regulations, guidelines, positions, lines of command, and hierarchies that are designed to dictate, as much as possible, what people do within the system and how they do it. The consummate bureaucrat thinks little about what is to be done, but simply follows the rules, deals with incoming work, and passes it on to the next step in the hierarchy. To further limit human choice and error, paper forms are developed, and the employees need do little more than fill out the required form and pass it on, up, or across the bureaucratic hierarchy.

Bureaucracies control not only the people who work within them, but also those who are served by them. Rules, regulations, prescribed paperwork, and many other aspects of bureaucratic life are designed to get the bureaucracy's clients to behave in a prescribed manner.

Scientific management clearly had as one of its ends the creation of nonhuman technology designed to limit or replace human technology. The one best way was a series of steps that all workers were to learn and follow in a mindless fashion. More generally, Taylor believed that the most important part of the work world was not the workers, or even the managers, but rather the organization that must be constructed to plan, oversee, and control their work.

While Taylor wanted all employees to be controlled by the organization, he accorded managers much more leeway than manual workers. It was the task of management to study the knowledge and skills of workers and to record, tabulate, and, ultimately, reduce that knowledge and skill to laws, rules, and even mathematical formulas. To put this slightly differently, managers were to take a body of *human* skills, abilities, and knowledge and transform them into a set of *inhuman* rules, regulations, and formulas. Since human skills were then codified, it was no longer necessary to hire skilled workers. Unskilled workers were to be hired, trained by management, and then employed in accord with a set of strict guidelines. In effect, what Taylor championed, and did, was to separate "head" from "hand" work. In the past, they had been combined in the skilled worker. Taylor and his followers studied and learned what was in the heads of those skilled workers, and then translated that knowledge into guidelines that could be taught to, and followed by, virtually anyone. Workers were left with little more than "hand work." This principle remains at the base of the movement throughout our McDonaldizing society to replace human with nonhuman technology.

Behind Taylor's scientific management, and all other efforts to replace human with nonhuman technology, is a goal of employing human beings with minimal intelligence and ability. In fact, Taylor sought to hire people who resembled lower animals, which can seen as the precursor to the contemporary effort to reduce human activities to robot-like actions so that the humans can be replaced by nonhuman robots. Taylor did not have mechanical robots at his disposal, so all he could do was to hire humans who resembled lower animals and then to dictate to them in great detail what they were to do on the job. It is worth quoting Taylor at length on this issue:

> Now one of the very first requirements for a man who is fit to handle pig iron as a regular occupation is that he shall be so stupid and so phlegmatic that he more nearly resembles in his mental make-up the ox than any other type. The man who is mentally alert and intelligent is for this very reason entirely unsuited to what would, for him, be the grinding monotony of work of this character. Therefore the workman who is best suited to handling pig iron is unable to understand the real science of doing this class of work. He is so stupid that the word "percentage" has no meaning to him, and he must consequently be trained by a man more intelligent than himself into the habit of working in accordance with the laws of this science before he can be successful.

It is no coincidence that Henry Ford had a similar view of the kinds of people who were to work on his assembly lines:

> Repetitive labour—the doing of one thing over and over again and always in the same way—is a terrifying prospect to a certain kind of mind. It is terrifying to me. I could not possibly do the same thing day in and day out, but to other minds, perhaps I might say to the majority of minds, repetitive operations hold no terrors. In fact, to some types of mind thought is absolutely appalling. To them the ideal job is one where creative instinct need not be expressed. The jobs where it is necessary to put in mind as well as muscle have very few takers—we always need men who like a job because it is difficult. The average worker, I am sorry to say, wants a job in which he does not have to think. Those who have what might be called the creative type of mind and who thoroughly abhor monotony are apt to imagine that all other minds are similarly restless and therefore to extend quite unwanted sympathy to the labouring man who day in and day out performs almost exactly the same operation.

The same kind of person sought out by Taylor was the kind of person who in Ford's view would work well on the assembly line. Such people, in this view, were more likely to submit to external technological control over their work and perhaps even crave such control. This perspective, in turn, lies behind the effort in fast-food restaurants, and many other components of a McDonaldizing society, to hire teenagers and have them operate as human automatons.

Conclusion

This chapter deals with the fourth dimension of McDonaldization—increased control through the replacement of human with nonhuman technology. In food production, nonhuman technologies are becoming increasingly ubiquitous, especially in the form of aquaculture and factory farming. The retail purveyors of food are coming to be dominated by such technologies as automatic drink dispensers, supermarket scanners, and even foods that cook themselves. In the amusement area, we find employees acting as human robots, and in shopping, the malls are turning people into mall "zombies." Doctors are increasingly controlled by nonhuman technologies. Teachers are constrained by preset lecture plans or now the even more restrictive instruction books of "McChild" care centers. In the work world, people are controlled by bureaucratic constraints, Taylor's one best way, and the assembly line.

Clearly, the future will bring with it an increasing number of nonhuman technologies with greater ability to control people. For example, we already have such military hardware as "smart bombs," which adjust their trajectories without human intervention so that they are able to hit their targets. In the future, we can expect smart bombs that scan an array of targets and "decide" which one to hit. Perhaps the next great step will be the expansion of artificial intelligence and the computers that practice it. Artificial intelligence gives machines the apparent ability to think and make decisions as humans do. Artificial intelligence promises many benefits in a wide range of areas (in medicine, for example). However, it also constitutes an enormous step in taking skills away from people. In effect, more and more of peoples' ability to think will be taken from them and built into the technology. Clearly, this promises still greater control of nonhuman technology over people. Smart bombs of the future endowed with artificial intelligence may "decide" to hit targets that their inventors never envisioned. Whether or not such dire scenarios occur, it seems clear that the coming growth of artificial intelligence will be utilized in a McDonaldizing society to extend control over people.

7

The Irrationality of Rationality
Traffic Jams on Those "Happy Trails"

Although there has been much criticism of McDonaldization in the preceding chapters, it has swept across much of the social landscape because it offers increased efficiency, predictability, calculability, and control through the substitution of nonhuman for human technology. In addition, many more specific advantages are found in the numerous settings that have undergone, or are undergoing, McDonaldization. Despite these advantages, the preceding chapters have been critical of McDonaldization. This chapter deals more systematically with the great costs associated with McDonaldization under the heading of the irrationality of rationality. In other words, it is the thesis of this text, following Weber, that rational systems inevitably spawn a series of irrationalities that serve to limit, ultimately compromise, and perhaps even undermine, their rationality.

We can conceive of the irrationality of rationality in several ways. At the most general level, it is simply the overarching label for many of the negative aspects and effects of McDonaldization. More specifically, it can be seen as the opposite of rationality and its several dimensions. That is, McDonaldization can be viewed as leading to *in*efficiency, *un*predictability, *in*calculability, and *loss* of control. Most specifically, irrationality means that rational systems are *unreasonable* systems—they serve to deny the basic humanity, the human reason, of the people who work within them or are served by them. In other words, rational systems are dehumanizing systems. Whereas the terms *rationality* and *reason* are often used interchangeably in other contexts, here they are employed to mean antithetical phenomena.

Before we get to the main irrationality of rationality—dehumanization—we will deal with some of the lesser irrationalities, especially inefficiency.

Long Lines and That Familiar Lube Job

We begin with the observation that rational systems, contrary to their promise, often end up being quite inefficient. The most obvious manifestation of the inefficiency of the fast-food restaurant is the long lines of people that are often found at the counters or the parade of cars that snake by the drive-through windows. What is purported to be an efficient way of obtaining a meal can often turn out to be quite inefficient.

In recognition of this inefficiency, McDonald's is now considering introducing a private television network in its stores. The network would beam entertainment, news, and especially advertisements to a daily audience estimated to be 15 million people. (A similar effort, Checkout Channel for people waiting in supermarket checkout lines, is also under development.) On the one hand, this represents another forward step in rationalization because now people will be able to do two things at one time—wait in line *and* watch television. On the other hand, and of central interest here, is the fact that this represents a tacit admission that people *are* waiting in line for their fast food, that fast food isn't so fast, and that these efficient systems aren't so efficient. Thus, an executive of the firm developing the new television network says, "One of the biggest customer concerns is the problem of queuing. . . . Anything a retailer can do to lessen the perceived wait is going to be a benefit."

The fast-food restaurant (and the supermarket) is far from the only aspect of our McDonaldized society that exhibits inefficiency. Interestingly, even the vaunted Japanese industry has its inefficiencies. Previously, we have discussed the "just-in-time" system as an example of the rationality of Japanese industry. However, it turns out that there are enormous inefficiencies associated with this system. Because the just-in-time system often requires that parts be delivered several times a day, the streets and highways are cluttered with trucks. Thus, people are often late for work or for business appointments. The result is lost productivity or, more generally, irrationality. The situation is made even worse now because Japanese convenience stores, supermarkets, and department stores have also begun to use a just-in-time system. This brings even greater numbers of delivery trucks onto the streets of Japan's cities. But the irrationalities go beyond traffic jams and missed appointments. All these trucks are wasting fuel, which is very expensive in Japan, and making a major contribution to air pollution.

Here is the way columnist Richard Cohen describes the inefficiencies of the automated teller machines (ATMs), and in the process deals with a point covered in several discussions earlier in this book—the tendency in a rational society to use the consumer as an unpaid worker:

> Oh Lord, with each advance of the computer age, I was told I would benefit. But with each "benefit," I wind up doing more work. This is the ATM rule of life. . . . I was told—nay promised—that I could avoid lines at the bank and make deposits or withdrawals any time of the day. Now, there are lines at the ATMs, the bank seems to take a percentage of whatever I withdraw or deposit, and, of course, I'm doing what tellers (remember them?) used to do. Probably, with the new phone, I'll have to climb telephone poles in the suburbs during ice storms.

Cohen underscores at least three different irrationalities—rational systems are not less expensive, they force us to do a range of unpaid work, and, most importantly from the point of view of this discussion, they are often inefficient. The fact is that the rationalized system is often *not* the most efficient means to an end, especially from the perspective of the customer. Perhaps on a cold, snowy night, it might be more efficient to deal with a human teller, either in the bank or drive-through window than to wait in line at an ATM. For many, it would be far more efficient to prepare a meal at home than to pack the family in the car, drive to McDonald's, load up on food, and then drive home again. This may not be true of some meals cooked at home from scratch, but it is certainly true of TV dinners, microwave meals, or full-course meals brought in from the supermarket. Yet many people persist in the belief, fueled by propaganda from the fast-food restaurants, that it is more efficient to eat there than to eat at home.

The fact is that these and other elements of the rational society may be inefficient from the point of view of the customer, but are quite efficient from the viewpoint of the purveyor of goods and services. It is more efficient from the bank's perspective to have us line up at an ATM (which might add to its inefficiency by breaking down or running out of money) than it is to provide us with human services. It is efficient from McDonald's way of looking at things to have us load up the family and drive to, or through, one of its fast-food restaurants.

From the supermarket's perspective, it is efficient for it to pack itself full of foods of all types. A Giant supermarket in Virginia has about 45,000 different products strung out along 23 aisles. In addition, the store includes a "florist shop, a wine store, a Fanny May candy store, a deli, a soup-and-salad bar, and machines that dispense cold soda and hot coffee, just in case a shopper's strength starts to wane." Is it efficient for consumers in search of a loaf of bread and a quart of milk to wend their way through this labyrinth? Of course not, and it is this that helps account for the popularity of chains like Seven-Eleven.

Although the forces of McDonaldization trumpet their greater efficiency, they never tell us for whom the system is more efficient. Most of the gains in efficiency are on the side of those who are pushing rationalization upon us. We need to ask: Efficient for whom? Most often, we will find that such systems are *not* efficient for us. Is it efficient for us to push our own food over the supermarket scanner and then bag it ourselves? Is it efficient for us to pump our own gasoline? Is it efficient for us to push numerous combinations of telephone numbers before we speak, if even then, to a human voice?

Fast-food restaurants, and other components of our McDonaldizing society, suffer from low productivity. This means that, as a rule, workers in such settings produce relatively few goods or services per hour of work. In the main, these are labor-intensive work settings where large numbers of workers are needed to accomplish the organization's goals. The best example is the fast-food restaurant with its hordes of teenagers working relatively unproductively. The fast-food restaurant is able to tolerate this low level of productivity because it pays most of its employees the minimum wage. Of course, elements of the McDonaldizing society, for example banks that rely on ATMs, do not suffer from this problem. Further, it seems likely that this problem will be solved as more and more rational institutions utilize increasingly sophisticated technologies either to replace unproductive workers or to render them more productive.

McDonaldized institutions have also not been notably effective in new product development. We have discussed earlier Ray Kroc's failures in this realm, notably the Hulaburger. As a general rule, what such systems excel at is selling familiar products and services in shiny new settings or packages. The fast-food restaurant markets only the most familiar of foods, but wraps that prosaic hamburger in bright packages and sells it in restaurants that have a carnival-like atmosphere. This point extends to many other manifestations of McDonaldization. For example, Jiffy Lube or one its imitators is selling us nothing more than the same old oil change and lube job.

Previously, in discussing the relationship between the customer and the rational system, we asked: Efficient for whom? This same question can be asked when we look within most rational systems at their relationships to employees. The answer is that they are highly rationalized for those who work at or near the bottom of the system—the assembly-line worker, the counterperson at McDonald's. Rationalization is something that those at the top of the organization, the owners, the franchisees, the top managers, seek to impose on those who rank below them in the organization. They want to control subordinates through the imposition of rational systems. Those at or near the top of these systems, however, find the rationalization of their own positions anathema to them. They want their own positions to be as free of rational constraints—as nonrational—as possible. They need to be free to be creative, but creativity is not desired from underlings in the organization. Subordinates are simply to follow blindly the dictates of the rules, regulations, and structures of the rational system. Thus, the goal is to impose efficiency on subordinates while those in charge remain as creative as possible.

"Expense World"

Not only do some aspects of our McDonaldized society not save us time through greater efficiency, but many also do not ordinarily save us money. A fast-food meal for a family of four these days might easily cost $20. That sum of money would go further if spent on the ingredients for a home-cooked meal.

In the quotation in the previous section, Cohen complains about the economic costs associated with using ATMs. The fact is, we must pay extra to deal with the inhumanity and inefficiency of the various elements of a rationalized society. The great success and profitability of these McDonaldized systems, the fact that there is such a rush to extend them to ever new sectors of society, and the fact that so many people want to get into such businesses, indicates that these systems are swallowing up a great deal of money.

The expense of McDonaldized activities was noted by Bob Garfield in an essay in the *Washington Post* entitled "How I Spent (and Spent and Spent) My Disney Vacation." Garfield took his family of four to Walt Disney World and found that it might be more aptly named "Expense World." The five-day vacation cost $1,700; $551.30 of which was spent on admission to Disney World. He calculates that out of the five days, they had less than seven hours of "fun, fun, fun. That amounts to $261 c.p.f.h. (cost per fun hour)." Thus, what is thought to be an inexpensive family vacation turns out be quite costly. Along the way, Garfield also criticizes the supposed efficiency of the Disney operation. He found that most of his time in the Magic Kingdom was spent riding buses, "queuing up and shlepping from place to place, the 17 attractions we saw thrilled us for a grand total of 44 minutes."

"Fun, Fun, Fun"

If it really isn't efficient, and it really isn't cheap, then what does the fast-food society and, more specifically, the fast-food restaurant offer us? Why has it been such a worldwide success? For one thing, it offers us the *illusion* of efficiency and of being inexpensive. It matters little what the actual situation is, as long as we *believe* fast-food restaurants to be efficient and inexpensive. Perhaps more important, what fast-food restaurants really seem to offer us, as Stan Luxenberg has pointed out, is fun (or Garfield's "fun, fun, fun"). As another observer notes, "Restaurants have become a form of entertainment." Today's diner is looking for theater more than food. This is even true of those who frequent up-scale restaurants: "I would rather eat mediocre food in a fabulous room than sit somewhere dull and boring and eat fabulous food. . . . I'm looking for decor, scale, *theatrics*, a lot going on." Fast-food restaurants (and many up-scale restaurants as well) are really a kind of amusement park for food. The colors and the garish signs and symbols bring to mind a carnival or an amusement park. In the case of McDonald's, there is even the ubiquitous clown, Ronald McDonald, and an array of cartoon characters to constantly remind us that fun awaits us on our next trip to McDonald's.

Some outlets even offer playgrounds and children's rides as part of the amusement park setting. Going still further, and in its continuing attempt to diversify, McDonald's is moving beyond offering playgrounds with its food and going into the playground business. In a mall (of course) outside of Chicago, McDonald's is opening a test site called Leaps & Bounds. The playground equipment is derived from equipment developed for use in the playgrounds that are found in conjunction with about 4,500 McDonald's restaurants. A McDonald's spokesperson said that the idea grew out of the advertising theme of "food, folks and fun. . . .We just turned it around and put the fun first." Some would say that McDonald's *always* put fun before food.

In another recent development, McDonald's in Japan (there are 850 McDonald's restaurants in Japan) is joining forces with Toys R Us. (McDonald's owns 20 percent of the Japanese operations of Toys R Us.) A number of the new Toys R Us outlets to be built will include McDonald's restaurants. In aligning itself more closely with playgrounds and toys, McDonald's is making it increasingly clear that it is in the business of providing "fun."

Making them even more like amusement parks is the nature of the food served at fast-food restaurants. It is the kind of finger food one is accustomed to buying at the stands scattered throughout an amusement park. It is kind of the "cotton candy principle" applied to other foods. People will buy, and even pay comparatively high prices for, a few pennies worth of food as long as it has a strong, distinct, and obvious flavor. Indeed, again as Luxenberg shows, what fast-food restaurants often sell is "salty candy." One of the secrets of the McDonald's french fry is that it is coated with *both* salt and, surprisingly, sugar. One tastes the salt and the sugar, but rarely if ever the potato slice, which is little more than an excuse for the sweet-salty taste.

Taking a slightly different perspective, we can think of McDonald's as offering a kind of "public theater." Instead of offering a private, book-like menu, what McDonald's offers is a kind of "marquee" on which, like the movie options at the local cineplex, are offered the diner's alternatives. In this, and many other ways, dining is transformed from a private and very personal experience into a public spectacle. Greeted by the same kind of marquees, we are beckoned to have fun in a public setting in both the movie theater and the fast-food restaurant.

Supermarkets have also increasingly become entertainment centers, dispensing more and more "fun foods" such as Count Chocula and, more recently, Teenage Mutant Ninja Turtles cereals; Snausages in a Blanket dog food; and Funny Feet fruit snacks. As one observer said:

> When The Shopper was young, Americans used to sing, "There's no business like show business," but they don't sing it much anymore, probably because just about every business is like show business now. Supermarkets are certainly no exception. These days, supermarkets are like theme parks.

The owner of large supermarkets in Connecticut invested a half million dollars in cartoon characters for his stores and has humans dressed as Daisy Duck wandering through them. Said the owner, "This is a people business. Customers are happy here. People come here to shop together with friends because it's fun."

All of this is part of our national obsession with amusement. Neil Postman, in his book aptly titled *Amusing Ourselves to Death*, argues that Las Vegas has become the symbol of this obsession because it "is a city entirely devoted to the idea of entertainment, and as such proclaims the spirit of a culture in which all public discourse increasingly takes the form of entertainment." If Las Vegas, which by the way has McDonaldized gambling, is the city that has become the symbol of entertainment, then McDonaldization symbolizes the emphasis on entertainment in the fast-food restaurant.

Entertainment is also central to the shopping mall. Malls are designed to be fantasy worlds. They are theatrical settings in which is played out what Kowinski calls "the Retail Drama." The consumers are important actors in this drama as are mall employees. After all, for many Americans, their favorite form of entertainment is shopping. The mall, itself, can be seen as a huge stage setting loaded with lots of props, all with a backdrop of ever-present Muzak to soothe the savage shopper. Some of the props are there on a year-round basis, while others (for example, Christmas decorations) are brought in for special occasions and special promotions. Then there are the restaurants, bars, movie theaters, and exercise centers to add to the fun. On weekends there are often clowns, balloons, magicians, bands, and the like to further entertain those on their way from one shop to another. Faced by the threat of various shop-at-home alternatives, one expert said, "You've got to make your centers more fun." Thus, in the future we can expect shopping centers to become an even more integral part of show business.

That future will be upon us with the opening of the new Mall of America in Bloomington, Minnesota. Included in the center is a huge amusement park, including a full-size roller coaster, an arcade, and shooting galleries. There will be an aquarium, and visitors will be able to walk through the tank via acrylic tubes. Golf Mountain will provide an 18-hole miniature golf course on two levels. The largest Lego structure ever built will also be in the mall. There will be a huge sports bar and an entertainment center with a Michael Jackson theme. And, of course, there will be many movie theaters. Said one critic, "Mall of America is not a mall, it's a circus."

Not only is *Business Week* a rationalized magazine (as we have seen) designed to be more efficient to read than the *Wall Street Journal*, but it also aims to be more enjoyable than the newspaper it competes with. An ad for *Business Week* claims, "We don't just inform you but we entertain you." Two critics say of this advertisement: "Is *Business Week* really serious? Are we to expect the following: Ha Ha Ha, Ha! The stock market just crashed! What a laugh! . . . Your company is going down the tubes. What fun!" Television news is often described as "infotainment" because it combines news and show business.

The *Phantom of the Opera* and "Molly McButter"

The examples of false fraternization at Roy Rogers and Nutri/System discussed earlier may be seen as but a small part of what Daniel Boorstin calls the pseudoevents that increasingly dominate American society. Many other aspects of a McDonaldized society may be thought of as false and deceptive events or situations, including the package tour, the modern campground, the international villages at amusement parks such as Busch Gardens, the computer phone call, junk mail, and many other examples.

To take our analysis one step further, all of this may be viewed as part of what Ian Mitroff and Warren Bennis call the "unreality industry." By this, they mean the fact that whole industries are now in the business of producing and marketing unreality. Indeed, much of the McDonaldized society is involved in the production of a wide range of unrealities. McDonald's, for example, creates the illusion that we are having fun, that we are getting lots of french fries, and that we are getting a bargain when we purchase our meal. A notable, recent example of such unreality is the discovery that the singing group Milli Vanilli's two "singers" did not actually do the singing on their record album. Though there are a wide range of unrealities to choose from, let us look at a few examples from the supermarket where fewer and fewer things are what they appear to be:

- Sizzlean is made out of beef and turkey, and kosher bacon has no pork.
- Molly McButter and Butter Buds have no butter.
- the turkey flavor in the frozen turkey TV dinner may well be artificial since the natural flavor was removed during processing.
- the lemon smell in the laundry detergent probably did not come from lemons.

Such unreality, along with various pseudoevents, have come to be integral to our McDonaldized society.

Caution: McDonaldization Can Be Dangerous to Your Health

The main reason that we think of McDonaldization as irrational, and ultimately unreasonable, is that it tends to become a dehumanizing system that may become antihuman or even destructive to human beings. There are a number of ways in which the health, and perhaps the lives, of people have been threatened by progressive rationalization. One example is the high calorie, fat, cholesterol, salt, and sugar content of the food served in fast-food restaurants. Such meals are the last things many Americans need, suffering as they do from obesity, high cholesterol levels, high blood pressure, and perhaps diabetes. Fast-food restaurants also help to create eating habits in children that contribute to the development of these, and other, health problems later in life. It can be argued that with their appeal to children, fast-food restaurants are creating not only life-long devotees of fast food, but also people who will grow addicted to diets high in salt, sugar, and fat.

Attacks against the fast-food industry on the health issue have mounted in recent years. As a result, many of the franchises have been forced to respond in various ways. Salad bars, or salads on the menu, have been one response, although the dressings for these salads are often loaded with salt and fats. Some fast-food restaurants have ceased cooking french fries in beef tallow and instead are using less cholesterol-laden vegetable oil. Fast-food restaurants have been forced to adapt to the increasing health concerns of the public (see Chapter Nine), but the fact is that the typical McDonald's meal of a Big Mac, large fries, and shake has more than 1,000 calories and is loaded with salt, sugar, and fat. This might be a desirable caloric intake for citizens of less-developed countries, indeed it might have more calories than people in such countries ordinarily consume in an entire day, but it is hardly desirable for the already well-fed, if not overfed, population of the United States.

McDonaldization poses a more direct health threat. Regina Schrambling links various diseases, especially salmonella, to the rationalization of food production. She states:

> Salmonella proliferated in the poultry industry only after beef became a four-letter word and Americans decided they wanted a chicken in every pot every night. But birds aren't like cars: you can't just speed up the factory line to meet demand. Something has got to give—and

in this case it's been safety. Birds that are rushed to fryer size, then killed gutted and plucked at high speed in vast quantities are not going to be the cleanest food in the supermarket.

Schrambling also links salmonella to the more rational production of eggs, fruit (like cantaloupes), and vegetables. More generally, she traces a wide range of illnesses to various rationalized production systems.

One Marxist critic, Tim Luke, has recently attacked the invasion of Russia by McDonald's as well as other aspects of the McDonaldized society. He labels what is being created a "McGulag Archipelago." (The "Gulag Archipelago" was the name often used for the elaborate system of prison camps that was found throughout the former Soviet Union.) Luke is saying that McDonaldization is creating a new kind of system to imprison Russian citizens, in other words, a new kind of "iron cage." Luke also attacks McDonald's for a variety of other reasons, such as being "nutritionally questionable," "waste-intensive," and "environmentally-destructive."

Following up on the last point, the fast-food industry has not only run afoul of nutritionists, but also of environmentalists. It produces an enormous amount of trash, some of which is nonbiodegradable. Many people have been critical of the public eyesore created by litter from fast-food meals strewn across the countryside. It takes hundreds, if not thousands of square miles of forest to provide the paper needed each year by McDonald's alone. Whole forests are being devoured by the fast-food industry, even though some paper containers have been replaced by styrofoam and other products (although the current trend may be back to paper products). Even greater criticism has been leveled at the widespread use by the fast-food industry of virtually indestructible styrofoam. Styrofoam debris piles up in landfills, creating mountains of waste that simply remain there for years, if not forever.

Turnover and "Trough and Brew"

The fast-food restaurant offers its employees a dehumanizing setting within which to work. Few skills are required on the job. Said Burger King workers, "A moron could learn this job, it's so easy" and "Any trained monkey could do this job." Thus workers are asked to use only a minute proportion of all of their skills and abilities. At one level, this is irrational from the organization's viewpoint, since it could obtain much more from its employees for the money (however negligible) it pays them. This is one of the secrets of the success of Japanese industry. The Japanese have developed a number of mechanisms, such as quality circles, to elicit a wide variety of contributions from their employees.

At another level, the minimal skill demands of the fast-food restaurant are irrational from the perspective of the employee. Employees are not only not using all of their skills, but they are also not being allowed to think and to be creative on the job. This leads to a high level of resentment, job dissatisfaction, alienation, absenteeism, and turnover among those who work in fast-food restaurants. In fact, the fast-food industry has the highest turnover rate—approximately 300 percent a year—of any industry in the United States. That means that the average worker lasts only about four months at a fast-food restaurant; the entire workforce of the fast-food industry turns over three times in a year.

Although the simple and repetitive nature of the jobs makes it relatively easy to replace workers who leave, such a high turnover rate is still undesirable from the organization's perspective. It would clearly be better to keep employees longer. There are costs involved in turnover (for example, those of hiring and training) that are magnified when turnover rates are extraordinarily high.

The fast-food restaurant is also dehumanizing as far as the customer is concerned. Instead of a human dining experience, what is offered is eating on a sort of moving conveyor belt or assembly line. The diner is reduced to a kind overwound automaton who is made to rush through the meal. Little gratification is derived from the dining experience or from the food itself. The best that can usually be said is that it is efficient and it is over quickly.

Some customers might even feel as if they are being fed like livestock in a highly rationalized manner. This point was made a number of years ago on television in a *Saturday Night Live* skit entitled "Trough and Brew," a take-off on a small fast-food chain called Burger and Brew. In the skit, some young executives learn that a new fast-food restaurant called Trough and Brew has opened and they decide to try it for lunch. They are next seen entering the restaurant and having bibs tied around their necks. After that, they discover a long trough, resembling a pig trough. The trough is filled with chili and is periodically refilled by a waitress scooping new supplies from a bucket. The customers bend over, stick their heads into the trough, and begin lapping up the chili as they move along the length of the trough making high-level business decisions. Every so often they come up for air and lap some beer from the communal "brew basin." After they have finished their "meal," they pay their bills "by the head." Since their faces are smeared with chili, they are literally "hosed off" before they leave the restaurant. The young executives are last seen being herded out of the restaurant, which is being closed for a half-hour so that it can be "hosed down." *Saturday Night Live* was clearly pointing out, and ridiculing, the fact that fast-food restaurants tend to treat their customers like lower animals.

"Get Lost," *Wheel of Fortune*, and Fake Submarines

Another dehumanizing aspect of fast-food restaurants is that they minimize contact among human beings. Let us take, for example, the issue of how customers and employees relate. The nature of the fast-food restaurant turns these into fleeting relationships. Because the average employee stays only a few months, and even then only works on a part-time basis, the customer, even the regular customer, is rarely able to develop a long-term personal relationship with a counterperson. Gone are the days when one got to know well a waitress at a diner or the short order cook at a local greasy spoon. Gone are the days when an employee knows who you are and knows what you are likely to order.

Not only are the relationships with a McDonald's employee fleeting (because the worker remains on the job only a short period of time), but each contact between worker and customer is of a very short duration. It takes little time at the counter to order, receive one's food, and pay for it. Both employees and customers are likely to feel rushed and to want to move on, customers to their dinner and employees to the next order. There is virtually no time for customer and counterperson to interact in such a context. This is even more true of the drive-through window, where thanks to the speedy service and the physical barriers, the server is but a dim and distant image.

The highly impersonal and anonymous relationships between customer and counterperson is heightened by the employees having been trained to interact in a staged and limited manner with customers. Thus, the customers may feel that they are dealing with automatons who have been taught to utter a few phrases rather than with fellow human beings. For their part, the customers are supposed to be, and often are, in a hurry, so they have little to say to the McDonald's employee. Indeed, it could be argued that one of the reasons for the success of fast-food restaurants is that they are in tune with our fast-paced and impersonal society (see Chapter Eight). People in the modern world want to get on with their business without unnecessary personal relationships. The fast-food restaurant gives them precisely what they want.

Not only are the relationships between employee and customer limited greatly, but also other potential relationships. Because employees remain on the job for only a few months, satisfying personal relationships among employees are unlikely to develop. Again it is useful to contrast this to the Japanese case, where more permanent employment helps foster long-term relationships on the job. Furthermore, Japanese workers are likely to get together with one another after work hours and on weekends as well. The temporary character of jobs in fast-food restaurants largely eliminates the possibility of such personal relationships among employees.

Relationships among customers are largely curtailed as well. Although some McDonald's ads would have us believe otherwise, gone are the days when people met in the diner or cafeteria for coffee, breakfast, lunch, or dinner and lingered to socialize with one another. Fast-food restaurants are clearly not conducive to such socializing. If nothing else, the chairs are designed to make people uncomfortable and interested in moving on to something else. The drive-through windows are a further step toward McDonaldization, by completely eliminating the possibility of interacting with other customers.

To summarize the preceding paragraphs, fast-food restaurants greatly restrict, or even eliminate the possibility of genuine fraternization among and between customers and employees. Instead, to reiterate a point made earlier in this book, what we are left with is either no human relationships or "false fraternization." Rule Number 17 for Burger King workers is "Smile at all times." The Roy Rogers' employees who used to say "happy trails" to me when I paid for my food really had no interest in what happened to me in the future, on the trail. (In fact, come to think of it, they were really saying, in a polite way, "get lost!") This phenomenon has been generalized to the many workers who say "have a nice day" as one is departing. In fact, of course, they have no real interest in, or concern for, how the rest of one's day goes. Again, in a polite and ritualized way, they are really telling us to "get lost," to move on so someone else can be served.

At Nutri/System, counselors are given a list of things to do in order to keep dieters coming back. First, the counselors are urged to "Greet client by name with enthusiasm." Knowing the client's name creates a false sense of friendliness, as does the "enthusiastic" greeting. Second, the counselor is urged to give the client personal recognition. Later, there is the recommendation that the counselor "Converse with client in a *sensitive* manner." The counselors are also provided with a small card with a glossy finish entitled "Personalized Approach at a Glance." (The card, of course, serves to rationalize the personal greeting.) Included are pseudopersonalized responses to problematic situations. For example, if the client indicates that he or she is receiving little support for the diet, the counselor is urged to say: "I'm so glad to see you. I was thinking about you. How is the program going for you?" Is the counselor *really* glad to see the client? *Really* thinking about the client? *Really* concerned about how things are working out for the client? The answers to such questions are quite obvious.

Fast-food restaurants also tend to have negative effects on other human relationships. There is, for example, the effect on the so-called "family meal." The fast-food restaurant is not conducive to a long, leisurely, conversation-filled dinnertime. The family is unlikely to linger long over a meal at McDonald's. Furthermore, as the children grow into their teens, the nature of fast-food restaurants leads to separate meals as the teens go at one time with their friends, and the parents go at another time. Of course, the drive-through window only serves to reduce the possibility of a family meal. The family that gobbles its food while driving on to its next stop can hardly be seen as having what is called these days "quality time" with each other. Here is the way one journalist describes what is happening to the family meal:

> Do families who eat their suppers at the Colonel's, swinging on plastic seats, or however the restaurant is arranged, say grace before picking up a crispy brown chicken leg? Does dad ask junior what he did today as he remembers he forgot the piccalilli and trots through the crowds over to the counter to get some? Does mom find the atmosphere conducive to asking little Mildred about the problems she was having with third conjugation French verbs, or would it matter since otherwise the family might have been at home chomping down precooked frozen food, warmed in the microwave oven and watching "Hollywood Squares"?

There is much talk these days about the disintegration of the family, and the fast-food restaurant may well be a crucial contributor to that disintegration.

In fact, as implied above, dinners at home may now not be much different from meals at the fast-food restaurant. Families tended to stop having lunch together by the 1940s and breakfast together by the 1950s. Today, the family dinner is following the same route. Even when they eat dinner at home, the meal will probably not be what it once was. Following the fast-food model, people are growing more likely to "graze," "refuel," nibble on this, or snack on that, than they are to sit down to a formal meal. Also, because it is now deemed inefficient to do nothing but just eat, families are likely to watch television while they are eating, thereby efficiently combining two activities. However, the din, to say nothing of the lure, of dinner time TV programs such as *Wheel of Fortune* is likely to make it difficult for family members to interact with one another.

A key technology in the destruction of the family meal is the microwave oven and the vast array of microwavable foods it helped generate. It is striking to learn that more than 70 percent of American households have a microwave oven. A recent *Wall Street Journal* poll indicated that Americans consider the microwave their favorite household product. In fact, the microwave in a McDonaldizing society is seen as an advance over the fast-food restaurant. Said one consumer researcher, "It has made even fast-food restaurants not seem fast because at home you don't have to wait in line." As a general rule, consumers are demanding meals that take no more than ten minutes to microwave, whereas in the past people were more often willing to spend about a half hour or even an hour cooking dinner. This emphasis on speed has, of course, brought with it poorer taste and lower quality, but people do not seem to mind this loss: "We're just not as critical of food as we used to be."

The speed of microwave cooking, as well as the wide variety of foods available in microwavable form, make it possible for family members to eat at different times and places. To give even children independence, food companies are marketing products like Kid's Kitchen, Kid Cuisine, and My Own Meals. Children no longer need to wait for their parents; they can "zap" their own meals. As a result, "Those qualities of the family meal, the ones that imparted feelings of security and well-being, might be lost forever when food is 'zapped' or 'nuked' instead of cooked."

The advances in microwave cooking continue. There are already plastic strips on some foods that turn blue when the food is done. The industry is promising strips that communicate cooking information directly to the microwave oven. "With cooking reduced to pushing a button, the kitchen may wind up as a sort of filling station. Family members will pull in, push a few buttons, fill up and leave. To clean up, all we need do is throw away plastic plates." What is lost, of course, is the family meal, and we need to decide whether we can afford the loss:

> The communal meal is our primary ritual for encouraging the family to gather together every day. If it is lost to us, we shall have to invent new ways to be a family. It is worth considering whether the shared joy that food can provide is worth giving up.

To switch to another key site of McDonaldization, dehumanization is central to Garfield's critique of Walt Disney World. Let me quote at length from his description of the dehumanized Disney World:

> I actually believed there was real fun and real imagination in store— only to be confronted with an extruded, injection-molded, civil-engineered brand of fantasy, which is to say: no fantasy at all.
>
> From the network of chutes and corrals channeling people into attractions, to the chillingly programmed Stepford Wives demeanor of the employees, to the compulsively litter-free grounds, to the general-ized North Korean model Socialist Society sense of totalitarian order, to the utterly passive nature of the entertainment itself, Disney turns out to be the very antithesis of fantasy, a remarkable technospectacle. . . .
>
> Far from liberating the imagination, Disney succeeds mainly in confining it. Like the conveyor "cars" and "boats" that pull you along steel tracks through "Snow White" and "World of Motion" and the "Speedway" rides, Disney is a plodding, precise, computer controlled mechanism pulling an estimated 30 million visitors along the same calculated, unvarying, meticulously engineered entertainment experi-ence. It occupies its customers without engaging them. It appeals to everybody while challenging nobody. . . .
>
> Imagine, for example, a fake submergence in a fake submarine for a fake voyage past fake coral and fake seafood, knowing full well that there are two magnificent aquariums within a 70-minute drive of your house. . . .

Thus, instead of being a creative and imaginative human experience, Disney World turns out to be an uncreative, unimaginative, and ultimately inhuman experience.

Fast-Food Croissants and Fast Forwarding Through Fall

Another dehumanizing effect of the fast-food restaurant is that it has contributed to homogenization around the country and, increasingly, throughout the world. Diversity, which many people crave, is being reduced or eliminated by the fast-food restaurant. This decline in diversity is manifest in the extension of the fast-food model to all sorts of ethnic foods. The settings are all modeled after McDonald's in one way or another and the food has been rationalized and compromised so that it is acceptable to the tastes of virtually all diners. One cannot find an authentically different meal in any of these ethnic fast-food chains.

The expansion of these franchises across the landscape of America means that one finds little difference among regions and among cities throughout the country. Tourists find more familiarity and predictability and less diversity as they travel around the nation, and this is increasingly true on a global scale. Apparently exotic settings are likely to be overrun with both American fast-food chains as well as indigenous varieties. The new and world's largest McDonald's and Kentucky Fried Chicken in Beijing are but two examples of this. Furthermore, many nations are applying the McDonald's model to native cuisine. In Paris one may be shocked by the number of American fast-food restaurants one finds there, but even more shocking is the incredible spread of indigenous forms such as the fast-food *croissanterie*. One would have thought that the French considered the croissant a sacred object and would have found it obscene to rationalize its manufacture and sale, but that is just what has happened. While the fast-food system has demeaned the quality of the croissant, the spread of such outlets throughout Paris indicates that many Parisians are willing to follow Americans and sacrifice quality for speed and efficiency. (And, one may ask, if the Parisian croissant can be turned into a fast-food success, what food is safe?) In any case, the spread of American and indigenous fast-food throughout much of the world means that there is less and less diversity from one setting to another. The human craving for new and diverse experiences is being limited, if not progressively destroyed, by the national and international spread of fast-food restaurants. The craving for diversity is being supplanted by the desire for uniformity and predictability.

Just as the fast-food restaurants are leveling food differences, mail-order catalogues are eliminating seasonal differences. Ellen Goodman recently critiqued this particular aspect of rationalization: "The creation of one national mail-order market has produced catalogues without the slightest respect for any season or region. Their holidays are now harvested, transported and chemically ripened on the way to your home." What upset Goodman was receiving her Christmas catalogue just as fall was beginning, prompting her to say, "I refuse to fast forward through the fall." (In addition, those who buy things through catalogues find that their deliveries are often late or they never arrive at all. Said the President of the Better Business Bureau of Metropolitan New York, "With mail order, the biggest problem is delivery and delay in delivery.")

Demystification, Deprofessionalization, and Assembly-Line Medicine

As has been made clear throughout this book, medicine is growing progressively rationalized; that is, it is being dominated by structures and institutions characterized by efficiency, predictability, calculability, and control through the substitution of nonhuman for human technology. However, these rational systems bring with them a series of irrational (or unreasonable) consequences. The purpose here is not to romanticize medicine's past. Although we will focus on the irrationalities of contemporary medicine undergoing the process of McDonaldization, that is not to say that prerationalized medicine is some sort of ideal to which we ought to return. For one thing, it is difficult, if not impossible, to turn back the process of rationalization. For another, medical practice in the past was itself rife with various problems. Another caveat—although we focus on irrationalities here, it is clear that rational medical systems also have rational (reasonable) consequences. For example, advances in technology can bring with them improved medical practice and life-saving techniques. Control by third-party payers and the government may bring about greater control over spiraling medical costs and may work to the benefit of all those requiring medical care.

From the point of view of the physician, the process of rationalization carries with it a series of irrationalities. At or near the top of the list is the shift in control away from the physician and in the direction of rationalized structures and institutions. The private practitioner of the past had a large degree of control over his or her work, with the major constraints being peer control as well as the needs and demands of patients. In rationalized medicine, external control increases and shifts to social structures and institutions. Not only is the physician more likely to be controlled by these structures and institutions, but also by managers and bureaucrats who are not themselves physicians. The ability of physicians to control their own work lives is declining dramatically. External control may soon be a problem for physicians, and this is likely to be manifest in increased levels of job dissatisfaction and alienation (and perhaps a turn toward unionization).

Rationalization often brings with it demystification, the removal of mystery or excitement from the work lives of physicians. Instead of relying on personal medical judgment in deciding what to do in a given case, the decisions of the physician are increasingly likely to be guided by rules, regulations, decisions of superiors, or technological imperatives. This, too, is likely to increase job dissatisfaction and alienation among physicians.

The process of rationalization is likely to bring with it some degree of deprofessionalization (for example, loss of autonomy) of physicians, and such a decline is highly irrational from their point of view. In most modern thinking on professions, the key factor is power. Professions are occupations that have the power to win and keep professional status. As we saw earlier, rationalized structures and institutions are exerting more and more control (power) over the medical profession. More decisions are being structured and even made by these external agencies. The result is an erosion of the power of physicians, and this decline in power is, by definition, leading to a decline in their professional status.

From the patient's point of view, the rationalization of medicine causes a number of irrationalities. The drive for efficiency can make patients feel as if they are on a medical assembly line being hastened through the system. The effort to increase predictability is likely to lead patients to lose the feeling of a personal relationship with physicians and other health professionals. Rules and regulations lead physicians to treat all patients in essentially the same way, thereby reducing the personal element in medical practice. This is also true in hospital nursing, where instead of seeing the same nurse regularly, a patient may see different nurses from one day to the next. The result, of course is that such nurses never come to know their patients as individuals.

As a result of the emphasis on calculability, the patient is more likely to feel like a number in the system rather than a person. Minimizing time and maximizing profits may lead to a decline in the quality of health care provided to patients. Like physicians, patients are apt to be increasingly controlled by large-scale structures and institutions, which are likely to appear to the patient as distant, uncaring, and impenetrable. Finally, patients are increasingly likely to interact with impersonal technologies and technicians. In fact, more and more technologies may be purchased at the drug store (for example, blood pressure machines and pregnancy tests), and the patient can test himself or herself, thereby cutting out human contact with both physicians and technicians. One of the results of many aspects of the rationalization of medicine is the increasing dehumanization and depersonalization of medical practice.

The ultimate irrationality of the rationalization of medicine would be the unanticipated consequences of a decline in the quality of medical practice and a deterioration in the health of patients. It may be that increasingly rational medical systems, with their focus on lowering costs and increasing profits, will reduce the quality of health care. This is especially likely to be the case for the poorer members of society. It may be that at least some people will become sicker, and perhaps even die, because of the rationalization of medicine. It may even be that health in general declines as a result of the rationalization of medicine. These are possibilities that can only be assessed in the future as the health-care system continues to rationalize. However, we can be sure that the health-care system *will* continue to rationalize. Given this, health professionals and their patients need to learn how to control rational structures and institutions to ameliorate their irrational consequences.

Factory-Like Universities, Bureaucracies, and Planes That Almost Fly Themselves

The modern university has, in various ways, become a highly irrational place. Many students (and faculty members) are put off by the huge, factory-like atmosphere in these universities. They might feel like automatons to be processed by the bureaucracy and the computer, or even cattle being run through a meat processing plant. In other words, education in such settings can be a dehumanizing experience. The masses of students, large, impersonal dorms, and huge lecture classes make it difficult to get to know other students. The large lectures, constrained tightly by the clock, make it virtually impossible to know professors on a personal basis. At best, one might get to know a graduate assistant teaching a discussion section. Grades may be derived from a series of machine-graded multiple-choice exams and may be posted impersonally, often by social security number rather than name. In sum, students may feel like little more than objects into which knowledge is poured as they move along an information-providing and degree-granting educational assembly line.

Of course, technological advances are leading to even greater irrationalities in education. Even the minimal contact between teacher and student is being further limited by such advances as educational television, closed-circuit television, computerized instruction, and teaching machines. We may soon see the ultimate step in the dehumanization of education, the elimination of a human teacher and of human interaction between teacher and student.

The irrationalities associated with bureaucracies of all types are well-known. Such organizations are often critiqued for being dehumanizing settings in which to work. People employed in bureaucracies often must deal with or respond to nameless, faceless bureaucrats elsewhere in the organization. This is an even greater problem for the client who has trouble reaching, let alone developing personal contacts with, the bureaucrats with whom they must deal and from whom they are seeking some product or service. This has been complicated by the telephone and a number of recent advances in telephone technology. Telephones in large bureaucracies are now often answered by prerecorded voices that tell us how important our call is to them (another form of fake fraternization that we rarely fall for), and return over and over again (often interrupting the beloved strains of Muzak) to tell us to keep hanging on. Then there are the fully computerized systems in which we must push a number of buttons in response to instructions from a computer voice. When we ultimately reach the office we are seeking, we may hear yet another computerized message. Dealing with such computerized voices is obviously even more dehumanizing (no humans exist on the other end of the phone line) than dealing with the anonymous bureaucrat.

Bureaucracies, in spite of being set up to operate efficiently, are often notoriously inefficient. Trying to get anything out of a bureaucracy, especially something that is the least bit out of the ordinary, can be an endless process requiring innumerable contacts with the relevant bureaucrats. Even doing normal business with a bureaucracy can mire the clients in "red tape" from which it seems they will never be able to extricate themselves.

Modern, computerized airplanes, such as Boeing's 757 and 767, represent interesting cases of substituting nonhuman for human control. Instead of flying "by the seat of their pants," or using old-fashioned autopilots for simple maneuvers, modern pilots can "push a few buttons and lean back while the plane flies to its destination and lands on a pre-determined runway." Said one FAA official, "We're taking more and more of these functions out of human control and giving them to machines."

The new, automated airplanes are in many ways safer and more reliable than older, less technologically advanced models. However, there is a fear that pilots, dependent on these technologies, will lose the ability to find creative ways of handling emergency situations. Said one airline manager, "If we have human operators subordinated to technology, then we're going to lose that creativity. I don't have computers that will do that [be creative]; I just don't." Thus, in an emergency situation, these airplanes pose a threat of the ultimate in dehumanization, the death of large numbers of passengers because human pilots may lose the ability to deal with unforeseen circumstances.

"Sometimes I Felt Just Like a Robot"

It is undoubtedly the automobile assembly line that is the classic example of a rational system that has produced a seemingly never-ending string of irrationalities. For example, the mass-production of automobiles has led to our voracious need for gasoline which, in turn, has made us dependent on oil-producing nations and willing to go to war to protect our oil supplies and keep oil prices low. To take another irrationality, the automobile assembly line has been extraordinarily successful in churning out millions of cars a year. But all of those cars, created year after year, have wreaked havoc on the environment, which has been polluted by the emissions of those millions of automobiles. The countryside has been torn up and scarred by an ever-expanding number of highways and roads. Then there are the thousands of people who are killed and the far greater number who are injured each year in traffic accidents.

Another example of the irrationality of the rationality of the automobile assembly line relates to calculability. The emphasis on things that can be counted can lead to unreasonable actions. Take the famous case of the Ford Pinto. Because of competition from small foreign cars, Ford rushed the Pinto into and through production, despite the fact that preproduction tests had indicated that its fuel system would rupture easily in a rear-end collision. Because the expensive assembly-line machinery for the Pinto was already in place, Ford decided to go ahead with the production of the car without any changes. Ford's decision was based on a quantitative comparison of the costs to the company of the lives that would be lost as a result of the defective fuel systems versus the costs of repairing them. They estimated that the defects would lead to 180 deaths and about the same number of injuries. Placing a value, or rather a cost, to them of $200,000 per person, Ford decided that the total cost from these deaths and injuries would be less than the $11 per car it would cost to repair the defect. Although this may have made sense from the point of view of profits, it was an irrational and unreasonable decision in that human lives were sacrificed and people were maimed in the name of lower costs and higher profits. This is only one of the most extreme of a number of such decisions that are made daily in the automobile industry as well as in many other components of a society undergoing McDonaldization.

Although killing people in the name of rationality is the ultimate in dehumanization, the automobile assembly line is best known for the way it dehumanizes life on a day-to-day basis for those who work on it. We have seen earlier that Henry Ford felt that while he could not do the kind of repetitive work required on the assembly line, most people, with limited mental abilities and aspirations, could adjust to it quite well. Ford said, "I have not been able to discover that repetitive labour injures a man in any way. . . . The most thorough research has not brought out a single case of a man's mind being twisted or deadened by the work." However, we now know that the dehumanizing character of assembly-line work has profound negative effects on those who work on the line. The rationality of the line is purchased at the expense of the reasonableness of those who work on it.

The objective evidence on the destructiveness of the assembly line lies in the high rates of absenteeism, tardiness, and turnover among employees. More generally, most people seem to find assembly-line work highly alienating. Here is the way one worker describes the repetitive nature of his work:

> I stand in one spot, about a two- or three-feet area, all night. The only time a person stops is when the line stops. We do about thirty-two jobs per car, per unit, forty-eight units an hour, eight hours a day. Thirty-two times forty-eight times eight. Figure it out, that's how many times I push that button.

Another worker offers a similar view: "What's there to say? A car comes, I weld it; a car comes, I weld it; a car comes, I weld it. One hundred and one times an hour." Others do more than describe the work, they are quite sarcastic about it: "There's a lot of variety in the paint shop. . . . You clip on the color hose, bleed out the color and squirt. Clip, bleed, squirt; clip, bleed, squirt, yawn; clip, bleed, squirt, scratch your nose." One other assembly-line worker recognizes that he has been turned into a human robot by the work: "Sometimes I felt just like a robot. You push a button and you go this way. You become a mechanical nut."

These workers' observations are supported by many scientific studies that show high degrees of alienation among assembly-line workers. This alienation is traceable to the rationality of the line and the fact that it produces the unreasonable consequence of dehumanizing work for those who work there. This not only creates a problem for those who work on the automobile assembly line, but also for people in the wide range of settings that have been built, at least in part, on the principles of the assembly line. In our rapidly McDonaldizing society, that means it has implications for most of us and for many different settings.

Conclusion: The Future Is Now

Perhaps the ultimate irrationality of McDonaldization is the possibility that people could lose control over the system, and it would come to control us. Already, many aspects of our lives are controlled by these rational systems. However, it at least appears that these systems are still controlled by people. But these rational systems can spin beyond the control of even the people who occupy the highest positions within those systems. This is one of the senses in which we can talk of an "iron cage of rationalization." It can become a system that controls all of us.

There are also authoritarian and totalitarian possibilities associated with the process of McDonaldization: These interlocking rational systems can fall into the hands of a small number of leaders who through them can exercise enormous control over all of society. Thus, we may become increasingly controlled by the rational systems themselves or by a few leaders who master those systems.

This kind of fear has animated many science fiction writers and is manifest in such classics as *1984*, *Brave New World*, and *Fahrenheit 451*. These novels describe a feared and fearsome future world, but McDonaldization is with us now, has been with us for awhile, and is extending its reach throughout society.

Thus, it is the argument of this text that contrary to McDonald's propaganda, and the widespread belief in it, fast-food restaurants and their rational clones are *not* reasonable, or even truly rational, systems. They spawn problems in the health of their customers and the well-being of the environment; they are dehumanizing and, therefore, unreasonable; and they often lead to the opposite of what they are supposed to create, for example, leading to inefficiency rather than increased efficiency. All of this is not to deny the advantages of McDonaldization, but it is to point to the fact that there are counterbalancing and perhaps even overwhelming problems associated with this phenomenon. These problems, these irrationalities, need to be understood by people who have been exposed to little more than an unrelenting set of superlatives created by McDonaldized systems to describe themselves.

8

The Iron Cage of McDonaldization?

McDonaldization is clearly with us for the foreseeable future. However, the profound irrationalities associated with McDonaldization raise serious questions about the desirability of such a future. Because of these troubling questions, we might say that we face a future of, as Max Weber might have phrased it, an "iron cage of McDonaldization."

The Forces Driving McDonaldization

One may ask: Why, in light of the irrationalities, are we confronted with such a future? Why can't we back away from the further institutionalization of McDonaldization? In answering these questions, we need to discuss the factors that drive the process of McDonaldization. Three factors suggest themselves. First, McDonaldization is impelled by material interests, especially economic goals and aspirations. Second, it is driven by our cultural system and the fact that McDonaldization has come to be seen as a valued end in itself. Finally, McDonaldization continues apace because it is attuned to various changes taking place within society. Let us take a brief look at each of these three factors.

Higher Profits and Lower Costs

Returning to the ideas of Max Weber, he would argue that ultimately it is material, or more specifically, economic interests that animate the process of rationalization in enterprises found in capitalist societies. Profit-making enterprises pursue McDonaldization because it leads to lower costs and higher profits. Clearly, greater efficiency and increased use of nonhuman technology are often implemented in order to increase profitability. Greater predictability provides, at the minimum, a climate that is needed for an organization to be profitable and for its profits to increase steadily from year to year. An emphasis on calculability, on things that can be quantified, is related to decisions that can produce and increase profits and to the measurement of the profitability of the organization.

While they are not oriented to profits and profit maximization, nonprofit organizations also press McDonaldization for material reasons, specifically because it leads to lower costs. Lower costs permit nonprofit agencies to continue to exist and perhaps even to expand their base of operation. Greater efficiency and the increased utilization of nonhuman technology tend to lower costs directly. A more predictable environment is one in which cost-reduction can be addressed more directly. Calculability allows the nonprofit organization to determine whether it is in fact lowering costs. Although it is not interested in profits, the nonprofit organization might well be interested in increasing revenues in order to cover rising costs. The elements of McDonaldization permit such an organization to act to enhance income. Thus, both for-profit and nonprofit organizations in capitalist societies pursue McDonaldization for economic reasons.

Interestingly, the dramatic changes currently taking place in Russia and Eastern Europe can be explained from the point of view of McDonaldization. One can argue that communism constituted a barrier to rationalization; as a result such societies failed to McDonaldize. Thus, Communist societies tended to be characterized by inefficiency, incalculability, unpredictability, and to be relatively backward (except in the military) in introducing advanced technologies. As a result, at least in part, of the failure to rationalize, Communist societies suffered the wide range of economic (and social) problems that forced them to abandon their economic system and move toward a more market-like economy, a system that at least resembles a capitalist system. In other words, Russia and Eastern Europe are now rushing headlong in the direction of greater rationalization. The race to rationalize is being animated by economic factors, by a desire to improve the economic situation in those nations.

McDonaldization for Its Own Sake

Although it is clear that economic factors lie at the root of McDonaldization, we should not ignore the fact that it has become such a desirable process that many people and enterprises of all sorts pursue it as an end in its own right. That is, many of us, either as individuals or as representatives of various institutions, have come to value efficiency, calculability, predictability, and control, and seek them out whether or not there are economic gains involved. For example, efficiency is something we have come to value in the modern world. We search out efficient undertakings even when they do not make good economic sense. Thus, eating in a fast-food restaurant, or having a microwave dinner at home, may be efficient, but it is more costly than if we prepared the meal ourselves. Because we value efficiency, we are willing to pay the extra cost.

At a more macroscopic level, while it may make economic sense for yet another entrepreneur to open still another McDonaldized institution, does it make economic sense at the societal level to have so many such institutions concentrated in given locales offering almost identical goods and services? After all, except for its square shape, the Wendy's burger is about the same as the McDonald's burger. Thus, McDonaldization does not always make economic sense, yet it continues to be pursued despite that fact. This means that we cannot explain McDonaldization solely in terms of material interests. It has become something we value in and of itself, and we are willing to accept it even when it does not make sound economic sense.

The reasons for the value placed on rationalization are not difficult to find. Since its proliferation in the late 1950s, McDonald's (to say nothing of the myriad other agents of rationalization) has invested enormous amounts of money and effort in convincing us of its value and importance. Indeed, it now proclaims itself as a part of our rich tradition rather than, as many people believe, a threat to many of those traditions. Almost all of us have eaten there in our younger years, gone out with teenage buddies for a burger, taken our children there at various times as they grew up, or had a cup of coffee there with our parents. There is a lot of emotional baggage wrapped up in McDonald's, which it has built on and exploited to create a large number of highly devoted customers. Their commitment to McDonald's is more emotional than it is rational, despite the fact that McDonald's built its position on rational principles. Thus, McDonaldization is likely to proceed apace both because it offers the advantages of rationality and because people are committed to it. This commitment leads people to ignore and overlook the disadvantages of McDonald's, and this, in turn, helps make the world open to even further advances in McDonaldization in the future.

McDonaldization and the Changing Society

A third explanation of the rush toward McDonaldization is that it meshes well with other changes occurring in American society as well as around the world. For example, there is an increasing number of dual-career families because the number of women working outside the home has increased greatly. In the old-fashioned nuclear family in which the husband worked and the wife stayed home to cook and tend to the house and children, an elaborate meal prepared from scratch and eaten in a leisurely manner was possible. But in the modern family, where both spouses are likely to work, there is less likely to be anyone with the time needed to do the marketing, prepare the ingredients, cook the food, eat it, and clean up afterward. There may not even be time, at least during the work week, for meals at traditional restaurants. Thus, the speed and efficiency of a fast-food meal fits in well with the demands of the modern, dual-career family. It also fits with the rise in single-parent families. If the parent is at work all day, there is little time for meal preparation (and many other things) with the result that a quick meal at a fast-food restaurant is alluring. Similar advantages are offered the single-parent and dual-career families by many other McDonaldized institutions.

A society that emphasizes mobility, especially by automobile, is one in which the fast-food model will thrive. Clearly, the automobile occupies an increasingly central place in the United States (and in much of the rest of the world). Automobiles are common, especially among the teenagers and young adults who are the most likely devotees of the fast-food restaurant. And automobiles are almost required in order to frequent most fast-food restaurants, except those found in the heart of large cities.

More generally, the fast-food restaurant suits a society in which people prefer to be on the move. Going out for a McDonaldized dinner, or any other rationalized activity, is in tune with the demands of such a society; even better is the use of the drive-through window so that one does not even have to stop to eat. Further serving McDonaldization is the increasing number of people who frequently move from one part of the country to another, either on business or for vacations. People on the move seem to like the idea that even though they are in a different part of the country, they can still go to the familiar fast-food restaurant and eat the same foods they enjoy at home.

Increasing affluence and more discretionary money is another factor in the success of fast-food restaurants. As we have seen, those restaurants are not nearly as economical as they would have us believe. People need to have extra funds at their disposal in order to support a fast-food "habit." The increasing influence of the mass media is also contributing to the success of the fast-food restaurant. McDonaldized systems rely heavily on a barrage of advertisements, especially through television. Fast-food restaurants would not have succeeded as well as they have were it not for saturation advertising and the ubiquitous influence of television and other types of mass media. Similarly, the extensive advertising employed by such McDonaldized systems as H&R Block during tax season, Nutri/System, and Pearle Vision Centers has helped make them resounding successes.

Of course, it is technological change that has probably played the greatest role in the success of McDonaldized systems. Throughout this book we have touched on many technological advances that contributed to the initial development and later expansion of McDonaldization. Initially, it was technologies such as bureaucracies, scientific management, the assembly line, and the major product of that production system, the automobile, that contributed to the birth of the fast-food society. Over the years, innumerable technological developments have both spurred, and been spurred by, McDonaldization. Included in this list would be such technologies as the "fatilyzer," automatic drink dispensers, supermarket scanners, foods that cook themselves, the microwave oven, aquaculture, factory farming, the StairMaster, video tapes, domed stadiums, the 24-second clock, RVs, cash machines, voice mail, and health maintenance organizations. In recent years, the computer has come to play a central role in the growth of McDonaldization. Among other things, as we have seen throughout this book, we now find computers in fast-food restaurants, computer calls, computer letters, robots controlled by computers as well as the calculation of GPAs and instantaneous bank balances made possible by the computer. We can expect many more technological marvels in the future, and many of them will either be derived from the expanding needs of a McDonaldizing society or help to create new areas to be McDonaldized.

Thus, three main factors help us to understand the seemingly unstoppable spread of McDonaldization. It is impelled by economics, by the fact that it is regarded as valuable in and of itself, and because it is attuned to a range of specific changes in the larger society. For these reasons, the most likely scenario is for increased McDonaldization; the likely end-product is an iron cage of McDonaldization.

McDonaldization and Some Alternative Perspectives

McDonaldization is presented here as a central process in the *modern* world, and thus this book constitutes an analysis and critique of *modernity*. However, there are a number of contemporary perspectives—especially postindustrialism, post-Fordism, and postmodernism—that contend that we have already moved beyond the modern world and into a new, starkly different society. The cumulative implication of all of these views is that the focus of this book is retrograde since it deals with a "modern" phenomenon (McDonaldization) that is, or should soon be, disappearing with the emergence of a new (postindustrial, post-Fordist, or postmodern) societal form. The contention of this text, however, is that McDonaldization and its "modern" characteristics are not only with us for the foreseeable future, but also are spreading their influence at an accelerating rate throughout the rest of society. Other thinkers have been too quick to declare an end to modernity, at least in its McDonaldized form. Thus, this book constitutes a critique of these alternative perspectives: postindustrialism, post-Fordism, and postmodernism. Let us look briefly at each of these perspectives and the ways in which the theme of this book stands in contrast to them.

Postindustrialism

First, and most briefly, according to postindustrialists we have moved beyond the industrial era into the postindustrial epoch. The most important exponent of this viewpoint is Daniel Bell. One element of Bell's argument is that we have moved from a goods-production to a service society. This is undoubtedly true and is reflected in most aspects of McDonaldization, since they tend to involve the provision of services. He also points, correctly in my view, to the rise of new technologies and the growth in knowledge and information-processing. In fact, all of these play a central role in McDonaldized systems. It is also true that professionals, scientists, and technicians have increased in number and importance, as Bell observes. However, in contrast to Bell's thesis, low-status blue-collar and especially service occupations show no signs of disappearing, and, in fact, the latter group has been expanding and is central to a McDonaldized society. Above all, however, McDonaldization, as we have seen, is built on many of the ideas and systems of industrial society, especially bureaucratization, the assembly line, and scientific management. The growth of McDonaldization contradicts, at least in part and at least in the sectors of society in which it is important (and they are many), the idea that we have moved into a postindustrial society. Society is certainly post-industrial in many ways, but the spread of McDonaldization indicates that aspects of industrial society are likely to be with us for some time to come.

Post-Fordism

A similar issue is of concern to Marxian social thinkers, who claim that we have undergone a transition from Fordism to post-Fordism. Fordism, of course, refers to the ideas, principles, and systems spawned by Henry Ford.

A number of characteristics can be associated with the idea of Fordism. First, it involves the mass production of homogeneous products. The classic example is the original Model-T Fords, which were identical down to their black color. Even today's automobiles are largely homogeneous, at least by type of automobile being produced. Second, Fordism involves inflexible technologies, such as the assembly line. Though there have been some experiments with altering assembly lines, especially those undertaken by Volvo in Sweden, today's lines look much like they did in Ford's day. Third, Fordism involves the adoption of standardized work routines, or Taylorism. Thus, the person involved in putting the hubcap on the car does the same task over and over and in more or less the same way each time. Fourth, increases in productivity are derived from "economies of scale as well as the de-skilling, intensification, and homogenization of labor." Economy of scale means simply that larger factories producing larger numbers of products can manufacture each individual product more cheaply than small factories producing goods in small numbers. Deskilling means that productivity is increased if you have a number of workers doing jobs requiring little or no skill (for example, putting hubcaps on cars) rather than employing, as had been the case in the past, a few workers with great skill. Intensification here means the more demanding and faster the production process, the greater the productivity. Homogenization of labor involves great specialization (again the person putting on the hubcaps) so that each worker does the same kind of highly specialized work. This serves to make workers interchangeable. Finally, Fordism involves the growth of a market for the homogenized products of mass-production industries and the resulting homogenization of consumption patterns. In the case of the automobile industry, Fordism led to a national market for automobiles and similarly situated people bought similar, if not identical, automobiles.

Although Fordism grew throughout the twentieth century, especially in the United States, it reached its peak and began to decline in the 1970s, especially after the oil crisis of 1973 and the subsequent decline of the American automobile industry and the rise of its Japanese counterpart. As a result, it is argued by some that we are witnessing the decline of Fordism and the rise of post-Fordism with a number of distinguishing characteristics.

First, there is a decline of interest in mass products and the growth of interest in more specialized products, especially those high in style and quality. People are seen as wanting more customized products. Rather than drab and uniform products, people want flashier products that are easily distinguishable. Today's consumers are also seen as being more interested in quality and willing to pay extra for a quality product.

Second, more specialized products demanded in post-Fordist society require shorter production runs and result in smaller and more productive systems. Thus, we are supposed to be seeing a move away from huge factories producing uniform products to smaller plants turning out a wide range of different products.

Third, in the post-Fordist world we are supposed to be seeing more flexible production being made profitable by the advent of new technologies. For example, computerized equipment that can be reprogrammed to produce different products is replacing the old, single-function technology. Such technologies make it profitable to produce a range of different goods. This new, more flexible production process is to be controlled through more flexible systems, for example, a more flexible form of management.

Fourth, post-Fordist systems are supposed to require more from workers than their predecessors. For example, workers are seen as needing more diverse skills and better training in order to handle the new, more demanding and more sophisticated technologies. These new technologies also make it necessary for workers to be able to handle more responsibility and to be able to operate with greater autonomy. Thus, post-Fordism is seen as requiring a new kind of worker.

Finally, as post-Fordist workers become more differentiated, they come to want more differentiated commodities, life-styles, and cultural outlets. In other words, greater differentiation in the work place is reflected in greater differentiation in the society as a whole. This leads to more diverse demands and still greater differentiation in the work place.

It is argued here, however, that there has been *no* clear historical break with Fordism. We can acknowledge that elements of post-Fordism have emerged in the modern world, and yet it is equally clear that elements of Fordism persist and show no signs of disappearing. Most important for our purposes, "McDonaldism," a phenomenon which clearly has many things in common with Fordism, is growing at an astounding pace in contemporary society. McDonaldism shares many characteristics with Fordism, notably homogeneous products, rigid technologies, standardized work routines, deskilling, homogenization of labor (and customer), the mass worker, and homogenization of consumption. Let us look at each of these elements of McDonaldism; that is, let us look at McDonaldization from the vantage point of Fordism.

First, a McDonaldized world is dominated by homogeneous products. The Big Mac, the Egg McMuffin, and Chicken McNuggets are identical from one time and place to another. Second, technologies like Burger King's conveyor system, as well as the french-fry and soft-drink machines throughout the fast-food industry, are as rigid as many of the technologies in Henry Ford's assembly-line system. Further, the work routines in the fast-food restaurant are highly standardized. Even what the workers say to customers is routinized. In addition, the jobs in a fast-food restaurant are deskilled; they take little or no ability. The workers, furthermore, are homogeneous and the actions of the customers are homogenized by the demands of the fast-food restaurant (for example, don't dare ask for a rare burger). The workers at fast-food restaurants can be seen as a mass of interchangeable workers. Finally, what is consumed and how it is consumed is homogenized by McDonaldization.

Thus, in these and other ways Fordism is alive and well in the modern world, although it has been transformed into McDonaldism. Furthermore, classic Fordism, for example in the form of the assembly line, remains a significant presence in the American economy.

Postmodernism

Finally, there is the more general perspective known as "postmodernism." Its basic thesis is that we have entered, or are entering, a postmodern society that represents a break or rupture with modern society; postmodernity follows and supplants modernity. Had we the time and space, we could try to sort out the various images of postmodern society and the array of theories of that society. While there are long lists of characteristics that are supposed to differentiate modernism from postmodernism, modernism is generally thought of as highly rational and rigid, while postmodernism is seen as more irrational and flexible.

A number of writers, most notably Jean-Francois Lyotard, have explicitly labeled McDonald's a postmodern phenomenon. In a recent essay entitled "Writing McDonald's, Eating the Past: McDonald's as a Postmodern Space," Allen Shelton extensively analyzes the relationship between McDonald's and postmodernism. Shelton concludes, "I portray McDonald's as an emblem of postmodernism, a moral symbol that acts as a signpost for the times." Although he does associate McDonald's with elements associated with postmodernism (for example, time-space compression, which I discuss shortly), Shelton also links it to various phenomena that I would associate with modernity. For example, Shelton makes the excellent point that what McDonald's succeeded in doing was automating the customer. That is, when customers enter the fast-food restaurant or wend their way along the drive-through, they enter a kind of automated system through which they are impelled and from which they are ultimately ejected when they are "refueled." In his view, McDonald's looks more like a factory than a restaurant. However, it is not a "sweat shop for its customers, but a high tech factory." To my way of thinking, this indicates that McDonald's is better thought of as a modern than a postmodern phenomenon.

There is general agreement among postmodernists about the distinction between modern and postmodern society. It is, however, unclear whether there is a radical disjuncture between modernity and postmodernity, or whether postmodern society gradually emerges from modernity and is difficult, if not impossible, to distinguish from it at the edges. Because of this ambiguity, and others, some scholars reject the idea of a new, postmodern society. Says one, "Now I reject all this. I do not believe that we live in 'New Times,' in a 'postindustrial and postmodern age' fundamentally different from the capitalist mode of production globally dominant for the past two centuries."

The viewpoint adopted in this book is clearly in line with the above criticism of postmodernism. While there may well be some characteristics of today's society that are dramatically different from its "modern" predecessor, there is also great continuity between the two types of society. Clearly, McDonaldization is a modern phenomenon emphasizing rationality that is rigidly structured. Thus, the emphasis on McDonaldization here constitutes a rejection of the general thesis that we have moved on to a postmodern society in which such modern phenomena are fast-disappearing. The view of this text is that McDonaldization shows no signs of disappearing and being replaced by new, postmodern forms. Although some postmodern developments may be occurring, they exist side-by-side with McDonaldization.

David Harvey, a critic of postmodernism, makes a similar argument. While Harvey sees great changes and argues that it is these changes that lie at the base of postmodern thinking, he believes that there are many *continuities* between modernity and postmodernity. His major conclusion is that while "there has certainly been a sea change in the surface appearance of capitalism since 1973 . . . the underlying logic of capitalist accumulation and its crisis tendencies remain the same."

Central to Harvey's approach is the idea of time-space compression. He believes that modernism served to compress both time and space and that that process has accelerated in the postmodern era leading to "an intense phase of time-space compression that has a disorienting and disruptive impact. . . ." But this is *not* essentially different from earlier epochs in capitalism: "We have, in short, witnessed another fierce round in that process of annihilation of space through time that has always lain at the center of capitalism's dynamic." (Shelton also places great emphasis on time-space compression, but he associates it with postmodernism and disassociates it from modernism.)

As an example of space compression in the case of McDonaldization, foods once available only in foreign countries or large cities are now quickly and widely available throughout the United States because of the spread of fast-food chains dispensing Italian, Mexican, or Cajun food. Similarly, as an example of time compression, foods that formerly took hours to prepare can now be made in seconds in a microwave oven or purchased in minutes at a fast-food restaurant. Or, to take a very different example, in the 1991 war with Iraq, television, especially CNN, transported us instantaneously from one place to another—from air raids in Baghdad to SCUD attacks on Tel Aviv to military briefings in Riyadh. Viewers were able to learn about many military developments as they were occurring and at the same time as the generals or the president of the United States. Thus, to Harvey, postmodernism is *not* discontinuous with modernism; they are reflections of the same underlying dynamic. In the view expressed here, McDonaldization is not only a modern development that continues to be important in a postmodern world, but also one that is extending its reach throughout society. We thus have the seeming paradox of a modern phenomenon expanding in a postmodern world. If it is the case that modernity is expanding within postmodernity, then there cannot be a radical disjuncture between modernity and postmodernity.

In sum, the phenomenon of McDonaldization stands in contrast to the ideas of postindustrialism, post-Fordism, and postmodernism. While we may have witnessed some new, postmodern (postindustrial, or post-Fordist) developments in recent years, elements of modernity persist. McDonald's is a modern phenomenon and McDonaldization is a modern process. McDonald's and McDonaldization are strongly influenced by the ideas and structures of industrialism and Fordism. Even if we are willing to describe society today as postmodern, we must recognize the continued vitality of modernity as represented by the spread of McDonaldization. We might say that the ghost of Henry Ford is stalking the Earth and eating at McDonald's, having his taxes done at H&R Block, and losing weight at Nutri\System.

Conclusion

This chapter has sought to argue in two different ways that we confront a future of an iron cage of McDonaldization. First, it was argued that McDonaldization is impelled by economic and cultural factors and that it is in tune with ongoing social changes. Because of the forces behind it, and because it meshes well with the changing nature of society, we can anticipate a continuation of this trend toward greater and greater McDonaldization. Second, we discussed three theories that seem to run counter to the McDonaldization thesis—postindustrialism, post-Fordism, and postmodernism. Although there may be elements of postindustrialism, post-Fordism and postmodernism in contemporary society, elements of modernity, especially McDonaldism, coexist with them. Thus, at both an empirical and a theoretical level, a strong case can be made that we confront a future of accelerating McDonaldization.

No social institution lasts forever, and McDonald's is not immune from that dictum. While McDonaldization and McDonald's remain powerful forces in a postmodern world (if that is what we want to call today's society), there will come a time when they, too, will pass from the scene. McDonald's will remain powerful until the nature of society has changed so dramatically that McDonald's is no longer able to adapt to it. Even after it is gone, McDonald's will be remembered for the dramatic impact it had, both positive and negative, on the United States and much of the rest of the world. In Chapter Two we discussed, among others, bureaucracies, scientific management, and the assembly line as predecessors of McDonaldization. When McDonald's has, like its predecessors, receded in importance, or even passed from the scene, it will be remembered as yet another precursor to a still more rational world.

9

Coping With a McDonaldized Society
A Practical Guide

Having discussed esoteric topics such as post-Fordism and post-modernism in the last chapter, we make a dramatic shift in this final chapter to more mundane, practical, day-to-day concerns. Assuming a continuing trend in the direction of increasing rationalization, what can a person do to cope with an increasingly McDonaldized world? The answer to that question depends, at least in part, on one's attitude toward McDonaldization.

Attitudes Toward the Iron Cage: Velvet, Rubber, or Iron?

As it is presented in this book, and as it was presented by Weber, the imagery of an iron cage communicates a sense of coldness, hardness, of great discomfort. However, for many people, their view of the future might better be depicted as the "velvet cage of McDonaldization." That is, they might be willing to admit that we are steadily being encircled and encased by McDonaldization, but this is a quite comfortable situation as far as they are concerned. They like, even crave, the McDonaldized world and welcome its continued growth and proliferation. This is certainly a viable position, and one that is especially likely to be adopted by those reared since the advent of the McDonaldized world. This is the world they know, it represents their standard of good taste and high quality, and they can think of nothing better than an increasingly rationalized world. They prefer a world that is not cluttered with too many choices and options. They like the fact that many aspects of their lives are highly predictable. They relish an impersonal world in which they interact with human and even nonhuman robots. They seek to avoid, at least in the McDonaldized portions of their world, close, human contact. For such people, and they probably represent with each passing year an increasingly large proportion of the population, McDonaldization represents not a threat, but nirvana.

For many other people, McDonaldization may represent a cage, but its bars are seen not as being made of iron, but rather of rubber; there is adequate means for escape. Such people dislike many aspects of McDonaldization, but they find other of its dimensions quite appealing. Like those people who see themselves in a velvet cage, this type of person may well like the efficiency, speed, predictability, and impersonality of McDonaldized systems and services. Such people are busy with many other things and obtaining a meal (or some other McDonaldized service) is something to be done efficiently so that they can get on with other things that need to be done. However, these people are aware of the costs and liabilities of McDonaldization. Thus, they seek to escape from it when they can. Its efficiencies may even enhance their ability to escape from it. That is, getting a fast meal may allow them the time to luxuriate in other, nonrationalized activities. For these people the bars of the cage are rubber and can be bent, and such people can move in and out as they wish. When they do move out of McDonaldized systems, they tend to look for, and become involved in, nonrationalized settings as a counterpoint to their normally highly rationalized lives. These are the types of people who on weekends and vacations go into the wilderness to camp the old-fashioned way; go mountain-climbing, spelunking, fishing and hunting (without elaborate equipment), antique-hunting, museum-browsing; prepare elaborate home-cooked meals from scratch; and search out old-fashioned traditional restaurants, inns, and bed and breakfasts. To these people, the bars of the iron cage of McDonaldization are pliable enough to permit them a sufficient number of ways of escaping that they can tolerate the rationalization of the rest of society.

These are the types of people who are likely to try to humanize their telephone answering machines with creative messages such as, "Sorry I ain't home, don't break my heart when you hear the tone." (However, as is often true in a McDonaldized society, and as is to be expected from the perspective of the idea of an iron cage, a company has come into existence to rationalize this escape route by selling prerecorded, humorous answering machine messages. Thus, one can now buy a prerecorded tape with an impressionist imitating Humphrey

Bogart: "Of all the answering machines in the world, you had to call this one.")

The third type of person is one for whom McDonaldization is both iron and cage. Such a person is deeply offended by the process and sees few, if any, ways out. Unlike the second type of person, these people see escape routes (if they see them at all) providing only temporary respites that will soon fall under the sway of McDonaldization. They share the dark and pessimistic outlook of Max Weber, and, like Weber (and this author), see the future as bringing with it a "polar night of icy darkness." These are the severest critics of McDonaldization and the ones who see less and less place for themselves in modern society.

Given these three types of people, the issue of concern in this chapter is actions open to them in a McDonaldized world. Clearly, the different types of people will choose different types of action. People of the first type will do nothing, because they are fast-food enthusiasts. They will continue to frequent fast-food restaurants and their clones within other sectors of society and even actively seek out and McDonaldize new venues in need of rationalization. Some, especially of the third type, may want to work for the radical transformation of our McDonaldized society. This might involve efforts to return to a pre-McDonaldized world, or to create a new non-McDonaldized world out of the rubble created by the fall of the golden arches. Although I would not argue against such activities, I do not, given my view that we are in the midst of producing an iron cage of McDonaldization, think that they are likely to be very successful.

This chapter argues neither for the passive acceptance nor for the overthrow of our McDonaldized society. Rather it is directed primarily at those of the second and third types who see McDonaldization as a rubber or iron cage, who are not happy about the lives they live within it, and who are, as a result, interested in carving out a less rationalized life for themselves.

We begin by first presenting a wide range of often successful efforts to modify McDonaldized systems and to limit their negative effects. As a result of the efforts to be discussed in the next section, McDonaldized systems will continue to exist, but they will be slightly more palatable. Second, we will discuss some efforts aimed at the creation of non-McDonaldized institutions in society. To the degree that they succeed and can remain free of rationalization, they represent nonrationalized niches in an otherwise rationalized world. Third, we will discuss a few examples of other, more individual ways that people can carve out non-rationalized niches for themselves. Our major focus will be on the creation of such niches in the work world, but they can be created elsewhere as well. Finally, we will discuss a number of more personal dos and don'ts for surviving in a McDonaldized society.

Modifying McDonaldized Institutions: McLean Deluxe Burgers and Macheezmo Mouse

One course of action for those opposed to McDonaldization is to put pressure on McDonaldized institutions to change, to reduce or eliminate the irrationalities of these systems. In fact, there is considerable evidence that people have pressured McDonaldized systems and that these systems have responded by mitigating some of their worst excesses.

In spite of the fast-food restaurant's widespread acceptance, many people have rebelled against, and attacked, it on a variety of grounds. A few communities have fought hard, and at times successfully, against the invasion of fast-food restaurants. They have reacted against the garish signs and structures, the traffic, the noise, and the nature of the clientele that is drawn to fast-food restaurants. Most generally, they have fought against the various kinds of irrationalities and assaults on tradition that the fast-food restaurant represents. Thus, there are communities that would be highly attractive to fast-food chains (for example, Sanibel Island in Florida) in which one sees few, if any, fast-food restaurants.

The resort village of Saugatuck, Michigan, fought McDonald's attempt to take over the site of a quaint old cafe called Ida Red's. Said one local businessman, "People can see McDonald's anywhere—they don't come to Saugatuck for fast food." The owner of a local inn seemed to recognize that the town was really resisting the broader process of rationalization: "It's the Howard Johnson's, the McDonald's, the malls of the world that we're fighting against. . . . You can go to a mall and not know what state you're in. We're a relief from all that." Outside the United States, the resistance has often been even greater. The opening of the first McDonald's in Italy, for example, led to widespread protest involving several thousand people. The Italian McDonald's opened in the picturesque Piazza di Spagna in Rome adjacent to the headquarters of the world famous fashion designer Valentino. One Roman politician claimed that McDonald's was "the principal cause of degradation of the ancient Roman streets."

In response to such protests and criticisms, and as an attempt to forestall them in the future, McDonald's is building more and more outlets that fit better into the community in which they are placed. Thus, a McDonald's in Miami's Little Havana has a Spanish-style roof and feels more like a hacienda. Another in Freeport, Maine, looks like a quaint New England inn. The 12,000th restaurant, which opened in 1991, is located in a restored 1860s white Colonial House on Long Island. The interior has a 1920s look.

Although McDonald's has been forced to mute and adapt its physical symbols and structure in light of various attacks and criticisms, few communities have succeeded in keeping its franchises out completely. But it is no doubt the case that the fast-food restaurant is a less glaring and visually offensive structure today as a result of these criticisms and corporate responses to them.

As we saw earlier, fast-food restaurants have also begun to alter their menus as a result of the numerous criticisms of nutritionists. Even Johnny Carson picked up on this, labeling the McDonald's burger "McClog the Artery." By far the most notable and visible critic of fast-food fare has been Phil Sokoloff and his nonprofit organization, National Heart Savers Association. In 1990, for example, Sokoloff took out full-page advertisements in *The New York Times* and 22 other major newspapers with the headline, "The Poisoning of America." The ads singled out McDonald's for serving food high in fat and cholesterol. When Sokoloff first began running such ads in 1988, McDonald's responded to them by calling them "reckless, misleading, the worst kind of sensationalism." But Sokoloff persisted and in July 1990 he ran ads with the lead, "McDonald's, Your Hamburgers *Still* Have Too Much Fat! And Your French Fries *Still* are Cooked with Beef Tallow." With surveys showing that people were reducing their patronage of fast-food restaurants, McDonald's and other chains buckled. By the end of July 1991, Burger King, Wendy's, and McDonald's announced that they were switching to the use of vegetable oils in the cooking of french fries. Said Sokoloff, "I couldn't be happier. Millions of ounces of saturated fat won't be clogging the arteries of American people."

McDonald's has begun to respond more broadly to these criticisms; we undoubtedly will see less fat, salt, and sugar in its products of the future. In late 1990 McDonald's unveiled its Lean Deluxe burger.

Instead of the Quarter Pounders' 20 grams of fat and 410 calories, the Lean Deluxe burger has 10 grams of fat and 310 calories. Although still far from a diet food, the Lean Deluxe reflected the responsiveness of McDonald's on this issue. In 1991 McDonald's went even further and introduced the McLean Deluxe hamburger with about 9-percent fat (still considered far too high by many nutritionists), less than half the fat in a typical McDonald's burger. (Other chains sell hamburgers with as much as 25-percent fat.) To accomplish this, McDonald's adds carrageen, a seaweed extract, to the McLean Deluxe. This additive binds water to the meat, preventing it from being too dry because of its lower fat content. To make up for the loss of flavor, McDonald's is adding natural beef flavoring to the mix. Although the McLean Deluxe is not a fully adequate response, it is even more striking that other chains are not yet ready to jump on the low-fat bandwagon. Said one Hardee's spokesperson, "We're not going to sell a water-and-seaweed burger."

Some fast-food chains have responded to these kinds of criticisms in a far broader way. For example, there is a small chain of Mexican restaurants on the West Coast called Macheezmo Mouse. This chain's slogan is "Fresh-Fit-Fast." It specializes in low-fat, low-calorie dishes that are baked, steamed, or grilled instead of fried. The menu includes nutritional information on each item. A corporate executive calls it "fast food for smart people."

McDonald's is also showing signs of being responsive to environmentalists, and it is experimenting with packaging that is less harmful to the environment. In late 1990 McDonald's announced that it was eliminating its plastic foam "clamshell" hamburger box. The box had been attacked by environmentalists because pollutants were generated in the production of the boxes and, more important, they lingered for decades in landfills or on the sides of roads. These boxes were to be replaced by a paper wrapping with a cellophane-like outer wrapper. In 1991 Hardee's announced that it would use recycled polystyrene in its packages. Said one environmentalist, "I think that the public is pressuring these people into taking positive steps."

In fact, the responses to complaints by communities, nutritionists, and environmentalists indicate that the fast-food restaurant is quite an adaptable institution, although all of these adaptations remain within the broad confines of rationality. Thus, for example, there seems to be little that can be done about the poor quality of the food. This fact is reflected in a diner opened by McDonald's, the Golden Arch Cafe, in Hartsville, Tennessee, which is modeled after old-time diners and sells things like cola floats and Salisbury steak dinners with two vegetables. The diner includes traditional "chrome-glass decor, neon lights, spin-seat counter stools, cozy booths, and a jukebox that blares '50s and '60s hits." McDonald's is experimenting with the return to the diner in order to be able to operate in very small towns. The belief is that diners are more likely than fast-food outlets to be viable economically in small towns. However, the opening of the diner does not seem to have done anything to improve the quality of the food:

> Not until your meal arrives does the restaurant reveal its origins in the fast-food industry: virtually everything reeks of processing. On a recent visit, scraps of stale-tasting catfish were all but invisible in their heavy orange breading; the mashed potatoes had the slightly bitter flavor that bespeaks dehydrated and reconstituted; the pork "cutlet" was perfectly shaped, oblong, dry and flabby, and heaped with a pale, salty gravy so congealed you could have eaten it with a fork—if you could have eaten it. Apart from a breakfast biscuit, which tasted fresh, the baked goods were heavy and doughy. A dessert called banana pudding came with sliced bananas tucked into it, but otherwise had the artificial, perfume-sweet flavor of a packaged pudding mix. Only the fried chicken was, as described, "real." If you strip off its greasy, acrid coat, you get an acceptable dish; what's more, the startling sight of a plain, honest piece of chicken is enough to bring tears to your eyes. Now *that's* nostalgia.

Needless to say, despite the poor quality of the food, the diner is jammed, at least as of a few months after its opening.

Another of the limitations of the adaptability of the fast-food restaurant is that it must offer a simple and limited menu. Over the years, McDonald's has experimented with, and even expanded upon, its menu, but only within narrow boundaries. McDonald's found that although the restaurant was available in the morning, it had no food to offer for breakfast. Thus, it was concluded that a variety of simple breakfast foods following the traditional model (for example, the Egg McMuffin) could be offered in the morning and that this would increase business. A similar expansion was made in the direction of adding a few desserts to the menu. One franchisee was concerned about a decline in his outlet's business during Lent. The result was the creation of the Filet-O-Fish sandwich that was ultimately adopted by, and became highly successful throughout, the McDonald's chain.

Faced with the growth of the fried chicken business, McDonald's introduced Chicken McNuggets. Confronted by increasing numbers of people wanting healthier, more dietetic meals, it began to offer salads and then carrot and celery sticks. For those who complain about the boring sameness of McDonald's fare, there have been periodic experiments with different kinds of foods like the McRib sandwich and the Breakfast Burrito. While today's McDonald's menu is not nearly as limited as was the menu of the 1950s (as of this writing many outlets have 33 items), the diner in search of variety is not going to find it at McDonald's. The physical limitations of the restaurants and the skill limitations of the workers make it impossible for the fast-food restaurant to offer more than a limited menu of simple foods.

McDonald's has adapted in other ways: Some people have actually complained about the disappearance of the old-fashioned huge golden arches, and at least one McDonald's franchise has responded by bringing them back. On the other side, in response to complaints from up-scale clientele about a dehumanizing dining environment, a new McDonald's in Manhattan's financial district offers Chopin on a grand piano, chandeliers, marble walls, fresh flowers, a doorman, and hostesses who show people to their tables. The golden arches are virtually invisible. There are a few classy additions to the menu (espresso, capuccino, tarts), but in large part the menu is the same as in all other McDonald's (albeit with slightly higher prices). Said one recent visitor, underscoring the continuity between this franchise and all others, "A smashing place, and the best thing is you can still eat with your fingers."

In fact, McDonald's has been forced to pick up the pace of innovation because of flat and even declining sales and falling share prices. The 12 McDonald's in Bakersfield, California, experimented with a credit card system—McCharge. McDonald's is even being forced to accept a practice that capitalistic firms are notoriously unwilling to engage in—price competition. Up to now, McDonald's has followed the modern capitalistic practice of competing on the basis of advertising rather than on a price basis. But with its American sales declining, and other fast-food restaurants succeeding on the basis of price, McDonald's has had to adapt. This new development was ushered in by Taco Bell which introduced a "value menu"—tacos and other items for 59 cents. Price competition allowed Taco Bell to attract new customers without violating the basic principle of keeping its menu short and simple. As a result, Taco Bell has become the best-performing fast-food chain in the United States. Reluctantly, McDonald's has begun to offer discounts on food with 59-cent burgers and soft drinks.

McDonald's is not the only fast-food restaurant to adapt to changing conditions. For example, Burger King has experimented with mobile restaurants, Burger Kings on wheels. As the fast-food business grows more and more competitive, we can expect the pace of innovation and experimentation to increase.

What keeps the fast-food business on its toes is the knowledge that food fashions change, and even the giant franchises can find themselves on the brink of bankruptcy. Recently, the Chock Full o' Nuts chain of coffee shops in New York City was reduced to its last outlet; at its peak in the 1960s, it comprised about 80 restaurants. Its nutty cheese sandwich, "cream cheese and chopped nuts on dark raisin bread wrapped in plain, waxed paper" was described as "the original fast food."

While McDonald's is in no immediate danger of going the way of Chock Full o' Nuts, there are some troubling signs. In addition to flat sales and declining share prices, McDonald's is confronted by the fact that sales in Mexican fast-food restaurants (like Taco Bell) are growing at three times the rate of sales in hamburger restaurants and pizza sales are growing at twice the sales rate of burgers. In addition, such upscale franchises as Red Lobster are exhibiting greater profitability. Further, many people are moving away from the trend of high-fat, high-sodium, high-calorie food served at McDonald's. Given these and other problems, it is clear that McDonald's will continue to change and evolve, although it is out of the question that it will ever surrender the basic rational principles that made it such a success and such a revolutionary force.

One general adaptation that we can expect to see more of is an increase in the number of rationalized activities that can be undertaken in a single setting. This, after all, lies at the base of the success of shopping malls. We are likely to see an increasing number of businesses that combine two or more activities. Examples include beauty parlors or book stores that also serve lunch. In a rational society it is inefficient to simply eat; one should be able to do other things while eating.

One issue that fast-food restaurants have shown little inclination to deal with is dehumanizing working conditions. Burger King, for example, has fought hard against unionization in order, at least in part, to avoid improving such conditions. As long as there is a steady supply of people willing to work in such settings for even just a few months, McDonald's will not do much about the working conditions. In some locales McDonald's has been faced with an inadequate supply from its traditional labor pool—teenagers. Rather than alter and improve the work to attract teenagers and keep them on the job longer,

McDonald's has responded by broadening its hiring net and seeking out teenagers who live in distant communities, hiring retarded adults, and bringing in older employees, often retirees, into a program called "McMasters." In the past, McDonald's was unwilling to hire older people because its management believed that low wages and the nature of the work would be intolerable to an older person. However, there are older workers, such as those permanently laid-off from dying or declining "smokestack industries" (for example, steel), who are desperate enough for work that they will, at least for a time, tolerate these conditions. Kinder-Care is also interested in making up for the shortage in younger workers willing to work for low wages by hiring older people. In fact, one expert said, "For old people who need to be needed, it [Kinder-Care] sure beats working in McDonald's."

One can predict that McDonald's will not significantly alter its working conditions until it is unable to find a steady supply of new workers. Even then, it may simply move in the direction of eliminating human employees rather than humanizing the work. If this is the case, we can expect to see more automation and robotization in the fast-food restaurants of the future.

Modifying the Auto Assembly Line in Sweden

Other elements of our McDonaldizing society have changed in response to their critics, the best example being the automobile industry and its assembly-line technology. The automobile companies have sought, often only after considerable external pressure, to reduce some of the worst irrationalities associated with the automobile. Under pressure from environmentalists, the automobile companies have done a few things to help reduce the air pollution caused by automobiles. When the critics were joined by government pressure and severe competition from Japan and elsewhere, efforts were made to make the automobiles smaller and more fuel efficient.

However the major irrationality of the automobile assembly line, at least from the point of view of this book, is the unreasonable character of work on it. As we saw earlier, the demands of the high speed of the line and the ultraspecialization of the jobs made the work alienating and dehumanizing. For many years, the automobile companies were attacked by workers and their labor unions and pressed to do something about the nature of the work. However, the companies did very little except perhaps pay the worker more in order to compensate, at least in part, for the negative aspects of the work. Because plenty of people were available and eager to replace disgruntled workers on the assembly line, there was little need to humanize the work.

However, in the 1960s and 1970s, especially in Sweden, a number of factors coalesced to help lead to significant humanization of work on the assembly line. Swedish workers, like their American counterparts, did not like work on the automobile assembly line. Their distaste was even greater because they were more highly educated and had higher aspirations than their American counterparts. The usual problems associated with distaste for assembly-line work increased—absenteeism, tardiness, sabotage, and turnover. However, Swedish industrialists could not, like their counterparts in the United States, ignore these problems, especially the turnover problem. There was little unemployment in Sweden in the 1960s so that it was difficult, if not impossible, to replace workers who quit their jobs. Thus, the Swedes were forced to take steps to reduce the dehumanizing and alienating aspects of work on the assembly line.

The Swedish automobile companies, such as Saab and especially Volvo, greatly modified the assembly line in order to eliminate its worst excesses. The single long line was replaced by structures that broke the line up into smaller components with each subsection handled by a relatively small work group of about 25 to 30 workers. A sense of community was engendered among the members of the work group. Instead of performing highly specialized tasks, each member of the group was allowed to perform a number of more complex tasks. Instead of performing the same set of tasks over and over, workers were permitted to trade jobs. Instead of being told which tasks to perform and how to perform them, work groups and their members were allowed to decide for themselves, within limits, what to do and how to do it. These changes and many others were all aimed at reducing the alienating and dehumanizing aspects of assembly-line work. And they met with some considerable success, at least initially.

In the United States, with the absence of the pressure caused by the low unemployment rate in Sweden, there was considerable interest in the humanizing reforms undertaken in Sweden, but very few actual changes in the work. In fact the likely response in the United States, and, eventually, in Sweden too, is not to try to humanize work, but rather to eliminate more and more of the human beings. This means increasing use of automation and robotization. We already find some use of robots on the automobile assembly line. As the technology improves and the costs decline, we can expect to see many more robots in the future.

Thus, McDonaldized organizations do have some ways of responding to the critics of their excesses, but they are not anxious to respond and only do so when the external pressure becomes too great. The nature of the responses is limited, because McDonald's can only go so far before it begins to undermine the basic principles that have made it so successful. Thus, looking to the future, we can expect some modifications and reforms by McDonald's, but they will be of a relatively minor character, and they are likely to come about primarily as a response to external pressure. Nevertheless, critics of McDonaldization can take heart in the knowledge that their protests will be heard and that McDonald's will adapt, albeit within limits, to them.

Creating "Reasonable" Alternatives: Baguettes, Ben & Jerry's, and B&Bs

The excesses of McDonaldization have led to the birth and development of various kinds of alternatives to it, alternatives that reject rationalization in favor of reason. These are places that do not put a premium on the efficient production of goods and services or the efficient processing of customers. Instead of large quantities, they focus on producing high-quality products. They revel in the unpredictabilities of the products they serve and the services they offer. Instead of nonhuman technologies, they employ skilled human beings who practice their crafts relatively unconstrained by external controls. Hence, these are not rational places in which to work or to be served by. The creation of such alternatives is another route open to the critics of McDonaldization.

Marvelous Market: "Crunchy Crusts and Full Taste"

A good example is a relatively new, nonrational, reasonable business that has opened in Washington, D.C. Its name is Marvelous Market. I hasten to add that even it has not eschewed all aspects of the rational model. It is a take-out market that emphasizes that its foods can be picked up "quickly" and used to prepare an "effortless" dinner. Even in a business that was developed in reaction to McDonaldization, it is impossible to totally ignore the demands of a society that has grown accustomed to the fast-food model and system.

However, Marvelous Market is primarily oriented toward reason rather than rationality. This is most notable in the fact that its main emphasis is quality rather than quantity. Here is the way its newsletter talks about food: "Cuisine is not just a way of cooking; it is a way of life. Food is much more than the answer to hunger. Food triggers moods and memories, reveals needs and desires, releases tensions and stimulates creativity." (Compare this to what fast-food restaurants have to say.) The main product at Marvelous Market is bread and it, too, is described in terms of its quality:

> I [the owner] moved to Washington in 1961, and was told right away, "There is no good bread in Washington." I have heard that flat sentence over the years, thousands of times, probably. It is said commonly by people talking wistfully about the old days.
>
> I don't expect to hear it any longer. The old days have arrived. Marvelous Market's breads have crunchy crusts and full tastes. . . .
>
> Every day you will find round loaves of walnut bread and rye with currants, great batards of sourdough, chewy country loaves with big holes, bread with rosemary and black olives, baguettes baked once before lunch and, so that they will be perfectly fresh for dinner, again at 4pm.
>
> This bread may be a little startling to people accustomed to . . . soft pre-sliced loaves wrapped in plastic bags. You have not tasted breads like this before; they are . . . addictive.

Marvelous Market's newsletter concludes, "We are most of all determined to sell foods with great taste."

Marvelous Market is not an efficient operation. Its foods are unpredictable. One deals with people rather than human automatons or mechanical robots. Says Marvelous Market, "You will find a friendly store where the bakers and cooks talk and explain, and work on new recipes for breads and foods."

The fact is that stores and shops like this have existed all along, although many have been forced out of business by the fast-food outlets. What is new is the birth of new versions of these shops to provide an alternative for those people who are fed up with the excesses of McDonald's. But, can this counter-movement ever become anything more than a minor phenomenon that exists within the interstices of the marketplace?

For a variety of reasons, I think that places like Marvelous Market are doomed to be restricted to isolated pockets of the McDonaldized society. For one thing, the growth of such places is restricted by their very nature. Their expansion is limited, because with increasing size comes greater and greater threats to the ability to control quality. And there are just so many people with the skills and inclinations needed to open places like Marvelous Market. A second barrier is the fact that a population reared from infancy on fast foods is likely to regard fast-food products as the ultimate in quality. The McDonald's hamburger bun is apt to be that generation's standard of quality, not something called a "batard." Thus, for example, one mother of a four-year-old said, "One day I hope that Kevin will appreciate my cooking. . . . But for now, I can't even compete with a Big Mac and fries." Finally, and most important, if such markets and shops really show signs of taking over a significant share of the market, the forces of McDonaldization will take notice and seek to transform them into rationalized systems that can be franchised around the world. One could foresee Gulf and Western or some other large conglomerate buying out the highly successful Marvelous Market, rationalizing its products (much as Kentucky Fried Chicken did to poor old Colonel Sanders's recipes), and creating a worldwide chain of Marvelous Markets. Of course, at that point instead of being an alternative to McDonaldization, Marvelous Market would have become part of the process of McDonaldization.

Marvelous Market became a phenomenal success in the Washington area. It soon had to limit bread purchases to two loaves per person and close for several hours during the day because it could not handle the demand, and the quantity of bread produced and sold grew dramatically. The owner ordered new, larger ovens, expanded by opening another bakery devoted solely to production and not sales, bought a truck to dispense bread at various locations in the Washington area, and began selling his breads to supermarkets and restaurants. As this expansion took place, the owner claimed that his market continued to emphasize quality: "And certainly we're trying to attend to quality, refusing to increase our output faster than we can, refusing to give up our hand-shaping, pulling off our shelves each week hundreds of pounds of bread that don't meet our standards." However, in my view, and the view of many other customers, the quality of the bread *did* suffer; for example the store sold more burned loaves. The demand for quantity seemed to cause the quality to deteriorate.

In light of these problems the owner published an open letter to his customers on November 9, 1991, on the opening of his new bakery. On the one hand, the letter recognized that in various ways growth had created irrationalities:

> We are in transition. . . .
>
> In the process we have offended some of you because the *quality of our bread has been erratic,* and we haven't adhered to our schedule of breads. . . .
>
> On some days of the week, like Saturday, we *run out of products* before you can come. Many of you who might wish to be on the courts playing tennis or at the firm billing clients, now *stand in line* Saturday mornings. . . .
>
> Moreover, although you have been fairly tolerant over the months in *quality* variations, we have been offended by them consistently. (Italics added.)

On the other hand, the owner promised that expansion would not mean a decline in quality (and other irrationalities):

> So we built a large new bakery, putting into it the best equipment capable of producing our kinds of breads. It is *not automated* equipment; we make breads in the other bakery just as we make them here, *slowly, by hand* . . . we'll be able to get *far more quality and consistency* in our breads.
>
> In addition, we managed to attract as leader of the new bakery Paula Oland, one of the premier bakers of the country. . . .
>
> For those who think that we are going to follow the course of other Washington bakeries which began with promise and then compromised, it's not going to happen here. (Italics added.)

The owner of Marvelous Market was clearly aware of the dangers of rationalizing his operation and was trying to avoid them while he greatly expanded the market's business. Time will tell whether he can succeed in avoiding the iron cage of McDonaldization.

Ben & Jerry's: "Caring Capitalism"

A far more established and well-known alternative to rationalized business, at least in some ways, is the Ben & Jerry's ice cream company with headquarters in Waterbury, Vermont. In a conscious effort to differentiate itself from the cold impersonality of rationalized businesses, Ben & Jerry's has sought to be known as the "company that cares." Unlike most of its rationalized alternatives, Ben & Jerry's cares about quality, about its workers, and about the environment. The owners, Ben Cohen and Jerry Greenfield, customarily come to work in T-shirts and sneakers. Although he owns stock worth millions of dollars, the chairman of the board, Ben Cohen, earns "only" $83,000 a year. This is a result of the company policy that executives may earn no more than seven times the earnings of the lowest-paid worker. Practicing "caring capitalism," the company commits 7.5 percent of its pretax earnings to its foundation, which makes grants to organizations "committed to imaginative social change," pays premiums for milk in order to assist Vermont's ailing family farms, and purchases blueberries from local Indians, peaches from black Georgia farmers, and nuts from the natives of the Amazon rain forest. Its corporate shareholder meetings not only involve the usual election of directors, but also the videotaping of messages to Congress promoting shareholders' favorite causes.

Ben & Jerry's is very conscious of the environment and of avoiding and limiting damage to it caused by corporate activities. The company recycles plastic and cardboard, uses recycled paper in its offices, and conserves energy. Ben & Jerry's even acknowledges that its major product, its super-premium ice cream, is a danger to the health of at least some people. Its 1990 annual report stated that "Ice cream has nutritional value, despite its high fat and sugar content. People who should not eat it for health reasons are free to choose not to eat it." More concretely, in the last two years the company has begun to fully market both light ice milk and frozen yogurt. These products reflect Ben & Jerry's concern for health (although it continues to give to each of its employees three pints of ice cream *per day*) as well as the fact that an increasingly health-conscious public is growing resistant to eating ice cream with high fat content.

Ben & Jerry's has also sought to avoid some of the effects of McDonaldization on its employees. Employees are described as adoring their jobs. Workers have at least some choice over the tasks they will perform on any given day. The company has what is called a "joy gang" that seeks to take some of the drudgery out of work. One can watch "the employees cheerfully yuk it up during a public tour of the pastel-colored Waterbury facility"; an executive answering machine might tell the caller that the officer is unavailable because he or she is "off doing transcendental meditation"; and a letter to this author from the Ben & Jerry's public relations officer is signed by the "P.R. Info Queen." Then there are the many employee benefits, such as free massages, free health club membership, profit-sharing, and child care. Said one worker, "It's what a job should be." One journalist describes it as "the friendliest of employee-friendly firms."

But Ben & Jerry's, which was founded in 1978, showed early signs of McDonaldization. The first Ben & Jerry's franchised "scoop shop" opened in Vermont in 1981; the first out-of-state franchise opened in 1983. To meet demand, some of Ben & Jerry's ice cream began to be produced by others under license to the company. Sales, profits, and the number of employees grew dramatically. By 1982 Jerry Greenfield was conscious of the rationalization that was underway: "We'd started as this homemade ice cream parlor and evolved into a sort of a manufacturing plant. . . . Where it used to be that we made every batch of ice cream and scooped every cone, now there were people buying our ice cream who had never met Ben or Jerry." Greenfield left the company but returned a few years later to seek to combine economic success with the values that had built the company in the first place.

Having achieved nationwide success and doubled the number of employees in one year from 150 to 300, the company made a conscious policy to limit growth. The company has limited franchise growth (up from 80 at the close of 1989 to only 86 at the end of 1990) and focused on improving the company's ties to existing franchisees. Similarly, growth in the number of employees has been slowed. A consultant has been hired not only to improve job, but also product, *quality*. There are plans to begin construction in 1992 of a new plant that will return all ice cream production to the company, thereby eliminating the dangers posed by allowing licensees to manufacture the ice cream even when it is closely monitored by Ben & Jerry's own quality control inspectors.

Patricia Aburdene, coauthor with John Naisbitt, of *Megatrends 2000*, sees Ben & Jerry's as "most certainly . . . the new model of the corporate form that we will see created in the 1990s and into the 21st century." (Note that this view stands in contrast to the perspective of this book that it is the highly rationalized McDonald's and *not* the determinedly nonrationalized Ben & Jerry's that is the more likely current *and* future corporate model.) At the minimum, to represent a viable alternative, Ben & Jerry's must continue to be vigilant to traces of McDonaldization and demonstrate that it can both be successful and ward off McDonaldization over the long haul.

Alternatives to "McBed, McBreakfasts"

Another example of a nonrationalized alternative is the bed and breakfast (B&B). In fact, one news report on B&Bs was entitled, "B&B's Offer Travelers Break from McBed, McBreakfast." B&Bs are private homes that rent out rooms to travelers and offer them home-style hospitality and a breakfast in the morning. Traditionally, the operators live in the home and operate it while taking a personal interest in the guests. Although many existed long before, B&Bs began to boom at the beginning of the 1980s. Some people were fed up with the cold impersonality of rationalized motel rooms and sought out, instead, the types of nonrationalized accommodations offered by B&Bs. Said one visitor to a B&B, "It was marvelous. . . . The innkeepers treated us like family. It was so comfortable and friendly and charming and romantic."

But success, once again, has brought with it the early signs of McDonaldization. The range of amenities being offered is expanding, and the prices are rising. It is getting harder to distinguish B&Bs from inns or small hotels. Owners increasingly no longer live in the B&B, but hire managers to run things for them. Said one observer: "Your best B&B's are those where the owner is on the premises. . . . When the owner leaves and hires a manager, bad things start happening. Dust balls start accumulating under the beds, the coffee gets stale, and the toast is burnt." In other words, quality suffers. With the expansion of B&Bs, the American Bed and Breakfast Association (a national organization which began in 1981) developed, and guidebooks of B&Bs proliferated. Now inspections are being undertaken, standards developed, and a rating system implemented. In other terms, efforts are underway to rationalize the burgeoning B&B industry.

Other Alternatives: "It's Okay to Go Outside the Lines"

Alternatives to rationalized settings exist in other social institutions. In education, for example, alternatives to highly rational state universities are small schools like Hampshire College of Amherst, Massachusetts, whose motto is "Where It's Okay to Go Outside the Lines." (The fast-food restaurants are not above using similar mottos, for example, Burger King's "Sometimes You Gotta Break the Rules.") At such colleges there are no specialized majors and no quantifiable grade point averages. Another example is the food co-op that offers an alternative to the supermarket. Co-ops specialize in health foods and in providing a range of food options for vegetarians. The food is healthier than in supermarkets, the shoppers are often members of the co-op and therefore actively involved in its management, and the employees are frequently more involved in and committed to their work and have even been known to be found singing on the job.

As we have seen, as nonrationalized institutions become successful, pressures mount to McDonaldize them. Then, the issue becomes how to avoid the rationalization of these businesses. For example, one thing to avoid is too much expansion. At some point, any institution will grow so large that it requires increasingly rational principles in order to function. While size is a threat, the far greater danger is the possibility of franchising. Franchising, almost by definition, brings with it rationalization. However, greater size and franchising are difficult to resist because they hold out the almost irresistible lure of greater profits. The entrepreneurs behind a nonrationalized business must always keep the reasons for creating such a business in the forefront of their thinking. They also need to continue to think about the obligations they have to customers who frequent their establishments because they are *not* McDonaldized. However, being creatures of a capitalist society, they may succumb to greater profitability and allow their businesses to expand or to be franchised. If they do, one would hope that they would use their profits to begin new, nonrationalized enterprises.

Carving Out Nonrationalized Niches for Ourselves: Tenured Professors and Skunk Works

Although opening a business like Marvelous Market or starting a bed and breakfast might be considered a way of carving out a nonrationalized niche for oneself, such undertakings are primarily oriented to providing such niches for others. Marvelous Market provides breads that are a welcome alternative to those who are fed up with Wonder Bread and its rationalized clones. Ben & Jerry's Cherry Garcia, with its large and irregularly shaped pieces of chocolate and cherries, is a delightful alternative to the bland and uniform flavors one usually finds in the supermarket freezer. Bed and breakfasts provide a human and homey option for those who cannot bear the cold sameness of yet another night at Days Inn. In this section we will give a few illustrations of how people can carve out nonrationalized niches for *themselves* in otherwise rationalized systems. Our focus will be on the work world which, with few exceptions, is highly rationalized. However, similar niches can be carved out in every other social institution.

The ability to carve out such a niche tends to be related to one's position in the occupational hierarchy; those in high-ranking occupations have a greater ability to create such niches. However, there are some people in lower-ranking occupations who are in a position to be largely free of rationalization. One example would be taxi drivers who, because they work primarily on their own, are free to construct a nonrationalized work life. They can go where they want, pick up the passengers they wish, eat when they want, and take breaks when they wish. Thus, the ability to create a nonrationalized work life is not restricted to those in higher-ranking occupations. Indeed, well-educated and well-trained people may seek out an occupation such as taxi driving because it permits them a less rationalized work life. Other low-status occupations in which such possibilities exist would be a nightwatchperson and a maintenance worker in an automated factory. Low-status workers, indeed all members of the work world who work on their own or in relative isolation in an organization, are in a good position to create a nonrationalized work environment.

However, it is in higher status occupations that one is most likely to have the capacity to create a nonrationalized niche for oneself. Physicians, lawyers, accountants, architects, and the like, in private practice have a great ability to create such an environment for themselves. Within large organizations, those with power, those at the top of the organization, have the greatest ability to resist rationalization. The general (unwritten) rule for most organizational higher-ups seems to be to impose rationality on others while keeping one's own work as nonrational as possible. Rationalization is something to be imposed on others, especially those with little power.

Let me take my own position as college professor as an extreme example of a position that enables the creation of a nonrationalized work life in an otherwise highly rational university bureaucracy. This semester, for example, I teach on Monday afternoons from 3:00 to 4:15 and evenings from 6:30 to 9:00 and on Wednesday afternoons from

3:00 to 4:15. In addition, office hours (about two hours a week), an occasional faculty meeting (one hour, once a month, when I choose to attend), and an occasional committee meeting, are the only other pre-determined work hours associated with my job; they are the only times I must be at a given place at a set time to do a task set by the demands of the organization. I often will be on campus at other times, but they are for various appointments that are arranged at my convenience. Furthermore, the preset class hours are for only 30 weeks, or 2 full semesters, during the year. For the other 22 weeks virtually all of my hours are my own. Thus, for only a few hours a week for only a little more than half the year do I have to be at any particular place doing any particular thing at any particular time. The rest of the time is my own to do with as I wish. In other words, my work time is almost totally nonrationalized.

If I wanted, as a tenured full professor, I could idle my days away. However, I choose not to do that; instead I occupy myself with professional activities, such as writing books like this one. But how, when, and what I write is totally nonrationalized. I can write in the middle of the night or early in the morning. I can write on a word processor, a yellow pad, or even a stone tablet. I can write about McDonaldization or about metatheorizing in sociology. I can write clad in a suit and tie or in my bathrobe (my preference). I can take a break when I like; I can go for my daily walk with my dog, Brandy; and I can listen to my favorite book-on-tape whenever I please. I can take my nap, something I never miss, when I feel the need. In short, my work life is almost totally non-rationalized. I am lucky to be in a position where I am able to carve out a largely nonrationalized niche for myself in an otherwise highly rationalized system of higher education.

My case is obviously an extremely fortunate one, but it is possible for people who are so inclined to seek out work in organizations in which at least some degree of nonrationalization is possible. For example, some high-tech organizations are known for creating and encouraging the use of "skunk works" where people can be insulated from routine organizational demands and do their work as they see fit. The emphasis in skunk works is on creativity and innovation, *not* conformity. Thomas Peters and Robert Waterman describe skunk works as singularly nonrational, even irrational, work settings:

> They were creating almost radical *decentralization* and *autonomy*, with its attendant *overlap*, *messiness* around the edges, *lack of coordination*, *internal competition*, and somewhat *chaotic* conditions, in order to breed

the entrepreneurial spirit. They had *forsworn* a measure of *tidiness* in order to achieve regular innovation. (Italics added.)

The italicized terms in the preceding quotation would all be considered nonrational or irrational from the point of view of a McDonaldized society.

Even in highly rationalized organizations, it is possible for people to carve out a wider range of nonrationalized work space and time for themselves. For example, by finishing routine tasks quickly, a worker would leave himself or herself time to engage in nonrationalized, albeit work-related, activities.

I am not suggesting that it is easy to find nonrationalized occupations or to carve out nonrationalized space within McDonaldized organizations, and I am not suggesting that everyone can do it all the time. But it is possible for some people, some of the time, to carve out nonrationalized niches for themselves in their occupations and employing organizations. If this can be accomplished in the work world, it can be achieved in other institutional settings as well.

One thing to be underscored about nonrationalized times and places is that they are likely to be the source of great creativity. It is difficult to be creative in the face of incessant, externally imposed, and repetitive demands. That is why high-tech organizations set up skunk works. Thus, it is not only in the interest of the individual to work in a setting that is, to at least some degree, nonrationalized, but it is also in the interest of the employer and the larger society. Both need a steady influx of creative new ideas and products, and they are far less likely to emanate from rigidly controlled bureaucratic settings than they are from skunk works.

I would not want to push this idea too far. First, rationalized organizations can provide both what is needed to do creative work and the outlets for that work. In other words, nonrationalized niches of creativity need the support of rationalized systems. Second, no large-scale organization can exist if it is composed of nothing but such niches. The result would be organizational chaos. Third, not everyone wants to work in such nonrationalized niches; indeed many people prefer their work days to be highly routinized. Fourth, not everyone is capable of operating in a nonrationalized niche. Thus, this does not constitute an argument for a work world composed of nothing but creative occupational spaces. Instead, it points out the need for more nonrationalized niches in an otherwise highly rationalized occupational and organizational world.

Individual Responses: Subverting the Process of McDonaldization

Beyond the work world, those who are uncomfortable with or opposed to McDonaldization have a variety of other options open to them. Before we discuss those choices, it should be pointed out that such people (those who view the rationalized cage as rubber or iron) ought to try to extract the best of what the McDonaldized world has to offer without succumbing to its dangers and excesses. This will not be easy to do, because the lure of McDonaldized institutions is great, and it is easy to find oneself becoming a devotee of, and enmeshed in, rationalized activities. Thus, those who use rationalized systems for what they have to offer need to keep the dangers of McDonaldization always in the forefront of their thinking. But, being able to get one's bank balance in the middle of the night, to avoid hospital emergency rooms by having minor problems cared for at "McDoctors", and to lose weight quickly and safely at Nutri/System, among many other conveniences, are all attractive possibilities for most people. The secret is clearly to be able to take advantage of the best that the McDonaldized world has to offer without becoming imprisoned in that world.

How can one do this? For one thing, it would be advisable to use McDonaldized systems *only* when such use is unavoidable, when no alternatives are available, or when what they have to offer cannot be matched by nonrationalized systems. Perhaps we might think about putting warning labels on McDonaldized systems much like those found on cigarette packs. One possibility:

> Sociologists warn us that habitual use of McDonaldized systems are destructive to our physical and psychological well-being as well as to society as a whole.

Above all, people should avoid the routine and systematic use of McDonaldized systems. To avoid the iron cage, one must seek out nonrationalized niches wherever and whenever possible. Such a search for these niches is difficult and time-consuming. It is far easier to use the various aspects of our McDonaldized society than it is to find and utilize nonrationalized alternatives. Yet, it is precisely such efforts that are necessary if we are to avoid the worst effects of the iron cage. Avoiding McDonaldization requires hard work and vigilance.

The most extreme step would be to pack one's bags and leave the highly McDonaldized American society. The problem with moving to another society is that other societies are themselves likely to be well along in the rationalization process or soon likely to embark on the process. Thus, a move to another society might buy people some time, but eventually, McDonaldization would have to be confronted, this time in a less familiar context.

A less extreme step is to search out a wide range of nonrationalized niches in our McDonaldized society such as those described above in the work world, . But, as we have seen, it is not enough for people to search out such niches, it is also necessary for others to have created nonrationalized enterprises in those niches or with such niches built into them. Indeed, the creation of such enterprises is not only a good in itself, but the enterprises can also be quite successful. Since there will always be people (one hopes) who rebel against McDonaldization, there is success to be had, to say nothing of the undying gratitude of the rebels in the creation of nonrational enterprises. Thus, the founding and frequenting of nonrationalized enterprises in niches throughout society are mechanisms for coping with the excesses of rationalization.

The following list contains suggested actions that individuals can take to cope with McDonaldization. In most cases, they assume prior action by others to create nonrationalized enterprises in those niches.

- Avoid living in apartments or tract houses. Try to live in an atypical environment, preferably one you have built yourself or have had built for you. If you must live in an apartment or a tract house, humanize and individualize it. In fact, the residents of Levittown, the original tract house community, have done just that so that one now sees "the Levitt box disguised as a Tudor Manor, a Swiss chalet, a Pennsylvania Dutch barn."

- Avoid daily routine as much as possible. Try to do as many things as possible in a different way from one day to the next.

- More generally, do as many things as you can for yourself. If you must use various services, frequent nonrationalized, nonfranchised establishments. For example, lubricate your own car. If you are unwilling or unable to do so, have it done at your local, independent gasoline station. Do not, at all costs, frequent one of the franchised lube businesses.

- Instead of popping into H&R Block at income-tax time, hire a local accountant, preferably one who works out of an office in the home.

- Similarly, the next time a minor medical or dental emergency leads you to think of a visit to a "McDoctor" or a "McDentist," resist the temptation and go instead to your neighborhood doctor or dentist, preferably one who is in solo practice.

♦   The next time you need a pair of glasses, use the local store-front optometrist rather than the Pearle Vision Center.

♦   Avoid Hair Cuttery and other hair cutting chains; the next time your hair needs cutting, go to a local barber or hairdresser.

♦   At least once a week, pass up lunch at McDonald's and frequent a local greasy spoon. For dinner, again at least once a week, park the car, unplug the microwave, avoid the freezer, and cook a meal from scratch.

♦   To really shake up the clerk at the department store, use cash rather than your credit card.

♦   Send back to the post office all junk mail, especially that which is addressed to "occupant" or "resident."

♦   The next time you are phoned by a computer, gently place the phone on the floor, thereby allowing the disembodied voice to drone on and occupying the line so that others will not be bothered by such calls for awhile.

♦   When dialing a business, always choose the "voice mail" option that permits you to speak to a real person.

♦   Never buy artificial products such as Molly McButter and Butter Buds.

♦   Seek out restaurants that use real china and metal utensils; avoid those that use materials like styrofoam that adversely affect the environment.

♦   Organize groups to protest abuses by McDonaldized systems. As we have seen, these systems do adapt to such protests. If you work in such a system, organize your coworkers to create more human-ized working conditions.

♦   If you must frequent a fast-food restaurant, dine at one, such as Macheezmo Mouse Mexican Cafe, that has demonstrated some sensitivity to the dangers of McDonaldization.

♦   If you are a regular at McDonald's, develop personal ties with the counterpeople; try to get to know them. Also, do what else you can to humanize it. In fact, during the breakfast hours, cus-tomers have done just that; they have "subverted the process" of McDonaldization. Instead of hastening through their meal, many breakfast customers "come every day of the week to read their papers, chat, drink coffee, and gobble down an Egg McMuffin." If breakfasts can be de-McDonaldized, why not other meals? Other aspects of the fast-food experience?

- Make the effort and read *The New York Times* rather than *USA TODAY* once a week. Similarly, watch PBS news once a week with its three long stories rather than the network news shows with their numerous snippets of news.

- More generally, watch as little television as possible. If you must watch TV, keep the channel selector on PBS. If you must watch one of the networks, turn off the sound and avert your eyes during commercials. After all, most commercials are sponsored by rationalized enterprises and they tout the virtues of rationalization.

- Avoid most finger foods.

- For your next vacation, go to only one locale and get to know it well.

- Never enter a domed stadium or one with artificial grass; make periodic pilgrimages to Fenway Park.

- Avoid classes where tests are short answer and graded by computer. If a computer-graded exam is unavoidable, make extraneous marks and curl the edges of the exam so that the computer cannot deal with it.

- Seek out small classes; get to know your professors.

- Go to no movies that have roman numerals after their names.

Regina Schrambling has developed a variety of strategies similar to those in the previous list for dealing with the health threats (especially Salmonella) posed by the rationalization of food production. Interestingly, Schrambling recognizes that returning to the prerationalized manner of raising chickens is not the answer. She argues that the "lifestyles" of such chickens, including "worm-grubbing," led to the possibility of Salmonella even in the prerationalized days of chicken production. Nevertheless, she prefers to shop at farmers' markets and buy chickens raised the older way. She buys her eggs "in hand-packed boxes from the same New York State farmer." In her view such eggs are fresher and cleaner than mass-produced eggs. She also purchases cantaloupes from farmers' markets and refuses to buy them in supermarkets because they have been in transit so long that there is an increased risk of spoilage and disease. While rationalization has allowed us to eat fruits and vegetables year round, there is a cost and a danger. As she puts it, they have been raised "in countries where we would never dare drink the water, where pesticides banned here are used freely." Thus, of course, she only buys fruits and vegetables during their local seasons. In addition to carefully buying fruits and vegetables only from local markets, one may also raise them in private gardens.

More generally, Schrambling argues that we need to understand that there are limited seasons for fruits and vegetables:

> We would remember that the strawberry crop is really as fleeting as fireflies, that sweet corn waits for no one; it's best when eaten within hours of leaving the stalk. There's nothing like the farmers' market in January, with only potatoes and squash and apples for sale, to give a deep new appreciation of nature's cycles.

Because of this, we need to understand that "we can't have all of the food all of the time."

(Schrambling's position seems reasonable, even laudable, but we must remember that the forces of McDonaldization continue to press forward, overcoming the kinds of boundaries she articulates. For example, a recent scientific discovery is that genetically altered tomatoes can be prevented from producing the gas that causes them to ripen. This permits the tomatoes, and potentially many other fruits and vegetables, to be left on the vine until maturity [instead of being picked early as is often the case], shipped great distances without refrigeration, stored for weeks, and then ripened [through exposure to ethylene gas] when the retailer wishes to put them up for sale. Thus, if this technique proves viable commercially, we *will*, contrary to Schrambling, have many fruits and vegetables, and even cut flowers, "all the time." Similarly, the strawberry crop may now not be as "fleeting" as Schrambling seems to think. The Driscoll strawberry, grown in Watsonville, California ["the strawberry capital of the world"], is big, glossy, and, most important, available [because of the favorable climate] all year round. Surprisingly, the Driscoll strawberry is also described as "actually hav[ing] *some* flavor, too." [Italics added.])

It is particularly important that steps be taken to prevent children from becoming mindless supporters of McDonaldization.

♦   Instead of using a "McChild" care center, leave your child with a neighborhood parent interested in earning some extra money.

- Keep your children away from television as much as possible. It is especially important that they not be exposed to the steady barrage of commercials from rationalized institutions, especially on Saturday morning cartoon shows.

- Lead efforts to keep McDonaldization out of the school system.

- If you can afford it, send your child to a small, non-McDonaldized educational institution.

- Above all, when possible, avoid taking your children to fast-food restaurants or their clones in other areas of society. If no alternatives are present (for example, you're on a highway and the only options are various fast-food chains), blindfold your child until the ordeal is over.

There *are* steps that can be taken to cope with McDonaldization. However, I hold little hope that such actions, even if they were all to be employed by many people, would reverse the trend toward McDonaldization. Despite this seeming inevitability, I think the struggle is worthwhile. First, it will serve to mitigate the worst excesses of McDonaldized systems. Second, it will lead to the discovery, creation, and use of more niches where people who are so inclined can escape McDonaldization for at least a part of their day or even a larger portion of their lives. Finally, and perhaps most important, the struggle itself is ennobling. As a general rule, such struggles are nonrationalized, individual, and collective activities. It is in such struggles that people can express genuinely human reason in a world that in virtually all other ways has set up rationalized systems to deny people the ability to behave in such human ways.

Conclusion

Although I have emphasized the irresistibility of McDonaldization throughout this book, my fondest hope is that I am wrong. Indeed, a major motivation behind this book is to alert readers to the dangers of McDonaldization and to motivate them to act to stem its tide. I hope that we are able to resist McDonaldization and can create instead a more reasonable, more human world.

McDonald's was recently sued by the famous French chef, Paul Bocuse, for using his picture on a poster without his permission.

Enraged, Bocuse said: "How can I be seen promoting this tasteless, boneless food in which everything is soft." Nevertheless, Bocuse seemed to acknowledge the inevitability of McDonaldization: "There's a need for this kind of thing . . . and trying to get rid of its seems to me to be as futile as trying to get rid of the prostitutes in the Bois de Bologne." Lo and behold, two weeks later, it was announced that the Paris police had cracked down on prostitution in the Bois de Bologne. Said a police spokesman, "There are none left." Thus, just as chef Bocuse was wrong about the prostitutes, perhaps I am wrong about the irresistibility of McDonaldization. Yet, before we grow overly optimistic, it should be noted that "everyone knows that the prostitutes will be back as soon as the operation is over. In the spring, police predict, there will be even more than before." Similarly, it remains likely that no matter how intense the opposition, the future will bring with it more rather than less McDonaldization. Even if this proves to be the case, it is my hope that people will at least follow some of the advice outlined in this chapter for mitigating the worst effects of McDonaldization. In other words, faced with Max Weber's iron cage imagery of a future dominated by the polar night of icy darkness and hardness, the least the reader can do is to follow the words of the poet Dylan Thomas: "Do not go gentle into that good night. . . . Rage, rage against the dying of the light."

End Notes

Chapter One

For a similar, but narrower viewpoint to the one expressed on page 1, see Benjamin R. Barber, "Jihad vs. McWorld." *The Atlantic Monthly*, March 1992, 53–63.

The statistics on McDonald's sales on page 2 come from Stephen Levine, "McDonald's Makes a Play to Diversify." *Washington Post*, August 30, 1991: G4. In the next bulleted item, the information about the number of McDonald's outlets is courtesy of McDonald's, and the ratio of chain restaurants to Americans came from Anthony Ramirez, "In the Orchid Room . . . Big Macs." *The New York Times*, October 30, 1990: D1, D5.

European resistance to fast food (page 2, the sixth bulleted point) is discussed in Gregory Hall's "The Psychology of Fast-Food Happiness." In Marshall Fishwick, ed., *Ronald Revisited: The World of Ronald McDonald.* Bowling Green: Bowling Green University Press, 1983: 84. In the same bulleted point, the Moscow McDonald's was covered by Louis Uchitelle, "That's Funny, Those Pickles Don't Look Russian." *The New York Times*, February 27, 1992: A4, and the information about the Swiss comes from "Big Mac on Track." *Travel and Leisure*, December, 1990: 26.

The Beijing McDonald's (pages 2–3) was covered by Nicholas D. Kristof in "'Billions Served' (and That Was Without China)." *The New York Times*, April 24, 1992. The number of McDonald's openings was written about by Eben Shapiro in "Overseas Sizzle for McDonald's." *The New York Times*, April 17, 1992: D1, D4.

For a discussion of the Lebanese fast-food restaurant mentioned on page 3, see Alison Leigh Cowan, "Unlikely Spot for Fast Food." *The New York Times*, April 29, 1984: 3: 5. The Body Shop example (further down the page) comes from Eben Shapiro, "The Sincerest Form of Rivalry." *The New York Times*, October 19, 1991: 35, 46. Near the bottom of page 3, the material about Toys R Us is quoted from Timothy Egan, "Big Chains Are Joining Manhattan's Toy Wars." *The New York Times*, December 8, 1990: 29; Stacey Burling, "Health Club . . . For Kids." *Washington Post*, November 21, 1991: D5, is the source of the quotation about KidSports; and Tamar Lewin writes about "Kentucky Fried Children" in "Small Tots, Big Biz." *New York Times Magazine*, January 19, 1989: 89.

The quotations from McDonald's loyalists on page 4 appeared in E.R. Shipp, "The McBurger Stand that Started it All." *The New York Times*, February 27, 1985: 3: 3, and Pizza Hut's opening in Moscow was covered in "Wedge of Americana: In Moscow, Pizza Hut Opens 2 Restaurants." *Washington Post*, September 12, 1990: B10.

For more about *USA TODAY* (page 4), see Peter Prichard, *The Making of McPaper: The Inside Story of USA Today*. Kansas City: Andrews, McMeel and Parker, 1987; information about the *USA TODAY* television show comes from Richard Zoglin, "Get Ready for McRather." *Time*, April 11, 1988.

The essays in Marshall Fishwick, ed., *Ronald Revisited: The World of Ronald McDonald*. Bowling Green: Bowling Green University Press, 1983, have a great deal more to say about McDonald's central role (page 4, last paragraph). The Maryland high school student quoted in the same paragraph spoke to John F. Harris for his article "McMilestone Restaurant Opens Doors in Dale City." *Washington Post*, April 7, 1988: D1.

The material about McDonald's as icon on page 5 comes from a variety of sources. Conrad Kottak discusses this idea in "Rituals at McDonald's." In Fishwick, ed., *Ronald Revisited*: 52–8. Bill Keller covers the opening of the Moscow McDonald's in "Of Famous Arches, Beeg Meks and Rubles." *The New York Times*, January 28, 1990: 1: 1, 12. William Severini Kowinski elaborates about shopping malls in *The Malling of America: An Inside Look at the Great Consumer Paradise*. New York: William Morrow, 1985: 218. Finally, the quotation about Walt Disney World comes from Bob Garfield, "How I Spent (and Spent and Spent) My Disney Vacation." *Washington Post*, July 7, 1991: B5. See also, Margaret J. King, "Empires of Popular Culture: McDonald's and Disney." In Fishwick, ed., *Ronald Revisited*: 106–19.

Ronald McDonald's name recognition (further down page 5) was reported in Steven Greenhouse, "The Rise and Rise of McDonald's." *The New York Times*, June 8, 1986: 3: 1.

For more about new enterprises by McDonald's in small-town USA (page 6), see Laura Shapiro, "Ready for McCatfish?" *Newsweek*, October 15, 1990: 76–7. The quotation about Route 161 comes from N. R. Kleinfeld, "Fast Food's Changing Landscape." *The New York Times*, April 14, 1985: 3: 1, 6.

The material on page 7 about Domino's in the schools comes from Paul Farhi, "Domino's is Going to School." *Washington Post*, September 21, 1990: F3, and "Grade 'A' Burgers." *The New York Times*, April 13, 1986: 12: 15 is the source for the "A for Cheeseburger " program.

On page 8, the quotation about "McNuggets" comes from Prichard, *The Making of McPaper*, 232–3, and the quotation about the *Boca Raton News* comes from Howard Kurtz, "Slicing, Dicing News to Attract the Young." *Washington Post*, January 6, 1991: A1.

Nicholas D. Kristof discussed dial-a-porn (pages 8–9) in "Court Test is Likely on Dial-a-Porn Service Game." *New York Times*, October 15, 1986: 1: 16. *The New York Times* quoted the city official about the McDonald's of sex in its October 5, 1986, issue, section 3, page 6.

On pages 9–11, the basic components of rationality are drawn from the work of Max Weber, especially *Economy and Society*. Totowa, NJ: Bedminster Press, 1921/1968, as well as that of interpreters of Weber's work such as Stephen Kalberg in his essay, "Max Weber's Types of Rationality: Cornerstones for the Analysis of Rationalization Processes in History." *American Journal of Sociology*, 1980, 85: 1145–79.

It should be pointed out that the words *rational, rationality*, and *rationalization* are being used differently on page 12 and throughout the book than they are ordinarily employed. For one thing, we usually think of these terms as being largely positive; something that is rational is usually considered to be good. However, they are used here in a generally negative way. The positive term in this analysis is genuinely human "reason" (for example, the ability to act and work creatively), which is seen as being denied by inhuman, rational systems like the fast-food restaurant. For another, the term *rationalization* is usually associated with Freudian theory as a way of explaining away some behavior, but here it is employed to describe the increasing pervasiveness of rationality throughout society. Thus, in reading this book, one must be careful to interpret the terms in these ways rather than in the ways they are conventionally employed.

On page 12, the criticism of Euro Disney was reported in Alan Riding, "Only the French Elite Scorn Mickey's Debut." *The New York Times*, April 13, 1992: A13.

Among the critics (and their works) mentioned on page 13 are Georg Stauth and Bryan S. Turner, "Nostalgia, Postmodernism and the Critique of Mass Culture." *Theory, Culture and Society*, 5, 1988: 509–26; Bryan S. Turner, "A Note on Nostalgia." *Theory, Culture and Society*, 4, 1987: 147–56.

In the sense described further down page 13, this resembles Marx's critique of capitalism. Marx was not animated by a romanticization of precapitalist society, but rather by the desire to produce a truly human (Communist) society on the base provided by capitalism. Despite this specific affinity to Marxian theory, this book is, as we will see, premised far more on Theories of Max Weber.

Robert J. Samuelson is quoted on page 14 from his article "In Praise of McDonald's." *Washington Post*, November 1, 1989: A25.

I would like to thank my colleague, Stan Presser, for suggesting that I enumerate some of the advantages listed on pages 14–5. The notion of McDonaldization as increasing a consumer's options on page 14 is elaborated upon by Stauth and Turner, "Nostalgia, Postmodernism and the Critique of Mass Culture." The point further down the same page about voice mail comes from Patricia McCormick, "Finding Out by Voice Mail." *Washington Post*, October 29, 1991: C5.

Chapter Two

The precursors introduced on page 18 and discussed throughout this chapter do not exhaust the rationalized institutions that predated McDonald's. However, the precursors to be discussed in this chapter are the most important, at least in terms of understanding McDonald's and McDonaldization.

The discussion of Weber's ideas on pages 18–24 is based on Max Weber, *Economy and Society*. Totowa, NJ: Bedminster Press, 1921/1968.

Takaki's words on page 22 come from his *Iron Cages: Race and Culture in 19th-Century America.* New York: Oxford University Press, 1990: ix.

For a further discussion of escape routes, which are discussed on page 23, see Harvey Greisman, "Disenchantment of the World." *British Journal of Sociology*, 27, 1976: 497–506.

The discussion of Taylor's ideas on pages 24–5 is derived from Frederick W. Taylor, *The Principles of Scientific Management.* New York: Harper and Row, 1947. The idea that American industry has been outstripped by Japanese industry is elaborated on by George Ritzer and Terri LeMoyne, "Hyperrationality." In George Ritzer, *Metatheorizing in Sociology.* Lexington, MA: Lexington Books, 1991: 93–115.

Ester Reiter shows how the fast-food industry has employed Taylorism (page 25) in her book *Making Fast Food.* Montreal and Kingston: McGill-Queen's University Press, 1991: 112–4.

For more on Ford and the assembly line than page 25 and the rest of the book can describe, see Henry Ford's autobiography, *My Life and Work.* Garden City, NY: Doubleday, Page, and Co., 1922, as well as James T. Flink, *The Automobile Age.* Cambridge: MIT Press, 1988.

The quotation on page 26 about the relationship between the assembly line and fast food comes from Bruce A. Lohof, "Hamburger Stand Industrialization and the Fast-Food Phenomenon." In Marshall Fishwick, ed., *Ronald Revisited: The World of Ronald McDonald.* Bowling Green: Bowling Green University Press, 1983: 30. For more on the same point, see Reiter, *Making Fast Food:* 75.

The connection between the automobile and McDonaldization on page 27 is discussed in Marshall Fishwick, "Cloning Clowns: Some Final Thoughts." In Marshall Fishwick, ed., *Ronald Revisited:* 148–51. For more on the relationship described in the same paragraph between the automobile and the growth of the tourist industry, see Flink, *The Automobile Age.* On the GM divisional system, mentioned on the same page, see Flink, *The Automobile Age,* as well as Alfred P. Sloan, Jr., *My Years at General Motors.* Garden City, NY: Doubleday, 1964.

The Levittown statistics on page 27 come from "Levitt's Progress." *Fortune*, October 1952: 155ff.

Alfred Levitt's words, quoted on page 28, come from "The Most House for the Money." *Fortune.* October 1952: 152. The "boom, boom, boom" quotation on the same page is also taken from "The Most House for the Money." *Fortune:* 153.

Herbert Gans quotes the advertisement mentioned on page 29 in his *The Levittowners: Ways of Life and Politics in a New Suburban Community.* New York: Pantheon Books, 1967: 13. Sources for the quotations and other material further down the page about suburbia are as follows: the "split level trap" comes from Richard E. Gordon, Katherine K. Gordon, and Max Gunther, *The Split Level Trap.* New York: Gilbert Geis Associates, 1960; Georgia Dullea writes about customization of Levittown in "The Tract House as Landmark." *The New York Times*, October 17, 1991: C1, C8; Gans's quotation about the New Jersey Levittown comes from his *The Levittowners:* 432.

William Severini Kowinski writes extensively about the mall (pages 29–30) in *The Malling of America: An Inside Look at the Great Consumer Paradise*. New York: William Morrow, 1985. The information about America's largest mall comes from Kara Swisher, "A Mall for America?" *Washington Post–Business*, June 30, 1991: H1, H4.

The quotation on the mall as "postwar paradise" (page 30) comes from Kowinski, *The Malling of America*: 25.

The discussion of Kroc and McDonald's on pages 30–3 is based on, among other works, Ray Kroc, *Grinding It Out*. Chicago: Contemporary Books, 1977; Stan Luxenberg, *Roadside Empires: How the Chains Franchised America*. New York: Viking, 1985; and John F. Love, *McDonald's: Behind the Arches*. Toronto: Bantam Books, 1986.

The quotation about McDonald's limited menu on page 30 comes from Love, *Behind the Arches*: 18. The idea of a fast-food factory at the paragraph's end also comes from Love: 20.

The quotation about McDonald's uniformity on page 32 is taken from Love: 68–9. Like McDonald's Hamburger University, which is discussed in the next paragraph, Burger King set up its own Burger King University in 1978. See Ester Reiter, *Making Fast Food*: 68.

Chapter Three

Herbert Simon elaborates on his views about organizational efficiency on page 35, in his book *Administrative Behavior*, 2d ed. New York: Free Press, 1957.

Ray Kroc's reaction to first seeing the McDonald brothers' business, quoted on page 37, appears in *Grinding It Out*. Chicago: Contemporary Books, 1977: 8.

The quotations about inefficient restaurants on page 37, and the one further down the page about hot dogs, come from Max Boas and Steve Chain, *Big Mac: The Unauthorized Story of McDonald's*. New York: E.P. Dutton, 1976: 9–10.

On page 38, Ray Kroc's statement about McDonald's refinements is from *Grinding It Out*: 96–7.

The quotation about Taco Bell on page 39 comes from Michael Lev, "Raising Fast Food's Speed Limit." *Washington Post*, August 7, 1991: D1.

For more about the voice mail phenomenon (page 43), see James Barron, "Please Press 2 for Service; Press ? for an Actual Human." *The New York Times*, February 17, 1989: A1, B2. The humorous quotation in the same paragraph comes from Michael Schrage, "Calling the Technology of Voice Mail Into Question." *Washington Post*, October 19, 1990: F3. The postal service's request for typed addresses, cited in the next paragraph, was reported on National Public Radio's "Morning Edition," October 3, 1990.

Ford's words about car paint (page 44) come from Henry Ford, *My Life and Work*. Garden City, NY: Doubleday, 1922: 72.

It should be noted that supermarkets have sought to make shopping more efficient by institutionalizing ten-item limit, no-checks-accepted lines for consumers that might ordinarily frequent the kinds of convenience stores discussed on pages 44–5.

For more on the microwave (pages 45–6), as well as the array of foods it has spawned, see "The Microwave Cooks Up a New Way of Life." *Wall Street Journal*, September 19, 1989; "Microwavable Foods—Industry's Response to Consumer Demands for Convenience." *Food Technology*, 41, 1987: 52–63. The quotation near the bottom of page 45 about Hormel's biscuit sandwiches comes from "Microwavable Foods." *Food Technology*, 41: 54. Also see Eben Shapiro, "A Page from Fast Food's Menu." *The New York Times*, October 14, 1991: D1, D3, from which the quotation on page 46 about McDonald's-like foods appearing in grocers' freezers is drawn.

Full citation for the Luxenberg book mentioned on page 46 is Stan Luxenberg, *Roadside Empires: How the Chains Franchised America*. New York: Viking, 1985.

I would like to thank Dora Giemza for the insights on page 48 into Nutri/System. Material about diet centers is also drawn from "Big People, Big Business: The Overweight Numbers Rising, Try Nutri/System." *Washington Post Health*, October 10, 1989: 8. For suggesting to me some of the points about McDonaldization and health clubs made on the same page, I would like to thank Steve Lankenau.

The quotation about the mall (page 49) comes from William Severini Kowinski, *The Malling of America: An Inside Look at the Great Consumer Paradise*. New York: William Morrow and Co., 1985: 61. In the next paragraph, the material about the scanfone comes from Kara Swisher, "Companies Unveil 'Scanfone' Shopping Service." *Washington Post*, April 16, 1992: B1, B15.

In the paragraph about Blockbuster video on page 50, the opening sentence quotes Mark Potts, "Blockbuster Struggles with Merger Script." *Washington Post–Washington Business*, December 9, 1991: 24; additional material comes from Eben Shapiro, "Market Place: A Mixed Outlook for Blockbuster." *The New York Times*, February 21, 1992: D6.

The material on pages 51–2 about Disney's trash-removal system comes from Michael Harrington, "To the Disney Station." *Harper's*, January 1979: 35–9.

The quotation on page 52 about Busch Gardens comes from Lynn Darling, "On the Inside at Parks a la Disney." *Washington Post*, August 28, 1978: A10.

Much of the information in the section about medicine (pages 52–5) is derived from George Ritzer and David Walczak, "The Changing Nature of American Medicine." *Journal of American Culture*, 9, 1987: 43–51.

The quotation about Denton Cooley (page 52) comes from Julia Wallace, "Dr. Denton Cooley—Star of 'The Heart Surgery Factory.'" *Washington Post*, July 19, 1980: A6.

The description of eye surgery in Moscow on page 53 comes from "Moving Right Along." *Time*, 1985: 44.

Some of the material on page 57 about custom publishing comes from Michael Miller, "Professors Customize Textbooks, Blurring Roles of Publisher, Seller and Copy Shop." *Wall Street Journal*, August 16, 1990: B1, B4.

In the paragraph about *USA TODAY*'s precursors on page 58, the quotation about *Reader's Digest* comes from Daniel Boorstin, *The Image: Guide to Pseudo-Events in America*. New York: Harper Colophon, 1961: 135; the second quotation (about *Business Week*) comes from Ian Mitroff and Warren Bennis, *The Unreality Industry: The Deliberate Manufacturing of Falsehood and What it is Doing to Our Lives*. New York: Birch Lane Press, 1989: 12.

In the paragraph on page 58 about religion, the point about widespread "televangelism" is drawn from Jeffrey Hadden and Charles E. Swann, *Primetime Preachers: The Rising Power of Televangelism*. Reading, MA: Addison-Wesley, 1981. John Tagliabue, "Indulgences by TV." *The New York Times*, December 19, 1985: 1: 8 is the source for both quotations about TV in the Vatican.

The assembly line's principles outlined on pages 58–9 are elaborated on by Ford in his book *My Life and Work*. The quotation about the worker's singularity of effort comes from that book's page 80.

Taylor's words about efficiency (pages 60–1) are quoted from Frederick W. Taylor, *The Principles of Scientific Management*. New York: Harper and Row, 1947: 6–7; the steps described on page 60 come from page 117 of Taylor's book.

Chapter Four

Just as quality is equated with quantity, as page 62 points out, quality is also equated with other aspects of McDonaldization such as "standardization and predictability." See Ester Reiter, *Making Fast Food*. Montreal and Kingston: McGill-Queen's University Press: 107.

Eben Shapiro writes about the Campbell's Big Start breakfasts mentioned on page 63 in "A Page from Fast Food's Menu." *The New York Times*, October 14, 1991: D1, D3.

Barbara W. Tuchman expresses the concern for quality mentioned on page 63 in "The Decline of Quality." *New York Times Magazine*, November 2, 1980: 38. The quotation further down the same page equating a McDonald's burger to a Brillo pad comes from Marion Clark, "Arches of Triumph." *Washington Post–Book World*, June 5, 1977.

On page 64, the notion of a McDonald's meal as a refueling stop comes from A. A. Berger, "Berger vs. Burger: A Personal Encounter." In Marshall Fishwick, ed., *Ronald Revisited: The World of Ronald McDonald*. Bowling Green: Bowling Green University Press, 1983: 126. Colonel Sanders' story (further down the page) is drawn from Max Boas and Steven Chain, *Big Mac: The Unauthorized Story of McDonald's*. New York: Dutton, 1976. The quotation about "the durned chicken" appears on that book's page 121 as does the first gravy quotation; the next quotation ("goddamn mad") appears on page 117.

The statistic about Burger King fries and drinks on page 65 comes from Reiter, *Making Fast Food*: 84. Reiter details the speedy service at Burger King described further down the page in *Making Fast Food*: 85.

The page 67 quotation about Fannie Farmer is taken from Stuart Flexner, *I Hear America Talking*. New York: Simon and Schuster, 1976: 142.

For more about "fat farms" (page 67), see N. R. Kleinfeld, "The Ever-Fatter Business of Thinness." *The New York Times*, September 7, 1986: 3: 1ff. The quotations on the same page about Nutri/System are from official Nutri/System publications.

The quotation from the ABC vice president on page 68 comes from Frank Mankiewicz and Joel Swerdlow, *Remote Control: Television and the Manipulation of American Life*. New York: Time Books, 1978: 219. The quotation in the next paragraph about the Nielsen ratings come from Erik Larson, "Watching Americans Watch TV." *The Atlantic Monthly*, March 1992: 66. For more about the Nielsens, see Peter J. Boyer, "TV Turning to People Meters To Find Who Watches What." *The New York Times*, June 1, 1987: 1: A1, C16.

The detail about the Democrats streamlining their 1992 convention on page 70 was reported in Michael Oreskes, "Democratic Chief Considers Cutting Convention for TV." *The New York Times*, July 12, 1990: B4.

Allen Guttmann writes about the quantification of sports (pages 70–1) in *From Ritual to Record: The Nature of Modern Sports*. New York: Cambridge University Press, 1978. The long, first quotation on page 71 appears on that book's page 47; the quotation that closes the paragraph is on page 51.

The material about *USA TODAY* on page 73 is drawn from Peter Prichard, *The Making of McPaper: The Inside Story of USA Today*. Kansas City: Andrews, McMeel and Parker, 1987. The junk-food journalism quotation comes from that book's page 8, "fast-hard pace" from page 113, and "no bran, no liver" from page 196. That the newspaper can be read in a sitting at a fast-food restaurant reminds one of the line in the movie, *The Big Chill*, spoken by Michael (played by Jeff Goldblum), who writes for a magazine resembling *People:* "Where I work we only have one editorial rule: You can't write anything longer than the average person can read during the average crap."

The quotation about initials on page 74 comes from Susan Gervasi, "The Credentials Epidemic." *Washington Post*, August 30, 1990: D5.

Donald Kennedy's words on page 77 come from Kenneth J. Cooper, "Stanford President Sets Initiative on Teaching." *Washington Post*, March 3, 1991: A12.

Kathleen Jamieson writes about the impact of TV on political speeches (page 78) in *Eloquence in an Electronic Age: The Transformation of Political Speechmaking*. New York: Oxford University Press, 1988. See also Marvin Kalb, "TV, Election Spoiler." *The New York Times*, November 28, 1988: A25. The quotations about Lincoln and Douglas on the same page come from Jamieson, *Eloquence in an Electronic Age:* 11.

The somewhat romantic physician union leader's words on page 80 are drawn from Dan Colburn, "Unionizing Doctors: Physicians Begin Banding Together to Fight for Autonomy and Control Over Medical Care." *Washington Post–Health*, June 19, 1985: 7.

Frederick W. Taylor's quotation about how much iron (between 47 and 48 tons daily) a man could handle (page 80) comes from his book *The Principles of Scientific*

Management. New York: Harper and Row, 1947: 42. On the next page, Taylor's suggestion to congratulate and not pity the pig iron handler comes from his book's page 138.

Shoshana Zuboff elaborates on the computer's impact (page 81) in *In the Age of the Smart Machine: The Future of Work and Power.* New York: Basic Books, 1988.

Chapter Five

The quotation about McDonald's predictability on page 84 comes from Margaret J. King, "McDonald's and the New American Landscape." *USA TODAY,* January 1980: 46.

Conrad Kottak writes about fast-food rituals (page 85) in "Rituals at McDonald's." In Marshall Fishwick, ed., *Ronald Revisited: The World of Ronald McDonald.* Bowling Green: Bowling Green University Press, 1983: 52–8.

An aside to page 85 and its description of the Roy Rogers chain: Roy Rogers had been taken over by Hardee's, but declining sales by franchises using the Hardee's name has led some outlets to return to using the Roy Rogers name. See Paul Farhi, "Roy Rogers to the Rescue of Hardee's." *Washington Post,* February 21, 1992: F1, F3.

The wit speaking of Wonder Bread on page 86 was first quoted in Henry Mitchell, "Wonder Bread, Any Way You Slice It." *Washington Post,* March 22, 1991: F2.

Going to McDonald's school for managers (page 87) is written about in Sarah Sanderson King and Michael J. King, "Hamburger University." In Marshall Fishwick, ed., *Ronald Revisited:*94–105.

The long quotation on pages 87–8 about the increasing homogeneity of food comes from William Serrin, "Let Them Eat Junk." *Saturday Review,* February 2, 1980: 18.

For an early critique of tours like those offered by Cook and American Express, one that offers points like those on pages 90–1, see Daniel J. Boorstin, *The Image: A Guide to Pseudo-Events in America.* New York: Harper Colophon, 1961.

Conrad Hilton is quoted on page 90 from Daniel J. Boorstin, *The Image:* 98.

The quotation about old-fashioned camping on page 91 comes from Beth Thames, "In the Mists of Memory, Sun Always Shines on Family Camping." *The New York Times,* July 9, 1986: C7, and the next quotation about more modern camping is taken from Dirk Johnson, "Vacationing at Campgrounds is Now Hardly Roughing It." *The New York Times,* August 28, 1986: B1.

The moniker given KOA campgrounds (page 92) comes from "Country-Club Campgrounds." *Newsweek,* September 24, 1984: 90. The camper quoted just below spoke to Dirk Johnson for his article "Vacationing at Campgounds." The quotations about Busch Gardens at the bottom of the page and extending to page 93 come from Lynn Darling, "On the Inside at Parks a la Disney." *Washington Post,* August 28, 1978: A10.

Andrew Beyer writes about Wayne Lukas in "Lukas Has the Franchise on Almighty McDollar." *Washington Post*, August 8, 1990: F1, F8. The quotations on page 94 are drawn from that article.

Peter Prichard quotes the executive speaking about *USA TODAY* on page 95 in *The Making of McPaper: The Inside Story of USA Today*. Kansas City: Andrews, McMeel and Parker, 1987: 102. The quotation about malls on the same page comes from William Severini Kowinski, *The Malling of America: An Inside Look at the Great Consumer Paradise*. New York: William Morrow and Co., 1985: 27.

The quotation about objectivity in medicine on page 98 comes from Stanley Joel Reiser, *Medicine and the Reign of Technology*. Cambridge: Cambridge University Press, 1978: ix.

Malvina Reynolds' lyrics on page 98 are reprinted by permission of Schroder Music Co., ASCAP, © 1962.

Chapter Six

Richard Edwards writes about the use of technology in the work place (page 100) in *Contested Terrain: The Transformation of the Workplace in the Twentieth Century*. New York: Basic Books, 1979.

The quotation about bakeries on page 102 comes from William Serrin, "Let Them Eat Junk." *Saturday Review*, February 2, 1980: 23. Further down the page, for more on aquaculture, see Martha Duffy, "The Fish Tank on the Farm." *Time*, December 3, 1990: 107–11.

More information about factory farms (pages 103–4) can be found in Peter Singer, *Animal Liberation: A New Ethic for Our Treatment of Animals*. New York: Avon Books, 1975; the quotations about chicken farming on page 103 comes from that book's pages 96–7 and 105–6, respectively. The quotation on page 104 about veal appears on page 123 of Singer's book.

The details about Taco Bell at the top of page 106 come from Michael Lev, "Raising Fast Food's Speed Limit." *Washington Post*, August 7, 1991: D1, D4. Further down the page, Ray Kroc writes about McDonald's fries in *Grinding It Out: The Making of McDonald's*. Chicago: Contemporary Books, Inc. 1977: 131–2.

The quotations about the hamburger-serving robot on pages 106–7 come from William R. Greer, "Robot Chef's New Dish: Hamburgers." *The New York Times*, May 27, 1987: C3.

In the paragraph about new automating efforts, on page 107, the quotation about Taco Bell comes from Michael Lev, "Taco Bell Finds Price of Success (59¢)." *The New York Times*, December 17, 1990: D9, and the next one, about the drink dispenser, is taken from Calvin Sims, "Robots to Make Fast Food Chains Still Faster." *The New York Times*, August 24, 1988: 5.

The quotations about the self-checkout system in grocery stores (in the middle of page 108) come from Eben Shapiro, "Ready, Set, Scan that Melon." *The New York Times*, June 14, 1990: D1, D8.

To elaborate on my point on pages 108–9 about supermarkets increasing their control over shoppers, when the scanners were instituted at my local market, management announced that it was issuing markers to customers who were interested in writing the price on each item. This, again, is consistent with the trend toward getting the consumer to do work historically done by others, in this case by grocery clerks who worked deep into the night to mark each item. Furthermore, the markers did not last long, since few hurried shoppers had the desire to put in several additional minutes a day as grocery clerks.

The quotation about music in Seven-Eleven (page 109) comes from "Disenchanted Evenings." *Time*, September 3, 1990: 53.

On pages 109–10, the detail about fast-food restaurants posting a time limit comes from Ester Reiter, *Making Fast Food*. Montreal and Kingston: McGill-Queens University Press: 86. Further down that paragraph, the uncomfortable seats are described in Stan Luxenberg, *Roadside Empires: How the Chains Franchised America*. New York: Viking, 1985.

Super Boil soup (page 110) is described in "Super Soup Cooks Itself." *Scholastic News*, January 4, 1991: 3.

The mall zombies (page 111) are treated in William Severini Kowinski, *The Malling of America: An Inside Look at the Great Consumer Paradise*. New York: William Morrow, 1985: 359.

The quotation on page 112 about computerized phone calls comes from Gary Langer, "Computers Reach Out, Respond to Human Voice." *Washington Post*, February 11, 1990: H3. For more about junk mail (on the same page), see Jill Smolowe, "Read This!!!!!!!!" *Time*, November 26, 1990: 62ff.

Michael Schrage is the *Washington Post* journalist cited on page 113: "'Personalized' Publishing: Confusing Information with Intimacy." *Washington Post*, November 23, 1990: B13.

William Stockton writes about computerized medical diagnosis (page 114) in "Computers that Think." *New York Times Magazine*, December 14, 1980: 48.

The kindergarten as boot camp analogy (page 115) comes from Harold Gracey, "Learning the Student Role: Kindergarten as Academic Boot Camp." In Dennis Wrong and Harold Gracey, eds., *Reading in Introductory Sociology*. New York: Macmillan, 1967. Source for that paragraph's last sentence is Charles E. Silberman, *Crisis in the Classroom: The Remaking of American Education*. New York: Random House, 1970: 122.

On page 116, the quotation about the lesson on crabs comes from Silberman: 125; the quotation that ends that paragraph comes from Silberman: 137. Source for information on the Sylvan Learning Center (further down that page) is "The McDonald's of Teaching." *Newsweek*, January 7, 1985: 61.

The introductory material in the paragraph on pages 116–7 about TV religion is based on a discussion in Jeffrey Hadden and Charles E. Swann. *Prime Time Preachers:*

The Rising Power of Televangelism. Reading, MA: Addison-Wesley, 1981. The material on Vatican television in the same paragraph comes from E. J. Dionne, Jr., "The Vatican is Putting Video to Work." *The New York Times*, August 11, 1985: 2: 27.

The new method of checking in to a hotel described on page 117 is based on the article "Automated Check-in." *Washington Post*, December 18, 1988: E8.

Frederick W. Taylor is quoted on page 119 from his book *The Principles of Scientific Management.* New York: Harper and Row, 1947: 59. The quote just below it comes from Henry Ford, *My Life and Work.* Garden City, New York: Doubleday, 1922: 103.

For more about artificial intelligence, touched upon briefly on page 120, see Raymond Kurzweil, *The Age of Intelligent Machines.* Cambridge: MIT Press, 1990.

Chapter Seven

Negative effects other than the ones discussed on page 121, such as racism and sexism, cannot be explained by this process. See Ester Reiter, *Making Fast Food.* Montreal and Kingston: McGill-Queen's University Press, 1991: 145.

For more about "McD TV," mentioned on page 122, and for the source of that paragraph's end-quotation, see Paul Farhi, "McDonald's Customers: Made-to-Order Audience." *Washington Post*, November 19, 1991: B1, B5. For more of the Japanese inefficiencies touched on in the next paragraph, see Michael Schrage, "The Pursuit of Efficiency Can Be an Illusion." *Washington Post*, March 20, 1992: F3.

Richard Cohen is quoted on page 123 from his article "Take a Message—Please!" *Washington Post Magazine*, August 5, 1990: 5.

The quotation about Giant supermarket on pages 123–4 comes from Peter Carlson, "Who Put the Sunshine in the Sunshine Scent?" *Washington Post Magazine*, December 16, 1990: 21.

The Bob Garfield essay "How I Spent (and Spent and Spent) My Disney Vacation" quoted on pages 125–6 appeared in *Washington Post–Outlook*, July 7, 1991: B5.

In the paragraph just below the head "Fun, Fun, Fun," on page 126, the quotations come from "Fast Food Speeds Up the Pace." *Time*, August 26, 1985: 60. The source for the material about McDonald's playgrounds discussed at the bottom of the page is Stephen Levine, "McDonald's Makes a Play to Diversify." *Washington Post*, August 30, 1991: G1, G4.

The alliance between Toys R Us and McDonald's mentioned on page 127 was reported in "Allying Toys and Fast Foods." *The New York Times*, October 8, 1991: D15. The next paragraph describes the salt-and-sugar-coated McDonald's fry; Burger King does the same thing to its fries. See Reiter, *Making Fast Food:* 65. In the next paragraph, Allen Shelton elaborates on McDonald's as theater in his forthcoming article "Writing McDonald's, Eating the Past: McDonald's as a Postmodern Space." At the bottom of the page, I describe entertainment in supermarkets; the long quotation comes from Peter Carlson, "Who Put the Sunshine in the Sunshine Scent?"

Washington Post Magazine, December 16, 1990: 20, and the quotation that ends the paragraph is taken from Michael Ryan, "Fast Food vs. Supermarkets." *Parade*, November 13, 1988: 6.

The quotation about Las Vegas at the top of page 128 comes from Neil Postman, *Amusing Ourselves to Death: Public Discourse in the Age of Show Business*. New York: Viking, 1985: 3. In the next paragraph, William Severini Kowinski describes entertainment in malls in *The Malling of America*. New York: William Morrow, 1985. The quotation in my discussion comes from that book's page 371. The source for the discussion on the same page of the Mall of America is Kara Swisher, "A Mall for America?" *Washington Post–Business*, June 30, 1991: H1, H4.

Source for the material and quotation about *Business Week* on pages 128–9 is Ian Mitroff and Warren Bennis, *The Unreality Industry: The Deliberate Manufacturing of Falsehood and What It Is Doing to Our Lives*. New York: A Birch Lane Book, 1989: 12.

Daniel Boorstin discusses at length the notion of pseudo-events mentioned on page 129 in his book *The Image: A Guide to Pseudo-Events in America*. New York: Harper Colophon, 1961. Mitroff and Bennis treat the notion of the unreality industry mentioned on that page in their book *The Unreality Industry*, and Joel Achenbach writes more about Milli Vanilli in "The Age of Unreality." *Washington Post*, November 22, 1990: C1, C14.

The health risks of McDonaldization described on page 130 are elaborated on by Maryellen Spencer, "Can Mama Mac Get Them to Eat Spinach?" In Marshall Fishwick, ed., *Ronald Revisited: The World of Ronald McDonald*. Bowling Green: Bowling Green University Press, 1983: 85–93.

The long quotation about Salmonella on page 130–1 comes from Regina Schrambling, "The Curse of Culinary Convenience." *The New York Times*, September 10, 1991: A19.

Tim Luke writes about "McGulag," mentioned on page 131, in "Postcommunism in the USSR: The McGulag Archipelago." *Telos*, 84, 1990: 33–42. The detail about McDonald's paper needs further down the page comes from Max Boas and Steve Chain, *Big Mac: The Unauthorized Story of McDonald's*. New York: NAL 1976. The moron and trained monkey quotations at the bottom of the page come from Reiter, *Making Fast Food*: 150, 167.

One exception to the general rule discussed on pages 133–4 that diners do not linger is the tendency for retirees to use McDonald's as a social center, especially over breakfast or coffee.

Burger King's Rule 17 (page 134) comes from Reiter, *Making Fast Food*: 95.

The quotation about family meals on page 135 comes from Nicholas von Hoffman, "The Fast-Disappearing Family Meal." *Washington Post*, 1978: C4.

The general point about the microwave oven made on pages 136–7 is based on Margaret Visser, "A Meditation on the Microwave." *Psychology Today*, December, 1989: 38ff. The two quotations in that section's first paragraph come from "The Microwave Cooks Up a New Way of Life." *Wall Street Journal*, September 19, 1989:

B1. Subsequent quotations in the section come from Visser, "A Meditation," page 40 ("'zapped' or 'nuked' instead of cooked"), and page 42 ("a sort of filling station" and "the communal meal").

Bob Garfield is quoted again on page 137 from his article "How I Spent My Disney Vacation."

Ellen Goodman's words on page 139 come from "Fast-Forwarding Through Fall." *Washington Post*, October 5, 1991: A19. The material in parentheses in the same paragraph comes from Leonard Sloane, "Buying by Catalogue Is Easy: Timely Delivery May Not Be." *The New York Times*, April 25, 1992: 50.

The quotations about aircraft automation on page 143 are taken from Carl H. Lavin, "Automated Planes Raising Concerns." *The New York Times*, August 12, 1989: 1, 6.

Mark Dowie wrote about the Pinto case in "Pinto Madness." *Mother Jones*, September/October 1977: 24ff. His article is the source for material on page 144. Ford's words on the same page are taken from his book *My Life and My Work*. Garden City, New York: Doubleday Page & Co., 1922: 105, 106. In the next paragraph, on the negative aspects of the assembly line, the long quotation about repetitive work comes from Studs Terkel, *Working*. New York: Pantheon, 1974: 159.

The quotation about welding and painting cars (page 145) comes from Barbara Garson, *All the Livelong Day*. Harmondsworth, England: Penguin, 1977: 88. The human robot quotation comes from Terkel, *Working:* 175.

Chapter Eight

Source for the detail on page 151 about computers in fast-food restaurants is Ester Reiter, *Making Fast Food*. Montreal and Kingston: McGill-Queen's University Press, 1991: 165.

The postindustrialism thesis mentioned on page 152 is drawn largely from Daniel Bell, *The Coming of Post-Industrial Society: A Venture in Social Forecasting*. New York: Basic Books, 1973.

The quotation about increased productivity on page 153 comes from Simon Clarke, "The Crisis of Fordism or the Crisis of Social Democracy?" *Telos*, 83, 1990: 71–98.

On the general point of the relationship between people's social situation and their choice of goods (page 154), see Pierre Bourdieu, *Distinction: A Social Critique of the Judgment of Taste*. Cambridge: Harvard University Press, 1984.

For more on postmodernism, touched on in pages 156–7, see Jean-Francois Lyotard, *The Postmodern Condition: A Report on Knowledge*. Minneapolis: The University of Minnesota Press, 1984.

On page 156, Allen Shelton is quoted from his forthcoming essay "Writing McDonald's, Eating the Past: McDonald's as a Postmodern Space." The scholar quoted at the bottom of page 156 is Alex Callinicos from his book *Against Postmodernism: A Marxist Critique*. New York: St. Martin's Press, 1990: 4.

David Harvey is quoted on page 157 from his book *The Condition of Postmodernity: An Enquiry into the Origins of Cultural Change*. Oxford: Basil Blackwell. 1989. The first quotation, about capitalism's sea-change, comes from that book's page 189; the next ("time-space compression") page 284; and the final ("annihilation of space") page 293.

Chapter Nine

The quotation about the answering machine at the bottom of page 161 is from Vic Sussman, "The Machine We Love to Hate." *Washington Post Magazine*, June 14, 1987: 33.

The material about Saugatuck on page 163 comes from Isabel Wilkerson, "Midwest Village; Slow-Paced, Fights Plan for Fast-Food Outlet." *The New York Times*, July 19, 1987: 1, 16. Mary Davis Suro covered the Italian protests mentioned further down the page for *The New York Times* in her article "Romans Protest McDonald's." May 5, 1986.

On page 164, *Time* magazine wrote about the Freeport McDonald's ("Eating Out is in, and the chains add variety to lure new diners." *Time*, August 26, 1985: 60–1), and the source for coverage of the 12,000th McDonald's was Anthony Ramirez, "In the Orchid Room . . . Big Macs." *The New York Times*, October 30, 1990: D1, D5. The Johnny Carson witticism in the middle of the page comes from Anthony Ramirez, "When Fast Food Goes on a Diet." *Washington Post*, March 19, 1991: D1, D7; McDonald's response to Sokoloff's ad in the same paragraph comes from Marian Burros, "Fast-Food Chains Try to Slim Down." *The New York Times*, April 11, 1990: C1, C10; the other material in the paragraph is based on a *Time* magazine article, Leon Jaroff, "A Crusader from the Heartland." *Time*, March 25, 1991: 56, 58.

Ramirez, "Fast Food on a Diet," is the source of the material at the top of page 165 about the fat content of McDonald's hamburgers. The material about Macheezmo Mouse in the next paragraph comes from the same source.

John Holusha writes about McDonald's new packaging (page 165) in two articles: "McDonald's Expected to Drop Plastic Burger Box." *Washington Post*, November 1, 1990: A1, D19; and "Packaging and Public Image: McDonald's Fills a Big Order." *The New York Times*, November 2, 1990: A1, D5. The environmentalist cited at the end of the paragraph was quoted by Warren Brown in "Hardee's to Introduce Recycled Plastic in Area." *Washington Post*, March 22, 1991: B1, B3.

The description of the Golden Arch Cafe on pages 165–6 comes from Phil West, "Cafe's Decor, Not-So-Fast Food Evoke McMemories." *Washington Times*, August 30, 1990: C1; Laura Shapiro reviews the food served at the Golden Arch Cafe in "Ready for McCatfish." *Newsweek*, October 15, 1990. The quotation on page 166 comes from her article.

Source for coverage of the upscale McDonald's on page 167 is Ron Alexander, "Big Mac with Chopin, Please." *The New York Times*, August 12, 1990: 42. The McDonald's and Taco Bell's innovations mentioned on the same page are based on discussion in several sources: Richard Martin, "Bakersfield McD Units Test Credit Card System for Business Customers." *Nation's Restaurant News*, November 18, 1985: 3; Paul Baran and Paul M. Sweezy, *Monopoly Capital: An Essay on the American Economic and Social Order*. New York: Monthly Review Press, 1966; Michael Lev, "Taco Bell Finds Price of Success (59¢)." *The New York Times*, December 17, 1990: D1, D9; and Michael Lev, "California McDonald's to Cut Menu Prices." *The New York Times*, December 21, 1990: D3. Eric Schmitt covered the mobile Burger King (at the bottom of the page) in "Burger King on Wheels." *The New York Times*, November 23, 1985: 35, 37.

The quotations about Chock Full o' Nuts on page 168 come from Eric Maykuth, "Chock Full O'Nuts Restaurants Are Dying Quietly." *Washington Post*, September 16, 1990: H16. At the bottom of the page, the discussion of the opposition to unionization is derived from Ester Reiter, *Making Fast Food*. Montreal and Kingston: McGill-Queen's University Press, 1991: 70ff.

On page 169, James Brooke points out that McDonald's reaches into distant communities in "Two McDonald's in Darien Do Their Hiring in Bronx." *The New York Times*, July 13, 1985: 1: 24. The hiring of retarded adults is discussed by Michael Winerip in "Finding a Sense of McMission in McNuggets." *The New York Times*, August 23, 1988: 2: 1. Two other *Times* articles mention retirees and "McMasters," respectively "McDonald's Seeks Retirees to Fill Void." *The New York Times*, December 20, 1987: 1: 54.; and Jennifer Kingson, "Golden Years Spent Under Golden Arches." *The New York Times*, March 6, 1988: 4: 26. The quotation about Kinder-Care comes from Glenn Collins, "Wanted: Child-Care Workers, Age 55 and Up." *The New York Times*, December 15, 1987: 1: 1.

There are certainly many other examples of such shops as Marvelous Market, described on pages 171–4. See Marian Burros, "Putting the Pleasure Back Into Grocery Shopping." *The New York Times*, February 21, 1987: 1: 54.

The mother's plaint on page 173 appeared in "Eating out is in, and the chains add variety to lure new diners." *Time*, August 26, 1985: 60.

Ben & Jerry's operation (pages 175–7) is discussed at length in Elizabeth Kolbert, "An 'Inspirational' Ice Cream Factory." *The New York Times;* many of the details in the first paragraph on page 175 come from Suzanne Alexander, "Oh, Wow, Man: Let's, Like, Hear from the Auditors." *The Wall Street Journal*, June 28, 1991: A1, A6. The quotation on the nutritional issue in the second paragraph comes from Ben & Jerry's 1990 Annual Report, 1990, p. 7.

On page 176, the quotation about the unavailable officer is taken from Maxine Lipner, "Ben & Jerry's: Sweet Ethics Evince Social Awareness." *COMPASS readings*, July 1991: 26–7; the satisfied worker and the impressed journalist spoke to Carol Clurman for her article "More than Just a Paycheck." *USA WEEKEND*, January 19-21, 1990: 4. In the next paragraph, Lipner quotes Jerry Greenfield in "Sweet Ethics": 25. In the following paragraph, Eric J. Wiffering wrote about Ben & Jerry's efforts to maintain quality in "Trouble in Camelot." *Business Ethics* 5, 1991: 16, 19. Patricia Aburdene's quotation at the bottom of the page comes from Clurman. "Paycheck." *USA WEEKEND*, January 19–21, 1990: 4.

On page 177, the article entitled "B&B's Offer Travelers Break from McBed, McBreakfast" was written by June R. Herold for *Business First–Columbus*, 5, 15: 1: 1. Further down the same paragraph, the boon of B&Bs in the early 1980s was reported in Betsy Wade, "B&B Book Boom." *Chicago Tribune*, July 28, 1991: C16ff. The quotation at the paragraph's end comes from Paul Avery, "Mixed Success for Bed-Breakfast Idea." *The New York Times*, July 28, 1991: 12NJ, 8. In the next paragraph, Eric N. Berg quotes the observer of B&Bs in "The New Bed and Breakfast." *The New York Times*, October 15, 1989: 5, 21ff.

The material about food co-ops on page 178 comes from Andrew Malcolm, "Bagging Old Rules to Keep a Food Co-Op Viable." *The New York Times*, November 8, 1991: B7.

Skunk works (page 180) are described more fully in Thomas J. Peters and Robert H. Waterman, *In Search of Excellence: Lessons from America's Best-Run Companies*. New York: Harper & Row, 1982. The quotations on pages 180-1 come from page 201 of that book.

Postman has a similar set of recommendations to those listed on page 183ff for "resistance fighters" against "technology." See Neil Postman, *Technology*. New York: Knopf, 1992: 183ff.

The quotation in the middle of page 183 about Levittown appeared first in Georgia Dullea, "The Tract House as Landmark." *The New York Times*, October 17, 1991: C8.

The material about humanizing the McDonald's experience on pages 184–5 is based on a forthcoming essay by Allen Shelton, "Writing McDonald's, Eating the Past: McDonald's as a Postmodern Space." The quotation about breakfast appears on that essay's page 47.

Regina Schrambling's article "The Curse of Culinary Convenience" (page 185), appeared on page A19 of *The New York Times*, September 10, 1991.

The discovery on page 186 about tomato gas was reported in Warren Leary, "Researchers Halt Ripening of Tomato." *The New York Times*, October 19, 1991: 7. Further down the paragraph, the material about strawberries comes from John Tierney, "A Patented Berry Has Sellers Licking Their Lips." *The New York Times*, October 14, 1991: A8.

The Bocuse quotations on pages 187–8 come from Roger Cohen, "Faux Pas by McDonald's in Europe." *The New York Times*, February 18, 1992: D1; the material about the Bois de Bologne comes from Sharon Waxman, "Paris's Sex Change Operation." *Washington Post*, March 2, 1992: B1.

The words that close the book on page 188 come from Dylan Thomas, "Do Not Go Gentle into That Good Night," 1952.

Bibliography

Rather than repeating the citations listed in the end notes, I would like to use this section to cite some of the major academic works that served as a resource for this book. There are three categories of such resources. The first is the work of Max Weber, especially that dealing with rationalization. The second is the work of various neo-Weberians who have modified and expanded upon Weber's original ideas. Finally, there are a series of works that focus on specific aspects of our McDonaldized society.

Works by Max Weber

Max Weber, *The Protestant Ethic and the Spirit of Capitalism*. New York: Scribner's, 1904-5/1958.

_____, "Religious Rejections of the World and Their Directions." In H.H. Gerth and C. W. Mills, eds. *From Max Weber: Essays in Sociology*. New York: Oxford University Press, 1915/1958: 323–59.

_____, "The Social Psychology of the World Religions." In H.H. Gerth and C. W. Mills, eds. *From Max Weber: Essays in Sociology*. New York: Oxford University Press, 1915/1958: 267–301.

_____, *The Religion of China: Confucianism and Taoism*. New York: MacMillan, 1916/1964.

_____, *The Religion of India: The Sociology of Hinduism and Buddhism*. Glencoe, IL: Free Press, 1916-17/1958.

_____, *The Rational and Social Foundations of Music*. Carbondale, IL: Southern Illinois University Press, 1921/1958.

_____, *Economy and Society*, volumes 1 through 3, Totowa, NJ: Bedminster Press, 1921/1968.

_____, *General Economic History*. New Brunswick, NJ: Transaction Books, 1927/1981.

Works by Neo-Weberians

Rogers Brubaker, *The Limits of Rationality: An Essay on the Social and Moral Thought of Max Weber*. London: Allen and Unwin, 1984.

Randall Collins, "Weber's Last Theory of Capitalism: A Systematization." *American Sociological Review*, 45, 1980: 925–42.

_____, *Weberian Sociological Theory*. Cambridge: Cambridge University Press, 1985.

Arnold Eisen, "The Meanings and Confusions of Weberian 'Rationality.'" *British Journal of Sociology* 29, 1978: 57–70.

Harvey Greisman, "Disenchantment of the World." *British Journal of Sociology* 27, 1976: 497–506.

_____ and George Ritzer, "Max Weber, Critical Theory and the Administered World." *Qualitative Sociology* 4, 1981: 34–55.

Jurgen Habermas, *The Theory of Communicative Action*. Vol. 1, *Reason and the Rationalization of Society*. Boston: Beacon Press, 1984.

Stephen Kalberg, "Max Weber's Types of Rationality: Cornerstones for the Analysis of Rationalization Processes in History." *American Journal of Sociology*, 85, 1980: 1145–79.

_____, "The Rationalization of Action in Max Weber's Sociology of Religion." *Sociological Theory* 8, 1990: 58–84.

Donald Levine, "Rationality and Freedom: Weber and Beyond." *Sociological Inquiry* 51, 1981: 5–25.

Arthur Mitzman, *The Iron Cage: An Historical Interpretation of Max Weber*. New York: Grosset and Dunlap, 1969.

Wolgang Mommsen, *The Age of Bureaucracy*. New York: Harper and Row, 1974.

George Ritzer, "Professionalization, Bureaucratization and Rationalization: The Views of Max Weber." *Social Forces* 53, 1975: 627–34.

_____ and David Walczak, "Rationalization and the Deprofessionalization of Physicians." *Social Forces* 67, 1988: 1–22.

_____ and Terri LeMoyne, "Hyperrationality." In George Ritzer, *Metatheorizing in Sociology*. Lexington, MA: Lexington Books, 1991: 93–115.

Guenther Roth and Reinhard Bendix, eds. *Scholarship and Partisanship: Essays on Max Weber*. Berkeley: University of California Press, 1971.

Lawrence Scaff, *Fleeing the Iron Cage: Culture, Politics, and Modernity in the Thought of Max Weber*. Berkeley: University of California Press, 1989.

Wolfgang Schluchter, *The Rise of Western Rationalism: Max Weber's Developmental History*. Berkeley: University of California Press, 1971.

Alan Sica, *Weber, Irrationality and the Social Order*. Berkeley: University of California Press, 1988.

Ronald Takaki, *Iron Cages: Race and Culture in 19th-Century America*. New York: Oxford University Press, 1990.

Works on Various Aspects of a McDonaldizing Society

Daniel Bell, *The Coming of Post-Industrial Society: A Venture in Social Forecasting*. New York: Basic Books, 1973.

Max Boas and Steve Chain, *Big Mac: The Unauthorized Story of McDonald's*. New York: E.P. Dutton. 1976.

Daniel Boorstin, *The Image: Guide to Pseudo-Events in America*. New York: Harper Colophon, 1961.

Pierre Bourdieu, *Distinction: A Social Critique of the Judgment of Taste*. Cambridge, MA: Harvard University Press, 1984.

Simon Clarke, "The Crisis of Fordism or the Crisis of Social Democracy?" *Telos*, 83, 1990: 71–98.

Richard Edwards, *Contested Terrain: The Transformation of the Workplace in the Twentieth Century*. New York: Basic Books, 1979.

Marshall Fishwick, ed. *Ronald Revisited: The World of Ronald McDonald*. Bowling Green: Bowling Green University Press, 1983.

James T. Flink, *The Automobile Age*. Cambridge: MIT Press, 1988.

Henry Ford, *My Life and Work*. Garden City, NY: Doubleday, Page, and Co., 1922.

Herbert Gans, *The Levittowners: Ways of Life and Politics in a New Suburban Community*. New York: Pantheon Books, 1967.

Barbara Garson, *All the Livelong Day*. Harmondsworth, England: Penguin, 1977.

Richard E. Gordon, Katherine K. Gordon, and Max Gunther, *The Split Level Trap*. New York: Gilbert Geis Associates, 1960.

Harold Gracey, "Learning the Student Role: Kindergarten as Academic Boot Camp." In Dennis Wrong and Harold Gracey, eds. *Reading in Introductory Sociology*. New York: MacMillan, 1967.

Allen Guttmann, *From Ritual to Record: The Nature of Modern Sports*. New York: Cambridge University Press, 1978.

Jeffrey Hadden and Charles E. Swann, *Primetime Preachers: The Rising Power of Televangelism*. Reading, MA: Addison-Wesley, 1981.

David Harvey, *The Condition of Postmodernity: An Enquiry into the Origins of Cultural Change*. Oxford: Basil Blackwell, 1989.

Kathleen Jamieson, *Eloquence in an Electronic Age: The Transformation of Political Speechmaking*. New York: Oxford University Press, 1988.

William Severini Kowinski, *The Malling of America: An Inside Look at the Great Consumer Paradise*. New York: William Morrow, 1985.

Ray Kroc, *Grinding It Out*. New York: Berkeley Medallion Books, 1977.

Raymond Kurzweil, *The Age of Intelligent Machines*. Cambridge, MA: MIT Press, 1990.

John F. Love, *McDonald's: Behind the Arches*. Toronto: Bantam Books, 1986.

Stan Luxenberg, *Roadside Empires: How the Chains Franchised America*. New York: Viking, 1985.

Jean-Francois Lyotard, *The Postmodern Condition: A Report on Knowledge*. Minneapolis, MN: The University of Minnesota Press, 1984.

Frank Mankiewicz and Joel Swerdlow, *Remote Control: Television and the Manipulation of American Life*. New York: Time Books, 1978.

Ian Mitroff and Warren Bennis, *The Unreality Industry: The Deliberate Manufacturing of Falsehood and What it is Doing to Our Lives*. New York: Birch Lane Press, 1989.

Thomas J. Peters and Robert H. Waterman, *In Search of Excellence: Lessons from America's Best-Run Companies*. New York: Harper & Row, 1982.

Neil Postman, *Amusing Ourselves to Death: Public Discourse in the Age of Show Business*. New York: Viking, 1985.

_____, *Technopoly: The Surrender of Culture to Technology*. New York: Knopf, 1992.

Peter Prichard, *The Making of McPaper: The Inside Story of USA Today*. Kansas City, MO: Andrews, McMeel and Parker, 1987.

Stanley Joel Reiser, *Medicine and the Reign of Technology*. Cambridge: Cambridge University Press, 1978.

Ester Reiter, *Making Fast Food*. Montreal and Kingston: McGill-Queen's University Press, 1991.

George Ritzer, "The McDonaldization of Society." *Journal of American Culture* 6, 1983: 100–7.

_____ and David Walczak, "The Changing Nature of American Medicine." *Journal of American Culture* 9, 1987: 43–51.

Allen Shelton, "Writing McDonald's, Eating the Past: McDonald's as a Postmodern Space." forthcoming.

Charles E. Silberman, *Crisis in the Classroom: The Remaking of American Education*. New York: Random House, 1970.

Peter Singer, *Animal Liberation: A New Ethics for Our Treatment of Animals*. New York: Avon Books, 1975.

Alfred P. Sloan, Jr., *My Years at General Motors*. Garden City, NY: Doubleday, 1964.

Frederick W. Taylor, *The Principles of Scientific Management*. New York: Harper and Row, 1947.

Shoshana Zuboff, *In the Age of the Smart Machine: The Future of Work and Power*. New York: Basic Books, 1988.

Credits

Quotations on the following pages are reprinted by permission. They are listed according to their original source.

The New York Times

Page 3, ". . . McDonald's of toys."

Page 4, "Pleas don't tear it down! . . . ."

Page 5, "ultimate icon" and "Cathedral of Chartres."

Page 6, "You want something the stomach? . . . ."

Page 9, "cookie-cutter cleanliness. . . ."

Page 46, "Instead of having a breakfast sandwich. . . ."

Page 58, "Indulgences are a release. . . ."

Page 91, "Of course it began to pour. . . ." and "All they wanted . . . was a space in the woods. . . ."

Pages 106-7, "The robot looks like. . . ."; "a computer-driven machine. . . ."; and "Orders are punched in at the cash register. . . ."

Page 108, "within five years, self-service groceries. . . ."

Page 117, "The big advantage to the Vatican. . . ."

Pages 130-1, "Salmonella proliferated in the poultry industry. . . ."

Page 143, "push a few buttons. . . ."; "We're taking more and more. . . ."; and "If we have human operators. . . ."

Page 163, "People can see McDonald's anywhere. . . ." and "It's the Howard Johnson's. . . ."

Page 164, "the principal cause of degradation. . . ." and "reckless, misleading, the worst. . . ."

Page 167, "A smashing place. . . ."

Page 169, "For old people who need. . . ."

Page 177, "It was marvelous. . . ." and "Your best B&B's are those. . . ."

Page 183, "The Levitt box. . . ."

Page 186, "We would remember that the strawberry crop. . . ." and "actually has some flavor, too."

The Washington Post

Page 4, "Nothing this exciting ever happens. . . ."
Page 8, "a sort of smorgasbord. . . ."
Page 14, "openly worship McDonald's"; "the greatest restaurant chain. . . ."; and "can't stand the food. . . ."
Page 39, "Inside, diners in a hurry for tacos. . . ."
Page 43, "The party you are trying to reach. . . ."
Page 50, "considers itself the McDonald's. . . ."
Page 74, "the more you tend to put after your name. . . ."
Page 77, "that nearly half of faculty. . . ." and "First, I hope we can agree. . . ."
Page 80, "the only ones who think of patients. . . .
Page 86, "I thought they just blew up library paste. . . ."
Page 113, "By dropping in people's names. . . ."
Page 122, "One of the biggest customer concerns. . . ."
Page 123, "Oh Lord, with each advance. . . ."
Page 128, "Mall of America . . . it's a circus."
Page 139, "The creation of one national mail-order. . . ." and "I refuse to fast-forward. . . ."
Copyright © 1987/88/88/89/90/91 by The Washington Post. Reprinted with permission.

TIME

Page 53, "In many ways the scene resembles. . . ."
Copyright © Time Warner Inc. Reprinted by permission.

USA TODAY

Page 84, "Replicated color and symbol, mile after mile. . . ."
Reprinted from USA TODAY MAGAZINE, January 1980, copyright © 1980 by the Society for the Advancement of Education.

Schroder Music Company

Page 98, "Little boxes on the hillside. . . ."
From the song "Little Boxes." Words and music by Malvina Reynolds. Copyright © 1962 Schroder Music Co. (ASCAP), renewed 1990 N. Schimmel. Used by permission. All rights reserved.

PSYCHOLOGY TODAY

Pages 136-7, "Those qualities of the family meal. . . ."; "With cooking reduced to pushing a button. . . ."; and "The communal meal. . . ."
Reprinted with permission from Psychology Today magazine. Copyright © 1989 (Sussex Publishers, Inc.).

Newsweek

Page 166, "Not until your meal arrives. . . ."
Copyright © 1990 Newsweek magazine. Reprinted with permission.

Dylan Thomas

Page 188, "Do not go gentle. . . ."
From "Do Not Go Gentle Into That Good Night," The Poems, Dylan Thomas. Reprinted with permission of David Higham Associates.

Saturday Review

Pages 87-8, "Regional and ethnic distinctions are disappearing. . . ." and "Sophisticated processing and storage. . . ."
Page 102, "The most advanced bakeries. . . ."
Copyright © 1980 Saturday Review. Reprinted with limited permission on "as is" basis by Omni International, Ltd.

Wall Street Journal

Page 136, "It has made even fast-food restaurants. . . ." and "We're just not as critical. . . ."
Copyright © 1989 Wall Street Journal. Reprinted with permission.

Index